Bond Book

MILLER'S

kitchenware

MILLER'S KITCHENWARE BUYER'S GUIDE

Created and designed by
Miller's Publications
The Cellars, High Street,
Tenterden, Kent TN30 6BN
Tel: 01580 766411
Fax: 01580 766100

Managing Editor: Valerie Lewis
Production Co-ordinator: Philip Hannath
Editorial Co-ordinator: Deborah Wanstall
Project Co-ordinator: Léonie Sidgwick
Editorial Assistants: Melissa Hall, Joanna Hill
Production Assistants: Caroline Bugeja, Mel Smith, Charlotte Smith, Ethne Tragett
Senior Advertising Executive: Jill Jackson; **Advertising Executive:** Emma Gillingham
Advertising Co-ordinator & Administrator: Melinda Williams
Designer: Nick Harris; **Advertisement Designer:** Simon Cook
Indexer: Hilary Bird
Production: Jane Rogers
Jacket Design: Alexa Brommer
Additional Photography: Emma Gillingham, Dennis O'Reilly, Robin Saker
North American Consultants: Shelia & Marilynn Brass

First published in Great Britain in 2005 by Miller's, a division of Mitchell Beazley,
imprints of Octopus Publishing Group Ltd,
2–4 Heron Quays, London E14 4JP

Miller's is a registered trademark of Octopus Publishing Group Ltd

© 2005 Octopus Publishing Group Ltd

A CIP record for this book is available from the British Library

ISBN 1 84533 071 4

Some of the material in this book has previously been
published in *Miller's Collecting Kitchenware* by Christina Bishop
Some images have appeared in previous editions of
Miller's Antiques Price Guide and *Miller's Collectables Price Guide*

Colour Origination: 1.13, Whitstable, Kent
Printed and bound: Toppan Printing, China

Front cover illustration:
L. **A pair of Salter scales,** c1920.
£65–75 / €100–115 / $120–140 ⊞ AL
R. **A set of Tala tin cake moulds,** 1950s.
£1–5 / €2–7 / $3–9 ⊞ DaM

Contents

Contributors

Storage and Cookware: Annie Marchant
Annie Marchant trades as Wenderton Antiques, specializing in 18th-century to very early 20th-century kitchenware. She regularly attends Olympia as well as selling her wares internationally. Annie has a personal interest in dairy-related items.

Biscuit Barrels: Glynis Braizer
Glynis Brazier has been the auction manager at Lambert & Foster, who hold general antiques auctions once a month, for 17 years and valuer for the last 10 years. Glynis' personal collections include furniture and porcelain figures.

Plastic Storage: Kevin O'Doherty
Kevin O'Doherty and his partner Luke Browne own Twinkled – a company dedicated to everything that will furnish a complete "retropolitan" living experience from the 1950s to the 1980s. Kevin can be contacted through his website www.twinkled.net

Storage Tins: David Huxtable
David Huxtable started selling old tins and advertising collectables at Alfies Antiques market 12 years ago. David believes that he has sold over 100,000 tins. He has appeared on television antiques shows both in the UK and abroad, and regularly contributes to Miller's titles. David now sells exclusively through fairs around the world and his website, www.huxtins.com, has up-to-date fairs information.

Dairy: Rose Smith
Rose Smith of Bread and Roses prefers antiques that have had a functional life instead of just ornamental. She has been buying and selling 1800 to 1950s kitchenware for about 12 years. Her extensive stock, which originates from Britain and France, can be found at the Ark Angel, Tetbury, Gloucestershire and at Zani Lady, Corfe Street, Ludlow, Shropshire. Rose is a regular stall holder at Shepton Mallet Antiques Fair in Newark and the National Exhibition Centre, Birmingham. She is always happy to buy and sell.

Baking: Jane Wicks
Jane Wicks, whose business grew from her own personal collection of kitchenware, has been trading from her shop in Rye for the last 10 years. She has a regular stall in the Abergevenny building at the Ardingly Antiques Fairs. Jane has contributed to other Miller's titles including the kitchenware section in *Miller's Buying Affordable Antiques Price Guide*.

Tableware: Sheila Kettle
Sheila Kettle has been dealing in English and Continental country antiques, kitchen and garden wares for the past 10 years. Sheila is a regular exhibitor at the National Exhibition Centre, Birmingham, the Scottish Exhibition and Conference Centre, Glasgow and occasionally at Shepton Mallet. A good selection of her stock can be found at Long Street Antiques in Tetbury, Gloucestershire and at Pennard House, East Pennard, near Shepton Mallet.

Scullery: Janie Smithson
Janie Smithson and her husband have been trading in antique kitchenware since 1988, and her particular enthusiasm is for early Victorian kitchenware and dairy items. The Smithsons show regularly at Olympia, the National Exhibition Centre, Birmingham and the Decorative Antiques and Textiles Fair, Battersea, London. Janie has contributed to many Miller's titles.

Books and Moulds: Sheila and Marilynn Brass
Sheila & Marilynn Brass are North American Consultants for *Miller's Antiques Price Guide* and *Miller's Collectables Price Guide*. They have been antique dealers and design consultants for 28 years. Their impressive collection of antique kitchenware, food moulds and cookbooks is considered one of the best in the US. They frequently act as consultants to universities, publications, television stations and dealers.

General Editor: Phil Ellis
Phil Ellis has a long-standing interest in antiques and collectibles. He has worked on various magazines and publications including *Antiques Magazine*, and has authored several books for Miller's including *Miller's Sci-Fi & Fantasy Collectibles* and *Miller's Antiques, Art & Collectibles on the Web*.

Christina Bishop
One of London's top kitchenware dealers for over 20 years, Christina Bishop attracts customers from as far afield as Japan, Australia and North America. Her enthusiasm for kitchenware stems from an interest in social and domestic history, as well as a passion for baking! She is the author *Miller's Collecting Kitchenware*.

How to Use

Every collector asks two key questions: "What should I look for?" and "What should I pay?". Both are answered in these pages. Nine main collecting categories are covered in both sections of the book which can be navigated by the colour-coded tabs. If you are looking for a particular item, turn to the contents list on p.5–6 to find the appropriate section, for example, Tableware. Having located your area of interest, you will see that the larger sections may be further sub-divided by subject, such as Cruets, Cutlery or Jugs & Boats. If you are looking for a particular factory, maker or object, consult the index, which starts on p.317. Cross reference boxes also direct the reader to where other related items may be found. Information on the different materials, media, and other key features is included on pp.12–15.

FINDING YOUR WAY AROUND
Use these running heads to see what sub-section you are in within each collecting category.

WHAT TO LOOK FOR
Key background and collecting information is covered in this section of the book.

INFORMATION BOXES
Additional historical, collecting or practical information is highlighted in these tint boxes.

Cutters

In Britain, the term "pastry cutter" refers to cutters designed for both pastry and biscuits. In continental Europe and North America, pastry cutters are used for pastry, and biscuit or cookie cutters are used to cut out biscuit shapes.

The earliest cutters were hand-carved and made of wood and they have a long history on both sides of the Atlantic. Early versions were known as imprint cutters, because they imprinted a design on the dough. They originated in Italy, and were used in Britain from the 15thC onwards to make gingerbread figures, often in the shape of popular contemporary personalities such as Queen Elizabeth I or the first Lord Wellington. By the 18thC they were used to make moulded sugar motifs to decorate cakes.

Later versions were outline cutters. They had a cutting edge, flat backs, and usually a handle. Made from square- or oblong-shaped wood, usually pear, walnut, or beech, both types of wooden cutters were produced in Britain until the mid-19thC, when they were replaced by mass-produced metal ones.

• **Promotional items** Cutters were sometimes used as promotional items. Davis Baking Powder issued a set of four animal cookie cutters, bearing the name of the firm on the side.

• **Sandwich cutters** Deeper cutters were designed for use to make attractively shaped sandwiches as well as biscuits.

Identification
The firms of Tala and Nutbrown dominated the market in Britain and were fierce rivals; their rivalry was such that they would often produce identical products. The only way to tell them apart is to check for a maker's mark. Both companies marked every item with their name.

SETS
Sets of pastry cutters were produced by Tala in green-painted tins with hinged lids in the early 1930s. Later in the 1930s, pastel colours became available with a glossier finish. In the 1950s, they were made of light aluminium rather than tin and came in garish colours. The cutters were available with crinkly or plain edges for the same price, and each tin contained four different-sized cutters, fitting neatly into each other, as above.

NOVELTY CUTTERS
Cutters made in novelty shapes were always popular for making biscuits in more interesting forms.

In the late 1940s and into the 50s, Tala made this particularly appealing set of six cutters in the shape of a pelican, seal, horse, elephant, penguin, and hippo (shown left).

It is rare to find a complete set like this with its original box. The base of the box has recipe instructions for biscuits.

PLASTIC
Less durable and more brittle than metal, plastic was regularly used to make pastry cutters by the 1950s. Commonly sold through Betterwear salesmen, the cutters were available in a variety of pastel shades, including pink, blue, yellow, and green.

Cream & Milk

DAIRY

◄ A brass cream skimmer, with an iron handle, c1760, 23in (58.5cm) long.
£170–190
€260–290
$310–350
⊞ F&F

A brass cream skimmer, c1780, 27in (68.5cm) long.
£310–350 / €470–530
$570–640 ⊞ SEA

A brass cream skimmer, c1780, 18in (45.5cm) long.
£85–95 / €130–145
$160–180 ⊞ F&F

Further reading
Miller's Collectables Price Guide,
Miller's Publications, 2004

◄ An elm dairy bowl, 19thC, 9in (23cm) diam.
£310–350 / €470–530
$570–640 ⊞ SEA

PURE MILK

A ceramic two-handled milk pail, with printed and hand-painted enamel decoration, repaired, 19thC, 12½in (32cm) diam.
£800–960 / €1,200–1,450
$1,450–1,700 ✗ SWO

A ceramic milk pan, 1880–1900, 10½in (26.5cm) diam.
£80–90 / €120–135
$110–125 ⊞ MSB

Cross Reference
Tableware see pages 247–287

COLOUR-CODED TABS
Each subject category is identified by a coloured tab allowing easy cross-reference between the two sections of the book.

FURTHER READING
Suggestions about where to go for further research are listed here.

SOURCE CODE
The codes refers to the 'Key to Illustrations' on p.313 that lists the details of where the item was sourced. The ✗ icon indicates the item was sold at auction. The ⊞ icon indicates the item originated from a dealer.

PRICE GUIDE
Prices are based on actual prices realized at auction or offered for sale by a dealer, shown in £sterling, €, and $US. Remember that Miller's is a PRICE GUIDE not a PRICE LIST and prices are affected by many variables such as location, condition, desirability and so on. Don't forget that if you are selling, it is quite likely you will be offered less than the price range. Price ranges for items sold at auction tend to include the buyer's premium and VAT if applicable. The exchange rate used in this edition is 1.87 for $ and 1.5 for €.

CROSS REFERENCES
These boxes direct the reader to where other related items may be found.

WHAT TO PAY
Each collecting area includes a cross-section of items, each one captioned with a brief description of the item including the maker's name, medium, date, measurements and in some instances condition.

Introduction

Kitchen antiques are as popular today if not more so than a decade ago. This is partly because there is plenty of scope for collectors with much that is easily affordable and also because they conjure up a sense of nostalgia as everyone can identify with these familiar household wares. Items are also readily available – car boot sales, yard sales, antiques fairs, charity shops, auctions and ebay are all equally good sources.

There are plenty of pieces of interest and areas which can be focused on – from objects originally made for dairy, scullery and baking purposes to those which are more decorative such as tableware and novelty tins. Much of the appeal for kitchenware is that the items can have a variety of uses. For example bread boards are very decorative and can be used as place mats or even for cutting bread on – these are particularly popular in the United States and Japan, although the Japanese market has slowed down, especially because of the number of reproductions appearing. Items that have unusual labels or colours always command a premium. Cornish Ware jars with labels for everyday ingredients like rice, sugar and currants still only reach around £40/€60/$75 but those printed with unusual contents like coconut, starch or dried fruit can still make up to £400/€600/$750 with the serious collector.

Many antique kitchenware items can still be used today, although it is always important to check the materials from which they are made conform to current safety standards as some items are no longer suitable – those containing lead for example. Some larger and more unusual items still have a market, although not necessarily the one they were intended for originally. Some items such as mangles, which can be very ornate, are given a new lease of life in the garden. Milk churns are also very popular for the garden today, and the later aluminium churns are often painted.

As with antiques and collectables in general the good quality items continue to hold their value (a rare Huntley and Palmer's delivery lorry tin reached £2,700/€4,050/$5,000 in it's original box at auction), however the more ordinary items are struggling and prices are even falling. The American market is still managing to hold its own, however Japanese buyers are notably absent across the board.

The buying and selling of antiques and collectables has changed dramatically in recent times due to the continued growth in the use of home computers. People are finding it much easier, convenient and rewarding to shop online at home, on the auction site ebay for example, than visit their local antiques centre or favourite weekend antiques fairs, as each evening one can view thousands of items from all over the globe and participate in a live auction with just a click of one's mouse. A particularly sought after biscuit tin in the form of a golf bag may struggle to reach £350/€530/$650 in a top London auction room, or remain unsold on the shelf of a stall in the prestigious Portobello Road Market, but they regularly reach £500+/€750/$1,000+ online, week in, week out!

what to look for

Media & Materials

The materials and methods of manufacture used to make an object can tell us a lot about its history and can also help to date it and to assess its value. This is as true for kitchenware as for anything else and the following pages describe some of the materials you are most likely to encounter.

Aluminium

Although aluminium is a common element, its existence was not established until 1808. In 1825 Hans Christian Oersted of Denmark produced the first small quantities of this metal. It was considered a precious metal until advances in technology in the late 19thC made mass production possible. From then on, it was widely used to make domestic hollow ware and was especially popular in North America. Its main advantage was that it was lighter and more versatile than the cast-iron pans it replaced.

Bakelite

Bakelite is an early form of plastic and was invented by Leo Baekeland in 1909. It was used for a variety of domestic objects. In the kitchen, its heat-resistant properties made it particularly useful for handles. It was seldom used in items associated with food preparation because it tended to give off an unpleasant smell and taint food. Bakelite often becomes very brittle with age. Bakelite was only made in dark colours, such as brown, red, or green and it is very desirable today.

Brass

An alloy of copper and zinc, the first brass foundries in Europe appeared in medieval times. Until the 18thC, "brass" was also used to describe what is now known as bronze (an alloy of copper and tin). Advances in technology in the 19thC made mass production possible and brass became more widely available. Victorian brass preserving pans are much sought after today and can be expensive. As well as its use in such pans, brass was also used for ladles, colanders, forks, graters, and especially – along with cast iron – in weights for scales. Beware of any metalwork that shows signs of soldering or repairs. Antique brass acquires a mellow, coppery-brass colour and overpolishing can lead to small holes, which reduce the value.

Cast Iron

Along with steel, this material was commonly used in the 19thC for pots and pans, before being superseded by aluminium in the 20thC. From about 1840, cast-iron items were available with enamelled surfaces. It was also used for a range of objects from egg stands to trivets. Cast-iron objects were traditionally made by pouring molten iron into a mould made in wet sand, contained in a wooden frame. This material is not as indestructible as is often supposed and can be quite brittle, so do take care.

Copper

Its excellent conduction of heat is one of the properties that has made copper a popular material for pans and kettles. Its big disadvantage is that copper reacts with acidic food, unless it is tinned on the inside. Copper pans were phased out in the early 20thC as they were costly and time-consuming to produce, expensive to buy, and impractical for the modern kitchen. The use of metal utensils with copper pans can damage the tinning. There should be evidence of tinning on the inside and tinning is essential if an item is to be used. Copper kettles were made in vast numbers and can still be bought quite cheaply.

Copper jelly moulds were widely used in middle and upper-class households in the 19thC and they were produced in large numbers and many different designs. This reflected the increasing emphasis on the presentation of food at the time.

Earthenware

Earthenware is a type of pottery that is made with porous clay. It therefore requires a sealant glaze, unlike porcelain or stoneware. Colours can vary according to the colour of the clay and the metal oxide content.

Enamel

Enamel is coloured glass that is applied, in paste form, to metal, ceramic, or glass and then fired for decorative effect. Enamelled kitchenware includes bread bins and storage containers, saucepans, and pie plates.

Ironstone

Charles James Mason patented ironstone, a type of stoneware, in 1813. Slag from iron furnaces is added to the clay, hence the name. The resulting ware is toughened and hardened by this process.

Lead Glaze

A clear glaze generally composed of silicaeous sand, salt, soda, and potash, mixed with a lead component such as litharge (lead monoxide). It is an old process; the earliest British lead-glazed pottery dates back to the 10thC. Lead glaze fires at less than 1,200°C (2,190°F) and is very glossy, smooth, and transparent. Potentially hazardous to workers and users, it was replaced by boric acid in the 19thC. Some glazes still contain lead oxide, but within safe limits.

Plastic

Cheap and durable, plastic began to dominate the kitchenware industry by the middle of the 20thC and is still widely used today. Many items are small and reasonably priced, so this is a good area for those starting a collection. Condition is very important; avoid scratched and faded items. Examples from the 1950s are especially collectible. Objects are often marked on the base, typically with the maker's name, place of manufacture, and perhaps a model number. Plastic is generally not as indestructible as is often supposed, however. Harder forms of plastic can be brittle and can crack easily, and plastics can become brittle and sticky with age.

Pyrex

Pyrex is a type of glass that can withstand extremes of temperature and chemical attack. It was developed in the USA during WWI. Pyrex jugs are easily identified because the name is impressed into the base. Early Pyrex is generally cloudy in appearance.

Salt Glaze

Used for covering stonewares, salt glaze is a thinly-applied glaze. Salt is added to the hot kiln at the highest temperature during the firing process; it then fuses with the clay to create a glassy surface. Iron impurities present

in many stoneware clays cause most salt-glazed stonewares to be brown in colour. Red lead was sometimes added with the salt to make the glaze glassier in appearance. The glaze may have a slightly pitted surface, an effect known as "orange peel".

Slip

A creamy mix of clay and water, used to decorate pottery and also for slip casting and sprigged wares. Another type of decoration, known as marbling, could be achieved by partly mixing two different-coloured slips while they were still in a fairly liquid state. Pitchers and pie plates were often decorated using this method.

Stainless Steel

This highly practical form of steel was developed in 1910 and incorporates other metals, notably chromium, to prevent rust. It was first used for making cookware and other kitchen utensils in the 1920s and quickly became the favoured metal for cutlery. Not only is it resistant to rust, but it also does not react to acids in food and is therefore safe to use.

Stoneware

Stoneware is a type of ceramic that is impervious to liquids. It is fired at a higher temperature than earthenware. Its finish can range from rough and grainy through to silky smooth, if polished. Stoneware was made in large quantities and the most desirable items are generally those with the most unusual decoration.

Terracotta

Terrcotta is a lightly-fired red earthenware, usually unglazed, which takes its name from the Italian for "cooked earth".

Tinware

Tin has been widely available in Europe and North America since the mid-19thC. In North America, it was initially expensive and highly prized. Old baking tins can still be used today, but they should never be left to soak afterwards because they are prone to rust. Dry your tinware thoroughly and store items in a dry place.

Wood

One of our oldest manufacturing materials, wood has long been a popular choice for kitchenware from bread bins to spoons as well as handles for saucepans and various utensils. Everything from pine, sycamore, and teak to beech, ash, and olive has been used. Advantages include cheapness and availability, but a major disadvantage is its vulnerability to rot and insect damage. Small objects in wood, especially hardwoods such as box, are known as treen and are collected in their own right. Identification and dating of wooden items can sometimes be difficult, not least because many do not bear a maker's name, although patination can be a guide to age.

Care & Display

Most kitchenware is fairly robust – after all, many objects were expected to put up with heavy use, exposure to acids in food and fluctuations in temperature. A lot of kitchenware can be, and sometimes is, used today and many collectors consider that using old kitchenware is part of the pleasure of owning it. However, old kitchenware in general will need more looking after than its modern equivalent.

As a general rule, ceramics and glass can be safely washed in warm water and a little washing-up liquid. Avoid scourers or abrasives and avoid using the dishwasher; old kitchenware was not designed with dishwashers in mind. Ferrous metals are vulnerable to rust, so remember this if you need to wash metal items. They must not only be dried thoroughly, but they must also never be stored in a damp place. There is usually no need to soak items for any length

of time and this is best avoided anyway, especially with tinware and also items made of wood.

Most objects benefit from a stable environment, with low humidity. Exposure to strong sunlight can cause damage, especially fading, but the biggest danger to items such as ceramics and glass comes from breakage so take care and avoid picking up delicate objects by the handle.

If an item has suffered damage and you are tempted to try to repair it yourself, consider its value

and the likely effect of a botched job. Some things can be repaired quite simply, but if you are in any doubt whatsoever, always consult an expert.

How you wish to display your kitchenware is entirely a matter of personal taste. However, you may want to consider using them as part of an overall decorative theme. If your kitchen is in an appropriate style, then you could display them there, even if you have no intention of using them.

Major Makers

Aluminium Goods Manufacturing Co.
Established in 1909 and active today. Possibly one of the earliest North American kitchenware makers still in existence.

Ash Bros. & Heaton Ltd.
Makers of copper kitchen moulds in the 19thC.

Baldwin
19thC manufacturers of coffee grinders, based in Stourport, Worcestershire.

Betterwear
Founded in 1929, they were early pioneers of doorstep selling, producing various household items and gadgets. Still active as Betterwear UK Ltd., based in Birmingham.

Bird's
Major manufacturers of convenience foods, established in 1837 by Alfred Bird. The company is best known for their jellies and custards.

Joseph Bourne & Son
Established in 1812 and still going today. They are among Britain's major stoneware producers and are best known for their Denbyware range of household pottery.

Central States Manufacturing Co.
Based in St. Louis, USA, makers of the Speedo Super Juicers. Acquired by the Dazey Churn and Manufacturing Company in the 1930s, the name was changed to the Dazey Corporation and, in 1945, it became a subsidiary of Landers, Frary, and Clark.

Crown Merton
Producers of high-quality aluminium hollow ware from the 1920s to the 1950s.

Daleware
Trade name for a brand of aluminium hollow ware made between 1910 and the 1950s. The production of hollow ware was halted during WWII in favour of ammunition production.

Doulton & Co.
Founded in 1835 in Lambeth, south London, producing stoneglazed

sewage pipes, sanitary, and kitchenware. Production expanded to include terracotta sculpture from the turn of the century onwards. In 1902, the company was renamed Royal Doulton.

The Dover Stamping Company
Based in Boston, Massachusetts, they manufactured tin goods, cookie cutters, and the famous Dover Egg Beater after the American Civil War. They do not appear to be in business today.

Ecko
Manufacturers of baking pans. Ecko is still in business in the USA.

Enterprise Manufacturing Co.
Based in Philadelphia in the late 19thC they produced a range of gadgets including meat choppers, sausage stuffers, lard pressers, and raisin seeders.

H. J. Green & Co. Ltd.
Grocers' suppliers based in Brighton, Sussex from 1910 to 1960. They sold a range of cooking equipment embossed with the company name.

T. G. Green & Co.

Makers of household pottery since the 1860s, they are best known for their Cornish Ware series of blue-and-white striped pottery. Thomas Goodwin Green bought the pottery in 1864 and in 1897 the company was sold to Cloverleaf, part of the Tootal organisation.

Guardian Frigerator Company

Manufacturers of domestic refrigerators in North America since c1919, this company went on to become the Frigidaire Corporation.

Joblings

One of the largest mineral merchants and suppliers of glass-making chemicals in the north of England. From 1921 onwards, the company owned the sole rights to manufacture Pyrex products throughout the British Empire, apart from those made in Canada.

Kenrick

Archibald Kenrick established an iron foundry in 1815, specializing in a wide range of household products. Most famous for coffee grinders, patented in 1815 and widely copied by other makers throughout the 19thC, the firm later became Kenrick & Sons.

The Kreamer Company

Manufacturers of tin goods, kitchenware such as moulds, cookie cutters, and baking pans. They are no longer in business.

Lee & Wilkes

Major producers of kitchen moulds, established as Birch & Villers in 1780, becoming Villers & Wilkes in 1818. The firm joined with Charles Lee in 1907 to become Lee & Wilkes.

Lovatt's

Established in Nottingham in 1895, major British manufacturers of earthenware pottery.

Made Rite

Producers of a wide range of inexpensive kitchen gadgets in the 1950s, based in London and Blackpool. Called themselves "domestic equipment specialists" producing "kitchen aids for the modern housewife".

Meredith & Drew Ltd.

Based in Scotland, the leading biscuit makers from the late 19thC to the mid-20thC. In the 1940s they joined McVitie's, a division of United Biscuits. Provided grocery shops with biscuit stands, cake stands, and glass plates on which to advertise their products.

Nutbrown

Established in Blackpool in 1927 and dissolved in 1988, Nutbrown was the trademark of a major British kitchen gadget company. The trade name Nutbrown is now owned by Friskars UK Ltd.

Pride-O-Home

Pride-O-Home was the promotional slogan for Homepride, one of Britain's leading brands of flour. Established in the 1920s, Homepride, owned by Fosters, were originally called Tommy Homepride Mills, based in Cambridge, Coventry, and Birkenhead. Between 1922 and 1923, Homepride produced a range of promotional kitchenware all marked with the "Pride-O-Home" slogan. Fosters were taken over by Spillers in 1949, becoming Dalgety-Spillers Food Ltd. in the 1960s.

Platers & Stampers

Based in Burnley, Lancashire from the 1910s to the 1950s, Platers & Stampers are best known for the production of the Skyline range of utensils and gadgets, although they also made bathroom fittings and other household items.

Robertson's

One of Britain's most famous manufacturers of preserves and jams. Set up by James Robertson, a grocer, in the 1860s. Producing a wide range of jams, preserves, and mincemeat, they became virtually synonymous with their Golly trademark, introduced in 1910.

Salter

Leading makers of weighing scales since 1760.

Skyline

A brand name for the American Prestige Company, distributed through Prestige of England and still sold today through the Prestige Group UK plc.

Smith's Potato Crisps Ltd.

Established in 1920 by Frank Smith, it has become one of Britain's most successful potato crisps manufacturers.

Tala

Trade name of Taylor, Law, & Co. Ltd., established in the late 1890s, originally in Birmingham and later at Stourbridge. Major manufacturers of good-quality tin gadgets and utensils and fierce rivals to Nutbrown. The Tala name is today used by George East Housewares.

Glossary

Baller (**Melon Baller** in the USA)
A small tool used for making spherical shapes of fruit.

Beater
North American term for a rotary whisk.

Brandreth
An early implement for holding baking pots just off the direct heat of the fire. Later replaced by trivets.

Crimper *see* **Jigger**

Double Boiler *see* **Porringer**

Flour Dredger
A canister-shaped container for flour. It dredges (sprinkles) the flour when shaken upside down.

Flour Sifter
A cap with a mesh across the base. Flour is sifted (to remove the coarse particles) by turning a handle that moves revolving blades through the flour. The sifted flour then passes through the mesh base.

Forcer (**Pastry Bag** in the USA)
A cloth bag used to make meringues or decorative mounds of creamed potatoes in the 19thC. From the late 1800s, decorative-edged nozzles were available. The bag was triangular with the point cut off to accommodate the nozzle.

Frosting Tube *see* **Syringe (icing)**

Grater *see* **Rasp**

Graniteware
North American term for enamelware.

Griddle
A flat sheet of iron with a handle, on which to cook. Dating from Roman times, griddles were originally made from slate or sandstone.

Jagger *see* **Jigger**

Jigger or **Crimper** (**Jagger** in the USA) Tool that adds attractive decorated edges to pastry.

Melon Baller *see* **Baller**

Pancheon
A deep, usually earthenware, bowl traditionally used for mixing and rising yeast dough.

Parer (also known as **Peeler**)
A tool for peeling apples.

Pastry Bag *see* **Forcer**

Peeler *see* **Parer**

Pie Funnel or **Cup**
Sometimes in the form of a blackbird, this is placed in the centre of a pie dish and pokes up through the pastry to support the pie and let out steam. In the USA, pie funnels and cups are known as pie birds, whatever their shape.

Poacher (egg)
A shallow pan divided into four sections with a handle and cover. Individual cups fit into the holed sections, the base of the cup dropping into water in the shallow pan. The cups should be greased to allow the eggs to slip out when set.

Porringer (**Double Boiler** in the USA)
A double saucepan, mostly used for making custards, sauces, and porridge.

Rasp (**Grater** in the USA)
A device used for scraping the burnt bottoms of loaves and also for making breadcrumbs.

Reamer
The North American term for any domed fruit juice squeezer.

Redware
A type of American clay pottery that turns red-brown when fired.

Ricer
A device for turning mashed potato into rice-shaped grains.

Sieve *see* **Tamis**

Spurtle
A traditional Scottish kitchen utensil used for stirring porridge.

Squeezer
British term for all fruit juicers. In North America, this term is used for a juicer with hinged arms.

Strainer *see* **Tamis**

Syringe (icing) (**Frosting Tube** in the USA)
A metal tube with a plunger inside. A wide selection of screw-on nozzles are available, enabling delicate and intricate designs to be created. Primarily used for icing and still in production today.

Tamis (also **Strainer** or **Sieve** in the USA)
Another term for a cook's sieve, with either a hair, wire, or nylon base. Also known as a drum sieve.

Toasting Fork
A large fork in varying designs. Bread or crumpet is pierced by the prongs (tines) and held in front of an open fire until toasted brown.

Trimmer *see* **Jigger**

Trivet
A three-legged stand on which to rest a pan, cooking pot, or kettle.

Storage

Food has traditionally been stored in containers made from whichever material was both available and convenient, such as wood, pottery, and cloth. From the 19thC onwards, storage jars were mass-produced in various sizes to suit their contents. Enamelled metal jars were common too; they could be bought plain from a hardware store and the shopkeeper would stencil on the desired name such as "flour" or "tea" for a small charge. Enamel bread bins (see p.18) and flour bins were especially popular in Britain and designs have altered very little since.

Food safes – wooden cupboards for storing food – were widely used until the introduction of refrigerators in the mid-20thC. Wealthier houses had cool, stone-flagged walk-in larders where all kinds of food could be stored including meat, game, and fish.

Other types of storage included wirework baskets and containers (see p.29) used for carrying items such as fish, bottles, or vegetables and for storing eggs or fruit. They were often beautifully made by hand from twisted wire, but beware of lesser-quality modern reproductions. Also be aware that wirework can be artificially aged.

Biscuit Barrels

The biscuit has a long history, going back at least as far as Ancient Rome. The word biscuit itself comes from the Latin and means "twice baked". For centuries, biscuits were produced on a small scale, by local bakers or in the home. The Industrial Revolution, with its emphasis on the factory system and mass production methods, affected biscuits as it did most things and by the end of the 19thC, biscuits were being mass-produced by large commercial concerns. Biscuits were still a luxury item until well into the 20thC and were mostly consumed by the middle and upper classes who could afford such treats.

Biscuits were originally made in small quantities, often for specific occasions such as afternoon tea parties, so storage was not a problem. As large bakeries began to dominate the market, so they started to sell their wares in attractive tins, which could then be re-used for other storage. Containers that were specifically designed to store biscuits soon found a ready market and are just as popular today, particularly if their design typifies a particular era.

MATERIALS

Biscuit barrels were and still are made from a variety of materials including wood, silver, glass, and ceramics. Sometimes they are made from a combination, such as a glass barrel with a silver or silver plate lid and handle. (See p.88–90.)

• Condition Check that the handle, if present, is firmly attached. Ceramic or glass examples should be examined for signs of chips and tins for rust. All of these will affect value.

POTTERIES

Such was their popularity that most potteries have included biscuit barrels in their range at some point. Famous names including Wedgwood, Crown Devon, Moorcroft, Maling, and Royal Doulton have all made them in various designs and patterns.

• Collecting Collectors interested in biscuit containers as kitchenalia face competition from dedicated collectors of the products of these and various other factories.

Similarly, Whitefriars Glass made biscuit barrels, but there are many keen collectors of Whitefriars who seek out products of this factory.

DESIGN

Biscuit barrels have tended to follow design trends of the era and/or to reflect popular subject matter of the time. Scenes of the British Empire were popular in the 19thC and early 20thC, Art Nouveau styles were popular in the early 20thC, and Deco designs in the 30s.

• **Clarice Cliff** This leading ceramics designer of the Art Deco era included biscuit barrels in her range of pottery – they command high prices and are snapped up by Clarice Cliff enthusiasts.

• **Colours** The reds and oranges favoured by Clarice Cliff were again in vogue in the 60s, often used in stylized flower decoration to reflect the "flower power" era.

THE 1950S

In Britain, biscuits had still been available in WWII, though fewer varieties were available. The end of rationing in the 50s and increasing prosperity saw an enthusiasm for biscuits, along with many other non-essentials. The growth of television in the post-war era saw biscuits taking an important place as a family snack to accompany an

evening's viewing. The biscuit barrel shown below left, which is stamped "Torquay Devon Pottery Ltd." on its base, is a typical late 1950s/early 1960s design. The rubber ring on the flat wooden lid of this container would keep biscuits fresh for weeks.

ADVERTISING

Containers for biscuits have always been deemed suitable for advertising purposes. The biscuit jar shown above dates from the 1920s and was made to promote the firm of Meredith & Drew Ltd. Based in Scotland, the firm operated from the 1890s to the 1940s, when they joined United Biscuits. This glass jar would have been kept full of

biscuits and placed on a shop counter to promote them.

TINS

While containers for biscuits were made in various materials, tins are a collecting field in their own right. Quality British tins are particularly desirable.

• **Decoration** Advances in technology in the 19thC, especially the development of chromolithography, allowed manufacturers to print attractive designs that made them appealing enough to be kept.

• **Novelties** Novelty biscuit tins were produced towards the end of the 19thC and into the 20thC in various forms, including boats, buses, or even longcase clocks. Those made in the form of modes of transport were especially suitable as toys and were intended to be played with after the biscuits had been consumed. Some were extremely elaborate and would have been aimed at the top end of the market. Today, some of the rarer examples can fetch four-figure sums.

• **Makers** Several manufacturers including Crawfords, Carr's, and Peek Frean made novelty tins, but Huntley & Palmers were especially prolific and are much sought after.

Bread Bins

Bread was once commonly stored in large wooden frames, known as "bread flakes", which were suspended from the ceiling. This method, thought to date from the Middle Ages, had the advantage of keeping bread off the floor and away from rats and mice. By the mid-19thC earthenware crocks with lids were introduced (see p.91), as well as bins made from tinplate and enamelled iron. By the late 19thC, stoneware bread crocks were produced and as commercially-

made bread bins became popular in the 20thC, so enamelled iron bread bins in various colours and designs were introduced. Some bread bins were made as items in their own right, but some were made as part of a series of storage containers of different sizes, which might be labelled with its contents. Bread bins are always popular as they look attractive in a "country" kitchen style and they will appeal to decorators as well as more serious collectors.

VENTILATION

Ventilation is always important as air helps to keep bread fresh for longer. Early earthenware bread crocks had high domed earthenware covers with strap handles and ventilation holes beneath. Surprisingly, from the 1950s, bread bins were often made without the holes. As a result, bread would go mouldy in just a few days, especially when in plastic wrappers, in which bread would "sweat".

Collectibility

• Coloured bread bins are more desirable – the more unusual the colour, the higher the price. Green was a favourite 1930s colour.
• Labelled kitchenware of any kind is always more appealing. Sometimes, bread bins have unusual styles of lettering for the period and this can make them more interesting and desirable.

CONDITION

• **Ceramic bins** have often suffered chips or cracks, which can seriously affect the value. Some damage may be acceptable if the item is particularly interesting or rare.
• **Enamel bread bins** These are also prone to chips though this is less likely to affect value quite as much as long as it is not too severe. It is quite difficult to find antique enamel that has not been chipped in some way if it has been used. The area around the lid is particularly prone to damage, caused by the constant opening and replacing of the lid. If there are no chips inside enamel bins can still be used.
• **Lids** A missing lid can be a major problem, as replacements can be hard to come by. An example is the "Improved Bread Pan" shown above, produced by Doulton & Co.

from the 1880s and marked accordingly. It had a perforated steel lid, which is sometimes missing and not easily replaced. This is such an interesting example, however, that it is still desirable even without a lid. Occasionally, they are stamped with the name of the shop where they were bought, which adds further interest.

DOULTON & CO

Doulton & Co. was founded in 1835 in south London, and in 1902 received permission to change their name to Royal Doulton. The company, which continues to this day, produced many bread bins and is one of the most celebrated British ceramics firms.

EUROPE

Continental bread bins sometimes have distinctive designs that were not seen in Britain. A particularly robust form of bread bin (below) was developed in both Holland and Germany from the 1890s to the 1940s, and is still widely used in Holland today. As well as the colours shown, they were also produced in green and red. The interiors are white and most have a

nickel steel latch and ventilating holes at the back of the box. Later examples, from the 1950s onwards, do not have a carrying handle. The deep blue colour of the 1930s box on the right is unusual, making it especially desirable.

ADVERTISING

Some food manufacturers recognized the potential of bread bins for bringing advertising into the consumer's kitchen.
• **Homepride** "Pride-O-Home" was the slogan used by Homepride, a brand of the flour producers Fosters. Originally known as Tommy Homepride Mills, Homepride had factories in Cambridge, Coventry, and Birkenhead. The "Pride-O-Home" slogan appeared on bins produced in painted tin between 1922 and 1923 (as below); they are now highly collectible.

CARE & STORAGE

Care and storage is not a problem with most bread bins. They can simply be wiped clean with a damp cloth and perhaps a little mild detergent. Tinplate or enamelled iron bins that have suffered chips should be kept in a dry place to avoid the dangers of rust. Ceramic or enamelled bread bins that have been chipped should ideally not be used for reasons of hygiene. If you do plan to use your bread bin, remember that it must be washed out regularly as even the smallest breadcrumbs will attract mould.

Canisters & Jars

Canisters are often made of metal, but they can be made out of any material such as glass or ceramics and are associated with the storage of dry goods, as opposed to preserves, honey, or other foodstuffs. They are usually cylindrical, but many containers that are not are also sometimes referred to as canisters. Canisters often come in sets, in different sizes to suit their various contents and may or may not be labelled in some way, either with the full name or simply the initial of the contents. (See pp.92–97.)

COLOURS

In the 1950s, red and white were among the most popular colours for kitchenware. Shown above is a set of American canisters sold under the name of Gay Ware. Gay (in its original sense) was a popular word at the time and was used in many advertisements and trade names. These graduated canisters could be placed inside each other, rather like Russian dolls, when not in use.

• **Rarity** Complete sets of canisters like this Gay Ware example are rare.

THE 1960S

The rise of the hippy culture and its "flower power" design themes, were reflected in kitchenware as in many other things. The ceramic canisters shown below are decorated with an interpretation of the "Carnaby daisy", inspired by the Mary Quant motif.

• **Colours** Red and orange were the most popular colours.

• **Typography** The lower case lettering used was popular at the time and recalls the style used by Conran for Habitat.

COLLECTIBILITY

French enamel canisters are especially desirable because of the many colours and shapes available.

MAKERS

T. G. Green & Co. first produced the very collectible Cornish Ware in the 1930s. The firm had been making household pottery since 1864. The blue-and-white banded ware as shown below right has become very familiar and is avidly collected. The range includes all kinds of storage jars as well as jugs, teapots, and even rolling pins. Interest has been increasing in recent years and not only does it look like a sound investment, but it is quite usable as well as being decorative.

• **Colours** Blue is by far the most common, but gold, yellow, and red are also known. Red is the most rare. Other colours, such as black and green, were experimented with.

• **Labelled wares** in blue and white were made for many different types of contents. Unusual wording, such as Granulated Sugar, or Brown Sugar, sell for higher prices.

• **Fakes** There have been cases of rub-down transfer-type lettering being added to plain items to increase their value. This is usually obvious on close examination. Previously unknown lettered jars do turn up from time to time and unusual jars can fetch high prices. This, coupled with a recent rise in values, encourages fakers. Many reproductions exist, so take care.

• **Marks** Most Cornish Ware is marked with a backstamp (some small early pieces were unmarked), and these may also be faked. In the late 1920s, a shield mark was introduced and used until the late 1960s, mostly in green, but sometimes black. The other most familiar marks are a church and the "circular church mark", with the name of the company circling the church logo. The church marks were used from the 1930s to 1962.

Oils, Herbs & Spices

The use of oils, herbs, and spices in cooking has a very long history. They are known to have been used in Roman times in the preparation of both food and medicines. The Romans introduced many herbs to Britain, which is why many herbs grown in Britain and northern Europe today are of Mediterranean origin.

By the Middle Ages, herbs were grown and used extensively to add flavour to food, or to disguise the taste of tainted meat and game. Favourites included sage, parsley, fennel, mint, and garlic. Herbs would typically be placed in a muslin bag and used as a bouquet garni, being added to soups and stews as they were cooked. Because herbs were widely available and were usually either picked straight from the garden or dried hanging in bunches, storage jars were not necessary.

By the 19thC, herbs had fallen out of fashion in the kitchen across much of northern Europe. In the 20thC, the famous British cook and writer Elizabeth David played an important role in restoring the popularity of herbs after WWII with her hugely successful travel cookery books (see p.84). These included *Mediterranean Food* and *French Country Cooking*, published in the 1950s. Her evocative descriptions of the way herbs were used in Continental cuisine struck a chord with a population recovering from rationing.

SPICES

Spices were much valued in centuries past and the first special containers for spices were made in the 17thC. They were often made in the form of wooden cabinets with drawers or small chests that stood on a table or hung on a wall.

• **Spice boxes** During the 18th and early 19thC these were made of painted tin and divided into compartments for the different spices (see p.98). Ginger, cinnamon, cloves, pepper, bay leaves, and allspice are some of spices known to have been included. They came complete with a small grater, which is often missing and should be present to achieve maximum value.

• **Spice towers** These are small, round boxes designed to stack on top of each other (see p.98). They became popular in the first half of the 19thC and are very collectible today. They often had paper labels to identify the contents of each box and these labels are often missing. If present, they will increase the value.

• **Combinations** This Dutch hand-painted herb and spice storage rack (below) was made from the late 1950s to the early 1960s and illustrates how attitudes changed. At one time, herbs and spices would have been stored separately, but visual appeal became a priority.

• **Labelling** The range of spices to choose from is vast and makers often made eccentric choices in their labelling of spice containers. The Dutch storage rack illustrated offers a curious selection; salt and pepper seems logical enough, but it is difficult to understand why only cloves and cinnamon should have been chosen to complete the set. A spice cabinet dating from the 1840s has drawers labelled "Lemon" and "Laurel" – both unusual choices, adding interest for the collector.

SETS

All of the containers in a set must be present to achieve maximum value. The attractive tin shown over the page was made c1860 and contains four black japanned tin spice containers and a nutmeg grater, neatly fitting into different compartments. Individual containers are often missing, so make sure they are all original and not replacements and that the lids fit snugly. The pots in these sets were often painted in other colours, including red.

LIDS

Metal lids were sometimes used on glass spice jars that were designed to be kept in the inside rack of a kitchen cabinet door. The lids screw

If tin boxes have been used without their liners, they are likely to have corroded through contact with salt and damp; this will always reduce the value.

onto the jars and had a wax-covered card liner under the lid for a closer seal. If the disc is missing, a double sheet of greaseproof paper cut to size can be used instead.
• **Condition** Rust is always a risk with such jars in the humidity of a kitchen, and will lower the value.

SALT
Salt is an important ingredient for flavouring and preserving food. It was a valuable commodity in times past and great care was taken to store it properly. Damp is the greatest threat to salt, so traditionally salt jars would be kept by the hearth and they therefore usually have hanging hooks.

MATERIALS
• **Earthenware** Salt jars made in this were popular in 19thC Europe.
• **Wood** This was the preferred choice in the USA. Most American salt jars in wood were plain in design, apart from those made by Dutch settlers in Pennsylvania, which were always elaborately carved and painted. British wooden salt jars are less common and were usually made in oak. Rarely elaborate or carved, the earliest ones were made with leather hinges to avoid corrosion.
• **Glass** This cannot be corroded by salt, so is an ideal material for storage. All glass kitchenware should be inspected for chips and cracks.
• **Pottery, china, enamel** These were the norm by the 20thC.

• **Tin** Painted tin salt boxes can be very attractive but are rarely found in good condition. Wooden liners help to prevent corrosion.

IDENTIFICATION
The shape of this curved fruitwood salt barrel helps to identify it as Scottish. English versions were usually square or rectangular. This one was made c1870, but the design was produced until c1910. The use of alternate light and dark woods helps to prevent shrinkage.

CONDITION
Ironically, salt boxes of the 19th/20thC were often made with metal hinges and have therefore suffered irreversible damage such as warping, while others have lost their lids. These factors will affect value.

• **Pig Jars** The reproduction glazed earthenware piece shown below is known as a pig jar (and also as a salt jar or a salt kit). It has white slip trailed decoration and was made in the 1920s as a copy of those made in Sunderland in northern England in the early 19thC. Originally, they fitted into ledges in a fireplace to keep dry. They are possibly named after their pig snout shape, which also made it easy for cooks to reach in for the contents, but some maintain that the name derives from a dense, orange clay, known as "pygg" from which they were originally made. Pig jars were not made outside England, so are rarely found in other countries today.

Packaging

Packaging as we know it today developed during the 19thC, with the development of methods of mass production, distribution, and communication, and the creation of the large food manufacturers. Food would previously be weighed out by the shopkeeper, and pre-packaged goods were initially viewed with suspicion by the grocery trade – probably because some unscrupulous grocers were known to add cheaper (and sometimes inedible or even dangerous) ingredients to make foodstuffs go further.

For the public, pre-packaged food meant peace of mind. Many producers were happy to boast of the purity of their products, and weights and quantities were standardized. Grocers also no longer had to weigh the food.

Most packaging, except decorative tins for example, was thrown away after the contents it stored had been consumed. For this reason, vintage packaging has become collectible and is a popular and growing field.

BRANDS

The 19thC saw the rise of well-known brands such as Bovril, Camp Coffee, Colman's Mustard, Bird's Custard, Robertson's Marmalade, and Lyle's Golden Syrup, and all are collectible.

LOGOS AND COLOURS

Many companies are proud to have kept their logos largely as they were a century or more ago. Radical design changes were comparatively rare because of the growing importance of advertising. It was important for customers to be able to recognize products they had seen advertised.

Brand recognition is important, but most commercial packaging changes regularly as companies try to follow the latest design trends.

Collectors particularly like packaging that is typical of the era in which it was produced.
• **The 1950s** Most goods were sold pre-packed after WWII. Strong colours attracted the attention of the housewife and simplified designs emphasized the name of the brand. The 1950s saw the introduction of much of the now-familiar convenience foods, ranging from the tea bag (introduced by Tetley's in 1953) to the fish finger, introduced by Birdseye in1955. Some products that were originally associated with austerity were re-packaged for a new generation. Powdered potato, known during WWII as "Pom", was renamed "Smash" by Cadbury/Typhoo in 1967, and promoted on television by "Martian" characters.

Care and condition
• **Paper and cardboard** This is particularly vulnerable to mould and rot. It can also be subject to insect attack. It should be kept away from damp and be well ventilated.
• **"Foxing"** These small brown spots that can appear on old paper may be caused by iron deposits from the manufacturing equipment, causing a chemical reaction in the presence of damp.
• **Fading** Direct sunlight bleaches colours, so should be avoided.

Plastic

Plastic is generally thought of as the "wonder material" of the 20thC. Early plastics were, however, in use in the 19thC and were developed partly due to the need to find a suitable substitute for ivory, widely used in billiard balls and piano keys for example. Perhaps the best known example is celluloid, which was originally developed as a potential material for billiard balls. This substance is flammable however, but the 20thC brought more stable forms of plastic.

By the 1950s, plastic was increasingly used in the home, where it became popular because of its flexibility, its affordability, and its associations with the modern world and the advent of the space age. From the 1950s onwards, plastic began to dominate the world of kitchenware. In spite of its reputation however, plastic is by no means indestructible and can deteriorate over time.

CONTAINERS

Plastic was ideal for storage as it would not taint the food and even the largest containers made in plastic would still be lightweight.

ADVERTISING

Because it was cheap and easy to mass-produce, plastic lent itself very well to the world of advertising, novelties, and merchandising. Television advertising came into its own in the 1960s and characters created for advertisements had great potential for merchandising. Some 1970s plastic spice jars feature Fred the flour grader and the Homepride men (see p.5), created in 1964 for a flour advert. In 1969, the company created its first plastic, Fred-shaped flour sifter, made by toy makers Airfix. Over 500,000 figures were sold in Britain, inspiring a wealth of merchandise including a salt and pepper set and spice jars and resulting in a collectors' club, the Friends of Fred.
• **Identification** Check for the Airfix mark on the bottom; this will tell you if it is indeed an early Fred.

DAMAGE

• **Colours** Some plastics can fade in colour over time, especially through exposure to sunlight. This is not unusual, but a badly faded piece will always be worth less than one retaining its original bright colours.
• **Physical damage** Bad scratching or cracks are a problem.

• **Chemical damage** This is far worse – plastic can become brittle and sticky with age, and if it gives off a sweet smell this is likely to be a sign of chemical deterioration. Chemical damage of plastics is irreversible, so any plastic object showing signs of this should be avoided. Some plastics are inherently unstable and will inevitably deteriorate over a long period of time.

CARE

• **If chemical damage** occurs with a plastic object in your collection, keep it away from other plastic items.
• **Keep away** from strong sunlight.
• **Do not use strong chemicals** or abrasives to clean items. A damp cloth should suffice.

Preserves & Ingredients

Storage jars for preserves and cooking ingredients have changed little since they were first commercially produced in the mid-19thC. Although large families would need to store ingredients in large quantities, most larders or pantries could only accommodate medium-sized jars, similar in size to the jam jars produced today. The range of ingredients has not changed much either, with flour, rice, and dried fruit among the most common. Tapioca and sago, however, are examples of ingredients less popular today.

Until WWII, containers were often bought plain locally, and labels for specific foodstuffs would be added at home or stencilled on by the shopkeeper for a small fee. Today, jars with homemade painted lettering are the least valuable, plain jars are more collectible, but it is the jars with the shop-made labels that command the highest prices.

LETTERING

• **Type** Unusual typefaces add interest to an item.
• **Rare labels** Labelled containers for rarer ingredients are also sought after, but some common ingredients rarely have dedicated storage containers. Breadcrumbs, for example, are often used but labelled jars are unusual because they need to be kept stale and crisp, whereas a jar would keep them fresh and moist.
• **Coloured lettering** Green is typical of the early 20thC, but was also popular in the 1930s. Brown

lettering is occasionally found on items such as 1920s flour bins, but the colour was very rarely used at this time, so an example such as that on the left would be valuable.

WOOD

Early English wooden flour barrels, also used to store butter, were produced in large numbers and were sometimes painted. By the 20thC, wooden barrels had been replaced by more durable and hygienic metal and pottery containers.

ENAMEL

Enamel containers were very popular from the 19thC onwards.

Metal flour bins were first used in the 19thC and early Victorian ones were made of enamelled iron, making them very heavy. As is often the case with kitchenware, the more elaborate or unusual examples are more desirable than simpler ones.

• **Practicality** Enamel containers are not always very practical for storage as their lids are not airtight.

• **Lids** The shape of a lid can add interest, for example if it is domed (as above) or has any other unusual features rather than being plain.

• **Large sets** of storage jars are particularly sought after, especially if they include containers for the more unusual ingredients. It is less expensive to buy them individually and build up a set gradually.

and the 1920s. Similar jars with raised white lettering and a pale blue interior were introduced in the 1930s; ones with flat lettering were available in the 1950s. Lids from both periods were self-coloured.

• **Stoneware jars** from late 19th/early 20thC make attractive sets, especially with ribbon design labels (above). They were made from the 1890s to the 1920s and the only way to date them is by looking at the colour carefully in good light. The buff colour became lighter over the years. Look out for ¼lb (100g) spice jars, as these are the most rare, and choose jars with lids.

POTTERY PRESERVE JARS

The jars shown below are all slightly different. The one on the left was made for James Keiller & Sons of Scotland, famous makers of marmalade. Established in 1797, they used this type of jar from 1873 until the late 1950s. The large jar in the centre can hold up to 2lb (900g) of Robertson's mincemeat and on

the right is a Flett & Co.'s apple and plum jam jar (a Scottish grocers).

The two on the right have their original labels, which is more desirable.

IDENTIFICATION

• **Marks** Later examples of the James Keiller & Sons jar can be identified by checking the mark under the crest. The one shown has a "Y", which dates it to pre-1945; jars made from 1945 onwards have an "L".

KILNER JARS

Kilner jars such as above were first launched to the British public in 1861 at the National Exhibition,

DATING

• **Interiors** The inside can provide a useful clue to the date. The one shown on the left of the picture above is self-coloured inside, which dates it from the early 1930s. It would have been bought plain and the lettering applied at home. The one on the right, with a white interior, was made between 1900

a showcase for contemporary designers. Used mainly for preserving fruit, the Kilner jar's main feature was a secure screw-top lid with a rubber ring seal to ensure extra freshness. Later versions included the "improved" Kilner jar, introduced in the late 1940s, whose improvement lay in the jar's ability to keep items fresh for longer.

EUROPE

Pottery dried fruit containers, including hand-painted examples (see right), were made in Austria for export from the late 1950s to the early 1960s. Sweden also produced similar containers during this period. The designs are more typically Scandinavian than Austrian. In both countries, sets could be built up to include jars for other ingredients.

Tea, Coffee & Sugar

Tea was first introduced to Europe and America from China in the 17thC and was initially a luxury product used only by the wealthy. It was stored in locked wooden tea caddies to stop the servants from stealing it.

By the mid-19thC, other countries were exporting tea and so the price came down, making it available to most people. Tea was being bought in larger quantities so larger, purpose-made containers were needed. Tea must be kept dry and away from the light.

From the mid-1850s, coffee was more commonly brewed at home so it too needed storage. Tins, japanned bins, wooden barrels, and sacks were used in both Europe and North America. Pottery, aluminium, and enamel were adopted in Europe after 1900.

Sugar was first imported into Europe and America in the 18thC from the West Indies. It began to replace honey as a sweetener and became an important cooking ingredient, especially in the cities.

• **Chicory** Although a popular drink in France, it is rarely found elsewhere. The roots of the plant are roasted and dried and used either as a coffee substitute or mixed with coffee to make it last longer. Sets of storage jars for coffee, sugar, and chicory were made in France (below) but there was also a fashion for chicory in Britain in the 1930s. This fashion was presumably short-lived, however, as no British chicory containers are known to have been made.

CONDITION

• **Enamel containers** These are not seriously devalued by chips, but the interior must be in perfect condition if it is to be used.

• **Gilt lettering** This rarely survives intact – such items are worth more.

RARE ITEMS

• **Cocoa** As well as for tea and coffee, storage containers were also produced for other drinks, such as cocoa and chocolate powder, from the mid-19thC onwards. Storage tins for cocoa are particularly rare, especially enamel tins from the 1930s like the one shown above.

THE 1960S

Storage jars generally became less imaginative in design from the mid-1960s onwards. By the 1980s, reproductions of early designs became fashionable, but they are not collectible today.

SETS

Tea, coffee, and sugar containers sometimes come in graduating storage sets, along with other items. Sets made in the 1930s, such as that above, are sometimes impractical, as they tended to be too small. However, the Art Deco styles in which they were made make them very attractive to collectors because this period is so popular. Larger graduating sets were made in the 1950s.

Toni Raymond

Among the most collectible of 60s wares is the hand-painted jar by the English potter Toni Raymond (see left) whose pottery was originally founded in Torquay, Devon, in 1951.
• **Marks** Toni Raymond pottery has a distinctive mark on the base, depicting a goose in flight. The wooden lid is attached by a rubber seal for airtight freshness.

Tins

The use of tins for storage is partly the product of the large scale commercial manufacture of food items. The 19thC saw the formation of many of the food companies that survived into the 20thC, some of which survive still. The manufacture of items such as cakes, which would previously have been made at home for almost immediate consumption, led to the need for containers for their storage. In the early part of the 19thC, tins often bore paper labels, though these were usually small as paper was taxed at the time. Advances in lithography then made it possible to print images onto the tins so it was easier and cheaper to produce colourful tins in large quantities. The manufacturers produced them with attractive designs, ensuring that their containers would be kept and re-used. Tins were also made with no particular product in mind, but simply for the storage of cakes, biscuits, confectionery, or whatever.

CONDITION

This is often the deciding factor in determining value. Look for scratches and dents, but also for rust, especially around the seams. If the tin has a hinged lid, check that it opens and shuts smoothly and fits snugly – some have been damaged through wear. Damaged tins can still be worth having, but you should pay accordingly and it must be a really exceptional and rare example.

The cake tin shown below, made from the 1900s to the 1920s, is part of a series of hard-wearing

enamel storage containers and is rarer than the rest of the set, which includes containers for tea, rice, sugar, and sago. The inside is white, which is typical of such containers from this period, and it has raised white lettering. A similar, but darker blue, cake tin with flat lettering was made in the 1950s.

THE 1950S

Painted aluminium cake tins such as

shown above were widely produced throughout the 1950s by firms such as Tala and Wessexware. Biscuit tins were also available as well as a stacking set for both cakes and biscuits, which was made in several different colour combinatiions.

• **Identification** A similar tin to this one was produced in the 1930s, but it is easy to tell them apart as the earlier ones are of painted tin rather than aluminium, they are heavier, and they have a hinged lid.

• **Designs** The selection of tins from the 1950s shown below illustrates some of the design themes that were popular at this time. The "pin up" tin was made for Thornton's toffee; the triangular box contained Huntley & Palmer's Cocktail Snacks. Keiller's "portable radio" (complete with twiddling dial) was designed to contain sweets, and the Rowntree's chocolate tin commemorates Queen Elizabeth's Coronation of 1953. The

pub tin tray at the back is decorated with a variety of popular beer labels.

THE 1960S

The 1960s saw a revival of interest in the Victorian era, which was both satirized and celebrated by the products of Dodo Designs Ltd., who specialized in tinware, giving a Pop slant to Britain's imperial heritage. Products included "Best Tea" tins emblazoned with a Union Flag design onto which was imposed sepia-tinted pictures of Boer War generals.

COLLECTIBILITY

• **Shape** This is important in both pre-war and post-war tins. The more interesting or unusual the shape, the more desirable the tin will be.

• **Images** These add value to a tin; the more decorative, the better.

• **Damage** Condition is crucial and the insides of tin containers need to be rust-free if they are to be re-used for storage.

SMITH'S CRISPS

Potato crisps evolved from a recipe brought over to Britain from France by Carters, a wholesale grocery company in London, and went on to become one of the most popular snacks ever produced. Frank Smith, the manager of Carters, liked the

idea and developed the product for the firm with Mr. Carter, the proprietor. In 1920, Smith branched out and formed his own company, Smith's Potato Crisps Ltd., which went on to become one of Britain's major crisp manufacturers. The Smith's crisps tin shown above was made in the late 1920s. It was intended for larger amounts of crisps and would have been bought for parties and picnics.

OXO

It was in 1899 that the name of Liebig's Extract, invented by the German Justus Liebig, was changed to Oxo. The origin of the name is unclear; legend has it that a dock worker chalked O-X-O on a crate of beef extract to distinguish it from others and the name stuck, but it seems as likely that it was chosen simply as a variation on the word "oxen". From 1910, it was available in cube form and in tins and became popular as an economical food for the poor, but became a staple in many households.

• **Collectibility** Oxo tins are collectible. They were produced in many different designs over several years. Like many manufacturers, special tins were sometimes produced for events such as Coronations and these are sought after by collectors of Royal memorabilia.

• **Rare items** These include a "zoo house" tin, made in the 1920s and printed to resemble a zoo. It came complete with cut out figures of animals, but these are unlikely to have survived.

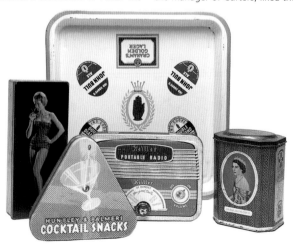

Wirework

Wirework is thought to have been invented by Slovakian tinkers in the 18thC. These nomadic people travelled throughout the Austro-Hungarian Empire and sold everyday objects made from carefully twisted wire. Once they had settled in countries such as Germany, France, and North America, they developed their craft locally, creating new variations in style and producing a wide variety of useful household items. Wirework products included baskets, glass carriers, and even dog muzzles.

Wirework from the 1700s to the early 20thC is beautifully made, with the wire twisted and turned into place. Highly desirable, they can make a wonderful collection.

EUROPE

Metal and wirework were widely used in France from the late 19thC onwards and were made in various shapes, as can be seen in the picture above. The 1930s item on the left is an unusual diamond shape. To the right is a later eight-hooped galvanized steel carrier from the 1930s to the 1940s. This is also an unusual shape and is larger than average. The 1920s four-bottle carrier next to it is a more common design. It has an attractive latticed bottom and is in good condition. The swing wire handle on the 1930s carrier on the right is unusual and its compact shape makes it much sought after, as it saves space.

Wirework was also used to make glass carriers for cafés and bars.

• **Baskets** Baskets such as that shown on the left were commonly used in France by kitchen staff from cafés and hotels to carry fresh fish back from the market. These baskets should always have a wooden handle – beware of a basket that does not, as it is likely that it has been sawn off to make it resemble a shopping basket.
• **Holland** The Dutch used galvanized steel and wire baskets, such as that above, in the potato fields during the 1920s and 1930s. These baskets were designed to help loosen the dirt from the potatoes as they were carried along. Similar baskets were also used in Britain.

VEGETABLE RACKS

Wirework makes an ideal material for use in racks, in particular those with open shelves, as it allows the free circulation of air, discouraging mould and helping keep vegetables fresh. One such example was made in England from galvanized steel wire, produced in several different sizes and also in green.

CONDITION

It is always wise to check for rust on wirework. Not only does it look unsightly, but it can make the wire brittle and prone to snapping when it is being cleaned. Rust also reduces the value of a piece considerably, although some collectors do like pieces to show some signs of wear.

DATING

Later items can easily be identified as the wire is heavier and usually welded or soldered together. Examples from the late 1930s are far less valuable than earlier pieces.

FAKES

Some wirework has been artificially aged. The clue is in the patina of the wire, which will not have the same depth of colour as earlier pieces.

Dairy

In the 19thC many families in the country kept a cow or two for their own dairy produce, which would be made in a dairy that was often adjacent to the house. Any surplus would be sold at the local market.

When the butter had been made and patted into shape, it was marked with special motifs, either using a carved stamp or rolling a roller over it to produce attractive designs.

Local farmers also delivered milk and cream to local homes in a handcart. As cities and towns grew, so a more sophisticated system for milk delivery was developed. By the late 19thC large dairies were established, such as the Express Dairy in Britain, which were able to deliver dairy produce every day.

Butter and cream were made at home in Britain until the 1950s, but cheese was usually bought from local grocers and markets. Interestingly, in continental Europe, there has never been a tradition of delivering dairy produce to the door.

Butter

Butter is made by agitating cream until it thickens. In the 19thC, on farms where butter was made in large quantities and sold at market, various types of rocker-action churns were used in the dairy. The simplest was made of wood, shaped like a child's cradle, and rested on carved rockers, while larger ones worked by means of a large wheel driven by a small dog or by water power from a nearby stream.

Once made, the butter was shaped into a slab (usually 1lb/450g in weight), using wooden butter pats dipped in warm water.

Curlers are used to shape butter into attractive individual curls by dipping the end into hot water and drawing it along the length of the slab. In the 19thC they were typically homemade out of horn or wood, but by the 20thC they were mass produced in metal. Butter ballers work in the same way.

Domestic butter-making equipment was first used in the 1890s in North America and was available in Europe by the early 20thC. Home butter-making remained popular until the 1950s, when most people preferred to buy their butter from the grocer.

By the 1930s, butter-making equipment had become quite advanced. The butter churn shown here features an unusual egg-shaped attachment on the lid. It is designed to allow air into the jar when the handle is turned.

BUTTER STAMPS & MOULDS
Traditionally, it was popular to decorate butter with attractive designs. Butter stamps, often made from sycamore, were more commonly used than moulds; they acted as a trademark when surplus butter was sold at the market, distinguishing it from the produce

of other farms. (See pp.127–134.)

• **Designs** Farm animals, crops, and plants found on farms were popular subjects. Stamps carved with a thistle and a rose are popular among collectors. The combination refers to the 1503 marriage of King James IV of Scotland to Margaret Tudor of England. The more detailed and unusual the print, the more sought-after the item.

• **Heart pattern designs** These are keenly collected in America.

• **Rarities** Other animal and bird stamps are relatively rare and therefore tend to be more valuable.

• **Collecting** Butter stamps' small

size makes them ideal for collectors with limited display space.

BUTTER CROCKS

Keeping butter cool was a major challenge in the days before refrigerators and many of the methods used were quite ingenious. Crocks are ceramic containers that would help to keep any food at a low temperature, partly by being stored somewhere cool. Butter crocks come in various sizes and were often transfer-printed with designs, often featuring the name of the place where the butter was sold. They are much sought after.
• **Stoneware** This was a favoured material for storing dairy products because it was thick and strong and so helped to keep the contents cool.

Cheese was often stored in stoneware jars in the home and in shops. Those bearing the name of a retailer are of particular interest.

COOLERS

This French butter cooler dates from the 1920s. The cover is hollow inside and has two holes at the top via which cold water is poured to keep the butter cool underneath.
• **Butter scoops** These were used to scrape the butter out of the churn, and were usually made in sycamore. Elm or mahogany scoops are rarer and are worth twice as much.

BUTTER DISHES

Some butter dishes were made for storing butter in the larder, others for serving at the table. In the

19thC, glazed white stoneware was very fashionable and was often used for butter dishes. Various potteries included them in their range and round dishes often came with a wooden surround. In the 1940s and 50s, glass dishes were used with such surrounds. Pyrex also became a popular material for butter dishes.

DAIRY

Milk & Cream

By the 1850s, in both Britain and North America, commercial dairies started to deliver milk to homes in towns and cities. Initially, the dairies were built in cities and milked herds of cows that were kept permanently indoors and fed on corn and hay brought in from the countryside.

By the 1920s, these city dairies had disappeared and farmers would send milk to town in large churns by train, as well as delivering milk to local homes. Billycans (small churns) were left outside the house, into which the farmer would ladle the milk.

The use of milk bottles dates back to 1879 when the Echo Farms Dairy Company of New York first sold milk in glass bottles. In Britain, the Express Dairy, founded in 1874, carried out experiments in selling milk in wired-cap bottles, but abandoned the idea as it was too expensive. However, the use of glass bottles for milk had become widespread throughout Britain by 1906.

STORAGE

Heavy ceramic jugs and jars were widely used for the storage of milk, which would be placed in a pantry or larder in the coolest part of the house. The thickness of the material would help to keep the milk cool.

MAKERS

The Dairy Supply Company, the utensil division of Express Dairies, was a major concern in Britain, producing all kinds of dairy

equipment such as churns, milk pails, and skimmers.

INNOVATIONS

The use of milk and cream in cooking has inspired many innovative items designed to make the cook's task quicker, easier, and less messy. In the 1930s, labour-saving devices became ever more popular and in 1933, the "Ideal" patented cream maker promised to make cream "in less than three

minutes". Cream was made by pumping a handle and, like many such devices, it clamped onto a table top for additional support.
• **Platers & Stampers** This Lancashire firm was one of many firms that produced ingenious equipment. Their popular Skyline range of kitchen utensils included a jug and beater set (see overleaf), introduced in the 1940s, which fitted together snugly, with a shield over the jug to prevent splashing.

• **Gadgets** Milk boiling over is the bane of many a cook's life and various methods of dealing with the problem have resulted in some interesting collectibles. In the 1930s and 40s, a French solution was an enamel milk boiler with holes in the lid; the milk bubbling through the holes would indicate that it was ready.

Another solution to the problem was marketed in the 1950s by the British firm Mirrorware, in the form of the "WHIS-I-MAGIC". This was a pan with a funnel at its centre, to which water would be added. When the water boiled, a whistle would blow to indicate that the milk should be taken off the heat. While it was ingenious, the pan proved clumsy to use and difficult to clean.

A similar solution was offered by the 1950s polished aluminium "milk saver" – essentially a large whistle that would be placed in the pan and triggered by the boiling milk.

Much simpler milk savers are the small glass or ceramic discs that are still being produced today. They are added to a pan of milk and as the milk approaches boiling point they vibrate, making a rattling sound and alerting the cook. Most are plain, but novelty ones bearing appropriate images (such as cows) do exist and appeal to collectors.

COLLECTIBILITY
The two 1930s cream makers shown below have similar names but were made by different companies. The blue-specked octagonal "Bel-Jubilee" has what the trade catalogue describes as a "Jacobean-style" glass receptacle. The "Jubilee Empire" next to it came in colours such as brown,

green, dark red, and bright red. In the 1930s, the "Bel" model was regarded as superior and was more expensive, but today the "Empire" is more sought after because of its desirable mottled Bakelite top. Bakelite generally has quite a large following among collectors.

• **Cream skimmers** These have long been popular with collectors. Basically a large, flat spoon with holes, it enabled thick cream to be skimmed from the surface while the milk dripped through. Those made entirely of brass, or perhaps with a brass handle are the most attractive (see p.135), although wooden versions are popular with collectors of treen.

CONDITION
All of the components should be present. Chips and other damage to ceramic items will always detract from their value. If it has survived with its original box, it will always be more desirable.

Eggs

Traditionally, eggs were stored in open wire or willow baskets and hung from the ceiling away from rats and mice. They were also kept on long wooden racks. From the mid-19thC onwards, egg racks became smaller, usually holding up to a dozen eggs, and new versions were made that could be stacked on top of each other.

Other types of egg storage included pottery hen nests. Introduced in the 1840s, they were produced in vast numbers by Staffordshire potteries (see opposite).

As more people moved to the cities, it became necessary to find new ways to transport eggs in large numbers without breaking them. One solution was a special box with felt pockets inside to hold the eggs. These boxes ranged in size, the smallest holding three dozen eggs and the largest 35 dozen. They were used from 1890 to the 1930s.

EGG CROCKS

Egg crocks, made from stoneware (see p.143), were used for pickling eggs in the days before refrigerators. Some are labelled with their contents, which is always more appealing to collectors, particularly if the typeface used is interesting or unusual.

EGG STANDS

• **Materials** Wirework was often used to make egg baskets in the 19thC and many were exceptionally well made and capable of holding several dozen eggs.

Cast iron, wood, or a combination of the two were also used to make egg stands at this time, found in both country and town larders.

• **Identification** Wooden egg stands were often made by local craftsmen and are extremely difficult to date, although the patina of the wood can be a clue. Large wooden egg stands may have belonged to a large household, but they may also have been made for commercial premises. Egg stands were also made commercially by a number of different manufacturers and painted tin stands became very popular between the 1930s and the 1950s. Those made by Wessexware are easy to identify because they have a wide handle. On Tala stands, the bottom tray can be removed. Stands by Worcesterware (as above) were made in blue, red, white, and green.
• **Condition** Some of these painted

tin egg stands have been repainted – avoid these as they are worth very little. Any item in its original box will be worth more.

PREPARATION

Collectible items connected with the preparation of eggs range from egg separators, used to separate the yolk from the white (some were also designed to lift boiled eggs from a pan), to egg wedgers. The egg wedger above was launched by Tala in the 1930s, a time when salads were becoming popular. As its name suggests, it was designed to cut eggs into wedge-shaped pieces.
• **Egg coddlers** These were designed for the preparation of coddled eggs, a dish that has gone out of fashion somewhat, largely because of concerns over the health risk. The method of preparation is similar to poaching, but the eggs are only very lightly cooked. They are broken into the buttered egg coddler, a container made of porcelain, glass, or pottery, and spices and seasonings are added if desired. The coddler has a lid which is then closed and the whole thing is placed into boiling water for a brief period. (See p.145.)
• **Identification** Egg coddlers can be easily confused with egg cups, especially if the lid is missing. The lid usually has a "lifting ring" to make its removal easier.
• **Makers** Manufacturers of egg coddlers include some of the most

famous potteries, such as Royal Worcester, Coalport, Spode, T. G. Green, and Wedgwood. The Syracuse China Company of New York made coddlers with metal lids but no lifting ring. They were also made in Pyrex. Commonly made for just one egg, larger coddlers designed to take two eggs were also made.
• **Egg cups** These have been made by many different firms and in a wide variety of materials. A collecting field in itself, egg cup collecting is known as pocillovy, and collectors as pocillovists.
• **Collectibility** Ceramic egg cups are often collected by enthusiasts interested in the factories where they were made, such as Spode, Royal Worcester, etc. Bakelite egg cups from the 1940s, however, are especially sought after.

HEN NESTS

Hen nests were used to keep boiled eggs warm at the breakfast tables of middle and upper-class Victorian homes. They were generally made from pottery, but glass examples are known, as well as bone china or Parian ware (unglazed, fine-grained porcelain). The example shown above, made from amber glass, is particularly interesting. It has been cast from a mould and the details are clearly defined, particularly on the feathers. Hen nests were originally filled with sweets as fairground prizes.

Ice Cream

Ice cream originated in the Far East, arriving in the West by the end of the 17thC. Early ice cream was made from ice, milk, and eggs in pewter pots with tight-fitting lids and stored in ice houses. By the early 19thC, it was possible to choose from a whole host of elaborate pewter moulds. In Britain one of the many famous ice cream makers of this time was Carlo Gatti, whose family firm made Italian-style ice cream. Known as "hokeypokey" it came in square slabs wrapped in wax paper and eaten in glasses called "penny licks" (see p.146). By the 1920s, many makers were competing for business. One of the most successful British firms is Wall's, founded in 1922 and the first in Britain to sell pre-wrapped ice creams from tricycles. Its slogan, "stop me and buy one" became a familiar household phrase. Now a multinational firm, Wall's merged with Bird's Eye in 1981. Ice cream was still made at home throughout the 20thC and the equipment has changed little over the past 100 years.

MOULDS
Pewter was widely used for making ice cream moulds and on p.48 is a particularly attractive 1868 example.
• **Identification and dating** The fact that pewter is marked aids identification. Because lead pewter was found to be poisonous and was banned in Britain in the late 1860s, any pieces bearing registration marks at around this time or earlier should be assumed to contain lead and should on no account be used.
• **Safety** It is also possible that pewter moulds may have been cleaned with chemical agents, so check if a mould has been treated before buying if you like to use your items for food perparation.

AMERICA
Ice cream has been popular in the USA since colonial times and in the 19thC and 20thC many firms produced equipment for making it. The design of the American ice cream freezer shown above was so successful that it has changed little. Produced by the Richmond Cedar Works, it has a wooden cylinder in the middle. The cavity between the wood and the cylinder is packed with ice and salt. The mixture is placed in the cylinder and rotated by a handle. Today, plastic parts are available to fit the original design.
• **Makers** Other American names and models worth looking out for include Reliance's "White Mountain Freezer" and Shepard's "Lightning Ice Cream Machine".

ICE CREAM SERVERS
By the mid-20thC, many designs of ice cream server had been developed.
• **Designs** In the picture above, both the mid-1930s server at the top, made by Reliance for commercial use, with a spring-grip action, and the 1930s Italian one in the centre, are still in production today. Beware of new ones as they are of much poorer quality. Tala made the spring-grip server with the green wooden handle from the 1930s to the 1950s – it was also available in cream and yellow. The picture below shows an American conical server from the late 1870s. When the small screw is turned, some integral blades scoop out the ice cream.

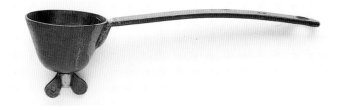

Baking

The kitchens in Victorian households lacked the built-in cupboards and work surfaces that we take for granted today. Instead, a typical 19thC kitchen had a table of pine or deal in the centre of the room on which food preparation would take place. Most antique pine furniture was originally painted and the paint was only removed because of the "stripped pine" fashions from the 60s onwards. Kitchen tables were always an exception to the painted rule because of hygiene; the top had to be regularly scrubbed to keep it clean. Victorian kitchen tables had shallow drawers for baking utensils and they were lower than modern work surfaces. This was better suited to strenuous activities such as kneading dough.

By the mid-19thC, when cast-iron coal or wood-burning ranges were introduced, there was a growth of equipment for baking because the new ranges allowed for more sophisticated cooking and baking techniques. Utensils available for baking from the 19thC included earthenware mixing bowls, flour dredgers, and rolling pins. Elaborate pies, jellies, and other desserts were created from exotic moulds, while simpler baking tins and patty pans were used for bread, cakes, and biscuits.

The early 20thC craze for tea parties gave rise to a host of implements and baking tins for making the accompanying treats.

Bowls & Basins

From the end of the Roman occupation in the 5thC until the 16thC, pottery was not widely made in Britain. Wood, such as elm or sycamore, was commonly used for household utensils instead.

By the mid-17thC, Staffordshire was the centre of British pottery. Different types were produced, especially earthenware, which is both durable and waterproof. The range of items was vast and included mixing bowls in various sizes as well as jars, plates, and jugs. Mixing bowls were also being exported to New England and Maryland in North America as early as 1653. Ceramics were not produced in any great quantity in North America until the early 19thC, when the industry developed mainly on the East Coast in Philadelphia and New Jersey.

19THC

By the 19thC, the simple wooden receptacles used in the Middle Ages had evolved into tin, earthenware, and metal bowls adapted to a range of uses including warming, cooling, salting, and storing food.

The British have long been known for their love of sweet and savoury steamed and boiled puddings, such as steak and kidney pudding and spotted dick. Popular since the mid-19thC, these are made in special china bowls to withstand the heat of steaming. The bowl is first lined with suet pastry and then filled with steak and kidney or shin beef. Basins can also be filled with syrup or stewed fruit at the base. The pudding is sealed with a lid of suet dough or sponge mixture, covered with a lining of greaseproof paper.

The top of the basin is then covered with a cloth, which is tied under the rim with string. The opposite ends of the cloth are knotted to make a handle for lifting the pudding in and out of boiling water. From the 1900s to the 1950s, you could buy special cotton or linen pudding cloths, which are collectible if unstained.

DESIGNS

• **Mixing bowls** These, on both sides of the Atlantic, were generally plain.

• **North America** Bowls of the early 19thC were often plain red, white, or yellow, with simple glazes.

• **Decoration** By the mid-19thC, stripes of colour were added in both Britain and the USA, as well as elements of decoration.

• **Late 19thC** Bowls often had lips added for pouring, especially useful for the batter mixture used in recipes such as Yorkshire Pudding. They were often made of cream earthenware or stoneware.

• **Price Kensington** This USA firm made some attractive bowls in the 60s with colours and abstract designs echoing contemporary textiles.

METAL

Some pudding basins were made of metal, including an aluminium one impressed with "Sutox, for all puddings" on the lid. Sutox was a type of suet used as one of the main ingredients in steam puddings and this basin would have been offered as a promotional item in the 1930s. A metal, clip-on lid is its main feature, avoiding the need for greaseproof paper and cloths.

PLASTIC

Plastic was increasingly used in the kitchen, thanks in part to firms like Tupperware. These plastic storage containers were invented by Earl S. Tupper, who marketed them through party plans. The range included a pudding basin with a lid that was suitable for steaming. Tupperware has avid followers and examples from the 1950s and 1960s are increasingly collectible.

PYREX

From 1921, glass firm Joblings acquired the rights to manufacture Pyrex throughout the British Empire, apart from in Canada. Pyrex products of the 1930s included bowls of various sizes as part of the "Pyrex Oven Table Glassware Series" and pudding basins, as well

as flat-sided glass dishes used for making soufflés or mousse.

• **Dating** Early Pyrex is distinctive because of its cloudy appearance.

IDENTIFICATION AND DATING

The mixing bowls shown above are all slightly different, which helps in dating. The buff colour dates to the 19thC, but over the years tone varied slightly. The insides changed from a pearly white to a creamy colour, while the outside became a deeper buff colour. Another 20thC feature is the gripstand, which makes it easier for a cook to hold a bowl steady. The bowls at the back of the picture have gripstands and date from the 1930s to the 1950s.

• **Victorian bowls** Generally these were not marked with a maker's name, making identification difficult.

• **White earthenware pudding basins** These vary in tone – by the 1950s, they had a creamier colour than those from the earlier 20thC.

• **Early basins** These are narrower and often have a curled edge, to allow string to be tied securely under the cloth, or they have a

deeper turned edge.

• **Mixing bowls** These are sometimes confused with pancheons, which are deeper bowls used for the mixing and rising of yeast dough.

• **Blue-and-white banded ware** Usually associated with the Cornish Ware of T. G. Green & Co., but Chefware also sold blue and white bowls as a less expensive alternative throughout the 1950s. T. G. Green products can be identified by their backstamp.

MANUFACTURERS

Names to look out for include Lovatt's Potteries (established in Nottinghamshire in 1895) as well as Mason & Cash and T. G. Green & Co. The latter two are the main manufacturers of the buff-coloured mixing bowls shown.

PATENTS

Since the late 16thC the British Crown has granted letters patent to inventors to protect their exclusive right to manufacture their products for a limited period, preventing others from copying them. The Patent Library in London has records of all the patents issued over the last 150 years, making it possible to check a patent number. Records will also show to whom a patent was issued and when. However, the date of a patent is not necessarily the same as the date of manufacture. Kitchenware products were often produced over long periods.

"QUICK COOKER"

The Staffordshire firm, Grimwade's, patented its ironstone china "Quick Cooker" (shown at the bottom of p36) in 1911, although the design was first patented and introduced in 1909. An impressive advertising piece, the basin promotes a whole host of other products by the firm, including pie dishes, "Safety Milk Bowls", and "hygienic household

jars". Directions on how to use the "Quick Cooker" are printed on the top of the lid, where it also claims to cook the contents quickly from the centre to the circumference with no need for pudding cloth. Notches on the four points of the lid correspond to the four notches on the underside base, where string is tied. These Quick Cookers are highly sought after today.

Before you buy
• Always test for cracks – a perfect bowl should give a clear "ping" when tapped with a pencil.
• Check enamel bowls for scratches – they are particularly prone to damage from utensils such as forks and whisks.

Cake Decorating

The history of cakes goes back many centuries. The Romans enjoyed various types of cake, mostly sweetened with honey, and cakes were popular gifts, especially as a part of religious festivals.

The tradition of cake as part of celebrations continued and in Tudor times a cake of "marchpane", a version of what we would call marzipan, would be at the centrepiece of many a banquet. The art of marzipan decoration and pastillage, the use of a form of sugar paste suitable for moulding and rolling, evolved and became an art form in itself. Therefore by Victorian times, the idea of an elaborately decorated celebratory cake was well-established.

BAKING

ICING SETS

In the 19thC, forcing bags inserted with small pipes were used to make meringues or decorative mounds of creamed potatoes. The modern icing syringe was introduced in the early 20thC and was a great improvement. It came with a selection of screw-on nozzles that would produce different patterns.

MAKERS

• **Tala** Based in Birmingham and later Stourbridge, Tala was one of the major manufacturers and produced a wide range of icing nozzles, related booklets, and recipe ideas from the 1920s through to the 1960s. Some icing sets included a turntable to put the cake on while it was being iced and which could be taken apart to be stored. The Tala name is currently used by George East Housewares.

• **Nutbrown** Established in Blackpool in 1927 and dissolved

in 1988, Nutbrown's trade name is now owned by Friskars UK Ltd. Nutbrown were fierce rivals of Tala.

DECORATIONS

The art of decorating cakes with figures and forms made from sugar is centuries old, and probably provided the inspiration for more permanent models. It seems a logical step to produce decorations that would not be eaten and could be reused countless times.

Cake decorations, those small figures made to brighten up celebratory cakes, are collectible and come in many different forms to suit the occasion. Weddings, birthdays, and Christmas are perhaps the most common events that are celebrated with a cake and there are various decorations to match.

Many figures were made from plaster or Bisque, a type of unglazed

porcelain, and Germany became a major centre of manufacture in the 19thC. Germany was already established as a manufacturer of children's dolls at this time.

What to look for
• Although simpler figures have a naïve charm, on the whole, the better the quality, the more desirable a piece will be.
• An unusual subject can also enhance appeal.
• Animated figures are more appealing to the collector than simple figures in sitting or standing poses.
• Original packaging is a bonus so look for boxed items in good condition.

IDENTIFICATION AND DATING
• **Nozzles** These can be a useful guide to the age of icing sets – pre-WWII ones are nickel-plated, while 50s ones are usually stainless steel.

Cutters

In Britain, the term "pastry cutter" refers to cutters designed for both pastry and biscuits. In continental Europe and North America, pastry cutters are used for pastry, and biscuit or cookie cutters are used to cut out biscuit shapes.

The earliest cutters were hand-carved and made of wood and they have a long history on both sides of the Atlantic. Early versions were known as imprint cutters, because they imprinted a design on the dough. They originated in Italy, and were used in Britain from the 15thC onwards to make gingerbread figures, often in the shape of popular contemporary personalities such as Queen Elizabeth I or the first Lord Wellington. By the 18thC they were used to make moulded sugar motifs to decorate cakes.

Later versions were outline cutters. They had a cutting edge, flat backs, and usually a handle. Made from square- or oblong-shaped wood, usually pear, walnut, or beech, both types of wooden cutters were produced in Britain until the mid-19thC, when they were replaced by mass-produced metal ones.

• **Promotional items** Cutters were sometimes used as promotional items. Davis Baking Powder issued a set of four animal cookie cutters, bearing the name of the firm on the side.

• **Sandwich cutters** Deeper cutters were designed in order to make attractively shaped sandwiches as well as biscuits.

Identification

The firms of Tala and Nutbrown dominated the market in Britain and were fierce rivals; their rivalry was such that they would often produce identical products. The only way to tell them apart is to check for a maker's mark. Both companies marked every item with their name.

SETS

Sets of pastry cutters were produced by Tala in green-painted tins with hinged lids in the early 1930s. Later in the 1930s, pastel colours became available with a glossier finish. In the 1950s, they were made of light aluminium rather than tin and came in garish colours. The cutters were available with crinkly or plain edges for the same price, and each tin contained four different-sized cutters, fitting neatly into each other, as above.

NOVELTY CUTTERS

Cutters made in novelty shapes were always popular for making biscuits in more interesting forms.

In the late 1940s and into the 50s, Tala made this particularly appealing set of six cutters in the shape of a pelican, seal, horse, elephant, penguin, and hippo (shown left). It is rare to find a complete set like this with its original box. The base of the box has recipe instructions for biscuits.

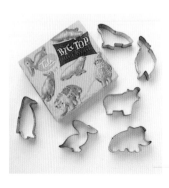

PLASTIC

Less durable and more brittle than metal, plastic was regularly used to make pastry cutters by the 1950s. Commonly sold through Betterwear salesmen, the cutters were available in a variety of pastel shades, including pink, blue, yellow, and green.

Dredgers & Shakers

Flour is an essential ingredient in baking. Flour dredgers and shakers have been used for more than a century and have changed very little in design. Shaped like canisters, they are turned upside down to shake the flour onto a rolling pin or pastry board before rolling out pastry. They could also be used for sprinkling sugar on top of pies or icing sugar onto cakes. They come in many different designs and colours and ceramic flour dredgers can make a particularly attractive collection. Tin flour dredgers are perhaps less attractive, but they are also collectible.

THE 1950S

The colourful flour dredger shown above is made of porcelain and dates from the 1950s, when polka dots were very fashionable. It is filled with flour from the base and has a special "Suba Seal" stopper.

MAKERS

Many firms produced dredgers and shakers, including potteries such as Maling, Bretby, and T. G. Green.

RARE ITEMS

• **T. G. Green** This company made shakers for flour and sugar in its famous Cornish Ware design (see p.164). They generally did not have handles, but they did make some with handles – these are rare.

• **Red-and-white sugar shakers** Made by T. G. Green, these Cornish Ware shakers are very rare indeed as they were only produced as an experiment and were not issued commercially.

PROMOTIONAL ITEMS

• **Quaker Oats** In the 1950s, Quaker Oats produced the sugar shaker shown below that could also be used for flour. It was made in the form of the Quaker gentleman used as the company logo. The logo was originally chosen as symbolic of the purity of living and honesty of character associated with the Quaker movement.

• **Homepride** In the 1960s, Homepride produced a variety of items, including a flour dredger, in the form of Fred, a bowler-hatted character introduced in a television commercial (see p.5). They were originally made by Airfix and should be marked as such.

CONDITION

• **Tin dredgers** Always check thoroughly for dents and signs of rust, especially around the seams.

• **Handles** These should always be examined carefully to check that they are still secure. Do not pick up ceramic dredgers by the handle, just in case they are vulnerable.

BAKING

Rolling Pins

Rolling pins are amongst the earliest flour utensils known to have been made. They have been used since at least the 17thC and were originally hand made from a variety of woods including sycamore, walnut, boxwood, beech, fruitwood, and ash. By the end of the 19thC they were mass-produced and, in 1902, the American firm Sears Roebuck introduced the revolving-handled rolling pin.

Different pins were designed for different jobs and can therefore be identified by shape and material; hollow glass pins were filled with crushed ice to keep pastry cool; ridged pins were used for crushing oats, salt, or bread crumbs; and pie crust pins (which are tapered at the ends) were used to make the edge of the pie crust thicker than the middle. Both functional and decorative, rolling pins are very collectible.

TYPES
Some of the many different types of rolling pin are shown above, dating from the 1890s to the 1950s. The smallest (bottom), from the 1920s, was used for candy-making. Above it is a Victorian pie-crust rolling pin – note the tapering edges. The long pin in the centre is also a pie-crust pin, but it was made in the 1950s.

By this time, it was also used for making pasta or noodles, an indication of changing eating habits.

GLASS
Hollow glass rolling pins were made to be filled with ice via openings in their ends. These would be closed with a cork or metal cap when in use. Glass rolling pins are not unusual, but although they must have been made in large numbers, they are not as commonly found as we might expect, possibly because of their fragile nature.

CONDITION
• **Ceramic-bodied** These rolling pins are prone to crazing and dis-colouration, which will affect value.
• **Wooden** These have a tendency to warp and split – unfortunately

this will always reduce value.
• **Painted handles** Any chipping and flaking of the paintwork should be taken into account when buying.
• **Handles** These are sometimes attached via a metal rod through the pin, which can be affected by rust.

Dating
A clue to the date of ridged rolling pins, which were used for crushing oats, is in the closeness and sharpness of the ridges. Ridges on older pins are very close and sharp because the oats were less refined. By the 1930s, refining techniques had improved, so rolling pins from this era have flatter ridges, more spaced apart.

Tins

Tin has been widely available in Europe and North America since the mid-19thC. It was initially quite expensive in North America, however, so it was greatly treasured.

Local tinsmiths were known as "whitesmiths" to distinguish them from iron-workers. Some tinsmiths would decorate the bases of tin items on request and these items are highly sought after today.

Use & Care
Early steel, tin, or cast-iron bakingware can usually still be used, but if you do intend to use them, they must be looked after properly. Never leave baking tins to soak in washing up water after use; they will rust if you do this. Instead, wash them carefully, dry immediately with a tea towel, and store them away in a dry place.

USAGE

Tins were often made for one specific purpose, but they could also be used for other purposes. For example, tins with four cups that were made for Yorkshire puddings could also be used to make individual sweet or savoury pies. Nine-cup embossed tins, such as those featured in the picture above, were designed for smaller items, such as mince pies and their distinctive features include raised seamless cups.

• **Manufacture** Considerable craftsmanship went into the manufacture of these tins. In the 1920s, the frame would be made separately with holes for the cups. Individual moulded cups were pressed into the frame and double-seamed in. By the 1950s, quality had declined and they would usually be stamped from a single sheet of metal. The detail in the embossing of 1950s pieces is generally less detailed and of lesser quality.

PATTY PANS

The term "patty pan" is derived from the French *pâte*, meaning paste, although they were used to make English tartlets. From the late 19thC onwards, they would be placed onto baking sheets made from iron or heavy steel to bake in the oven. Early ones (from the 1890s to the 1940s) are usually made from heavy tinned steel, while later ones are much lighter.

LOAF TINS

Loaf tins were first made from the early 19thC but were affordable only to large, wealthy households. In most homes, bread would be moulded by hand and baked in the oven on an iron sheet or in an earthenware dish.

• **Early 20thC** Tins were more widely available and were also used for cakes, such as fruit loaf.

• **Marks** Tins are sometimes stamped with the name of the manufacturer and some have a small hoop to hold when taking them from the oven. Marked tins are always more appealing.

• **Quality** Better quality tins are sometimes wired around the rims to give them extra strength.

OTHER TYPES

From the latter part of the 19thC to the 1950s, baking tins were produced in a wide variety of shapes to suit different types of baking and cooking – a selection can be seen below.

• **Oval tin** This large, heavy tin measures 11x8in (28x20cm) and could be used to make a large pie or to roast a piece of meat. It was also available in other sizes; 12x9in (30x22cm) or 13x10in (33x25cm).

• **Russian tin** To the right is a Russian cake tin by Tala. This tin has an additional piece that slots into the centre, enabling different coloured sponge cakes to be made – the basis of a Russian cake or Battenberg as it is also known.

• **Charlotte mould** The small oval tin was used to make a French Fruit or Charlotte Pudding (stewed fruit covered with layers of bread and butter), it was also available in a round shape and in various sizes. The one shown would make enough for two people.

• **Square tin** This large tin was primarily for making Yorkshire pudding, but could also be used to make parkin (a type of sticky cake). Baking tins are extremely versatile, as with many pieces of kitchenware.

MAKERS

• **Acme** This British manufacturer made all types of household utensils from the 1920s to the 1950s, including baking tins.

• **H. J. Green & Co. Ltd.** This firm of grocers' suppliers was based in Brighton, Sussex. In the late 1920s, they offered a range of promotional kitchenware, embossed with their company name and the name of one of their products. Today, they are still fairly easy to find and can be

BAKING

built up to make complete sets.
• **Look for** Other collectible names include Peter Pan, Tala, Ovenex, Evaware, and Bakejoy.

CONDITION
• **Patina** Tinware acquires an attractive patina as it ages. Remarkably, the two baking tins shown to the right both date from the 1930s. The one on the right looks brand new, as it has been stored in a cupboard unused.

COLLECTIBILITY
• **Quality** Good quality manufacture and design affects the desirability of baking tins. The selection of tins shown right date from the 1900s to the 1950s. The larger tins have cutter blades to help remove the cake more easily. The earliest cutter blades (top) from the 1930s are quite crudely made and are flimsy and thin, with the blade sticking out from the edge of the tin in an unattractive way. By the late 1930s, the design had been improved; the cutter blade on the bottom left tin is wide and folds neatly over the outline of the rim. The other sandwich tin is also from

the 1930s and has a fluted rim.
• **Tartlet tins** Two different kinds of these are also shown in the picture; the three darker ones at the top were made in the early 1900s.

They are of excellent quality, hardwearing and far more desirable than the two lightweight 1950s ones below.
• **Loaf tins** Early 20thC loaf tins, from the 1900s to the 1920s, tend to be of better quality than the later examples and so are more desirable.
• **Baking sheets** Early examples are very hard to find today and are highly sought after.
• **Other uses** Baking tins are not always bought for use or display – some tins are large and attractive enough to be used as planters.

Weights & Measures

Weighing devices of some sort or another have a very long history, dating back thousands of years. Weighing technology is and always has been important for commerce, because only by giving equal, fair, and universally agreed measures can trade prosper. Giving short measure has long been a serious offence and the weights and measures we use today stem from the need for standardization. In the home, accuracy was not as essential as it was for businesses, but it was nevertheless important to the busy cook seeking perfect results. Here you will see the different kinds of measures available.

NATIONAL SYSTEMS
• **England** Since the Middle Ages, the English system of weights and measures has been based on a single grain of wheat and, from the 17thC to the 19thC, a pound was equivalent to 7,000 grains. In 1824, the official standard was changed to the Troy pound, weighing 5,760 grains, but it was not popular and in 1878 the Imperial Standard Pound of 7,000 grains was re-introduced.
• **Continental Europe** The metric system has been in use since the 19thC and a kilogram is defined according to a prototype kept at the International Bureau of Weight

and Measures, established in 1875, in Sèvres, France.

• **North America** In the USA cooking ingredients were weighed out with special sized cups which, by the late 19thC, had been standardized to equal 8oz (225g).

SELF-INDICATING SCALES

Leonardo da Vinci (1454–1519) was the first to design this type of scale, where the weight could be read on a chart instead of having to make constant adjustments until a balance was achieved. As with many of his ideas, no practical application of the design was developed during his lifetime and it was not until the 19thC that such scales were put into production.

COUNTER BALANCE SCALES

Although we do not know who made these late 19thC counter-balance scales with tin pans, below, the principle of their design is well known. These types of scales were discovered by the mathematician Professor Gilles Personne de Roberval in France in 1669. Known as "Static Enigma", the machine oscillates above and below its normal level before coming to rest when it is balanced. The principle was widely adopted by scale makers and is still used today.

MAKERS

Of the many different makers that produced scales, two of the most famous names are Salters and Krups.

• **Salters** Based in West Bromwich in the West Midlands, they have been among the leading international designers and manufacturers since 1760. They first introduced spring balance scales, which did not need weights, in 1770. Salters is one of the most collectible names and produced many different designs, some of which are capable of measuring up to 28lbs (12.6kg).

• **Krups** This German company produced many attractive scales sought after by collectors. Their early 20thC range included some Art Nouveau designs, and in unusual colours made for export.

• **Look for** Other collectible names are Avery, often associated with commercial scales, and Tower.

RARE ITEMS

• **Quadrant balance** The example below is one of the most interesting inventions to come from Salters. It takes its name from its shape and appeared in the firm's catalogue of 1876. They are very rare and so were probably produced in smaller numbers than the more circular, oblong, or pedestal types.

WEIGHTS

Most Victorian weights were made from cast iron and brass, widely available, durable, and inexpensive

to produce. Stone was also occasionally used, mostly for heavier ranges. Weights were also made from pottery and they are highly sought after today because they are much rarer. In 1907, they were made illegal because of their tendency to chip, which would therefore make them lighter than their stated weight. Some sets of weights have the larger ones in cast iron and the smaller ones in brass.

• **Sets** Scales should always have a complete set of weights. If they do not, then it is often the smallest weights that will be missing. Larger ones are easier to find individually.

• **Replacements** Antique weights are often sold independently of scales, so scales that have weights missing are still worth considering if you can find some to suit.

Terminology

• **Beam scales** Scales in which pans are hung from the ends of a beam supported at the centre.
• **Self-indicating scales** Scales in which the weight is displayed on a chart.
• **Spring balances** These depend on springs as the resistant; often the weight is displayed on a dial.
• **Counter-balance scales** These use different-sized weights to counter-balance the weight of an object.

COLOURS

Most 19th and early 20thC household scales were painted in drab colours, so any that are more colourful are always desirable.

ACCURACY

Always test a set of kitchen scales for accuracy before buying. With counter balance scales, put equal sets of weights on both sides to check that they balance. If they are

METAL
Aluminium, being both hardwearing and lightweight, makes an ideal material for measuring jugs. One of the leading 20thC makers of this type of jug was Swan Brand.

GLASS
Glass was widely used for measuring jugs, such as those below. Valued for their ability to withstand hot liquids, Pyrex jugs are easy to identify because the name is always impressed on the base. (See p.36.)

spring-type, just put a weight into the pan.

METRICATION
Britain joined the European Union (then known as the European Economic Community, or Common Market) in January 1973 and had to adopt a directive on metrication. Recipes and packaging were printed with metric equivalents alongside the imperial, but the public were slow to adapt. Stylish kitchen scales appeared including the plastic metric 4000 model by Italian designer Marco Zanuso for the French firm Terraillon. Plastic scales are generally not as desirable as older models, but these would appeal to those interested in modern design.

Also on hand were various aids to help the public to adapt to the new measurements. These included plastic measuring spoons in metric quantities and handy aids like the Metricook by British makers Probus. This device had wheels that would be turned to convert imperial measurements into metric.

MEASURES
In early times, wooden mugs were commonly used to weigh out all kinds of foodstuffs, and were made in varying sizes. By the late 18thC, special measures for specific items were available. Pewter measures were used for ale and vinegar, while

earthenware was better suited to milk and cream. Tin measures were used for shellfish, while corn was measured in deep, round wooden containers. As household scales became more common in the mid-19thC, measures were used less, apart from wooden corn measures and measures for ale, milk, and other liquids.

The Cook's Measure shown above was made by Tala and provides "weights and measures at a glance", according to its makers. Each row of measurements lists the range of items that can be measured or weighed. Take care when cleaning this type of measure; the paint will come off if a scourer or abrasive cleaner is used. The measure on the right, called the Cook's Treasure Measure, is an earlier version, dating from the 1930s. Unpainted inside, it is slightly less easy to read, but contains the same kind of measuring information. Similar measures are produced today, but only in plastic.

DATING
Measurements on jugs have been in both metric and imperial since 1900. Few included American cups until the 1930s.

CONDITION & COLLECTIBILITY
• **Before buying** Always make sure that the measurements are clearly marked.
• **Enamelled jugs** Early 20thC examples are becoming more difficult to find, especially in good condition.
• **Bakelite** Some metal jugs have a bakelite handle, which is especially desirable.
• **Design** Collectors look for a good design – clumsy, poorly proportioned handles are not so desirable.
• **Commercially-used measures** These are collectible. Tin measures used by shop keepers were stamped with their size by British Customs & Excise officials.

Moulds

In the 19thC, moulds were commonly used in middle and upper class households, where cooks would prepare elaborate meals with a savoury or sweet jelly, blancmange, or mousse as an impressive centrepiece. The most attractive moulds were made of copper and Wedgwood creamware, but white earthenware ones were also made. By the turn of the 20thC, moulds were commercially made and were available in a much wider variety of materials. Swan Brand, Tala, and Nutbrown are among the most famous makers. In 1931, E. Selman invented the wire stand, which meant that manufacturers could produce moulds that could stand up, making it easier to pour liquid into them. An important figure in the history of moulds is the 19thC English businesswoman Mrs A. B. Marshall. Mrs Marshall ran a cookery school, a domestic staff agency, and also sold speciality cooking ingredients, such as pistachio compound and liqueur syrups. In 1886, she published her *Illustrated Catalogue of Moulds and Special Kitchen Equipment*, in which she illustrates and describes more than 1,000 moulds. This book is still available today and is an essential reference work for the mould collector.

POTTERY

The Victorians used earthenware moulds like those on the right to make a variety of savoury dishes. Images of vegetables and fruits were often embossed on the base to make attractive designs.

• **Fruits** Commonly found embossed fruits include a pineapple (which was a sign of welcome), and at harvest time a wheatsheaf, symbolizing prosperity.
• **Ceramic moulds** Made by many different potteries including Shelley, Maling, and Wedgwood.
• **Joseph Bourne & Son (est.1812)** Still one of Britain's major producers of stoneware pottery, from 1912 to the 1930s they produced moulds in leadless glass stoneware and made kitchenware known as Denbyware.
• **Shortbread moulds** Although wood was often favoured for these moulds, pottery versions also exist. Some of these carry advertising for baking powder and/or cornflour and are more collectible than plain moulds.

COPPER

Copper moulds are the most collectible of all on both sides of the Atlantic, being beautifully made in a vast array of designs and sizes. Their heyday was in the 19thC, from the 1830s onwards, but only the wealthy could afford them. During this time, developments in close-plating and tinning safeguarded them against verdigris poisoning. A collection of copper moulds makes a superb display. The two moulds shown below were produced from the 1860s to 1880 – the one on the right is the rarer design.

• **Marks** Many copper moulds bear impressed names – these almost always refer to the retailers rather than the makers. Best-known retailers' marks found on copper moulds are Jones Bros., Ash Bros. & Heaton Ltd., and Benhams. Benhams products, in both pewter and copper, were usually marked with an "orb and cross" symbol.

TIN

Tin moulds are often thought of as an inferior alternative to copper, but they can be extremely attractive. Above is a tin mould known as a "Solomon's Temple"; its name reflects the 19thC vogue for Ancient Egypt. This mould would have been used to make a large multi-coloured savoury jelly.

WOOD

• **Cheese moulds** Cheese has traditionally been made in home-made wooden rings. Now banned from use due to hygiene reasons they are still collectible for their decorative qualities. Cheese moulds were also made in pottery and tin.
• **Shortbread moulds** Shortbread has customarily been made by pressing the mixture into hand-made wooden moulds such as at the top of this page. Although usually associated with Scotland, the original recipe is believed to have originated in France. In Scotland, it is traditionally eaten on New Year's Day, or Hogmanay (or "Cake Day").

• **Sycamore** This was a favourite wood for making biscuit moulds.

BAKING MOULDS

• **Kugelhopf moulds** These were designed specifically for the rich, bready cake of that name that is popular in Europe. A Kugelhopf mould is hollow in the centre and the outer bowl is fluted and seamless. The picture below is one example. Versions for both commercial and domestic use exist, made in heavy tinned steel, enamel, aluminium, and earthenware.

• **Turk's head pan** So called because of its resemblance to a turban, this is similar to a Kugelhopf mould, and is also used for a cake, traditionally topped with almonds. Examples were made in ceramic, tin, copper, and graniteware.
• **Bundt pans** Also similar to Turk's head pans, but they are not as tall.
• **Dainties** Small fancy cakes were often referred to in Britain in the 1930s as "dainties" and it was common for people to go into a tea shop and order "a pot of tea and some dainties". Tala made a set of flan tins which advertised on the

Shapes
• **Ring moulds** These were used to make a mousse border for dishes such as a seafood platter or a sweet mousse for a fruit dessert.
• **Oval moulds** These are hard to come by and are highly desirable.
• **Fish-shaped moulds** These were generally used to make mousse.
• **Other animals** Popular shapes of glass moulds included tortoises (1910–40s) and rabbits and hares (1930s–50s).
• **Kosher marks** Moulds are occasionally impressed with the Star of David – this is to indicate that the contents are Kosher.

box that they produced "novel moulded dainties". The use of the word is a reasonable indication that the set dates from the 1930s, although these flan tins are still being made to this day. If you are interested in collecting any boxed sets, it is important to check that all the pieces are still intact.
• **Popover pans and dariole pans** These are small and round and it is easy to confuse the two as they are very similar. The former are for small batter puddings, whereas the name "dariole" refers to a traditional English cake of this shape, which was made from puff pastry and filled with custard. Both are collectible, especially in sets of six.
• **Brioche tins** These are flared with fluted sides – early versions (early 1900s) are more desirable than the later ones (1950s).
• **Éclair moulds** Often made from aluminium, these long, shallow tins could also be used for baking *langues de chats* (cats' tongues, a type of flat, oval biscuit).
• **Boat moulds** Also known as

bateau or barquette moulds, these are roughly boat-shaped. They are highly collectible today, especially when made of heavy tinned steel, as are many examples from the 1920s.

• **Raised pie moulds** These produce attractively decorated pie crusts and were traditionally used for poultry and game pies. From the late 18thC onwards, game pies were made in earthenware moulds or tureens. Some were embossed with hunting emblems (see p.181), and handles sometimes moulded in the form of a hare. Metal moulds appeared in the 1850s and 60s and

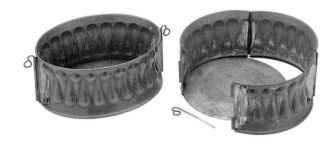

early ones were often elaborately decorated. Some are oval in shape, such as the French one above on the left, while others are round like the British one on the right.

• **Small cakes and tarts** A range of attractive tins such as those shown below were used to make

small cakes and tarts. Originally known as cornet moulds and later as cream horns, the jam and cream-filled pastries they produced were perennial favourites. Cream horn tins were made in boxed sets by both Tala and Nutbrown and both makes are collectible.

Chocolate & Fondant Moulds

Chocolate was enjoyed by the Aztecs and the Mayas of South America many centuries before the Spanish introduced it to Europe in the 16thC. In the 19thC, advances in cocoa refining together with the development of machinery and the factory system led to the

foundation of the chocolate industry as we know it today. In the kitchen, chocolate and chocolate-based desserts were very popular and moulds were widely used to make them, therefore there is plenty of scope for the collector. (See pp.183–185.)

SHAPES

Easter is of course a popular time with chocolate lovers so rabbit-shaped moulds are not uncommon. However, animal subjects in general were always popular and a whole

menagerie was created with moulds in the form of ducks, cockerels, pigs, tigers, swans, and fish.

EARLY MOULDS

• **Hand-carved iron** The early type

of mould made by craftsmen from hand-carved iron dies are more sought after than later, machine-made moulds.

• **How to identify** Older moulds are generally more detailed and made of a heavier metal than newer ones.

• **Marks** Antique moulds are often marked with the manufacturer's name or number, but newer ones are less likely to be marked.

• **Makers** The best known American maker is the American Chocolate Mould Co., founded in 1912 and still going today.

• **Hinged chocolate moulds** Designed to enable figures to be made in two halves, allowing three dimensional forms to be produced, these are quite common.

• **Reproductions** Moulds are being reproduced today, so be on your guard (see right).

Ice Cream

Ice cream has its origins in the Far East, but was known in the West by the end of the 17thC. In Britain, it was popularized by King Charles II, following a fashion for frozen dessert that had started on the Continent.

Ice cream moulds were commonly made in pewter and can be highly decorative. The fact that they come in so many different sizes and designs makes them attractive to the collector. They often come in two or three pieces, comprising the main body of the mould plus a lid or a lid and a base. Ice cream, made from ice, milk, and eggs, would be packed firmly into the mould and the lid and base fixed on tightly. The container would be stored in an ice house and when ready to serve, the mould would be taken apart to leave an attractive dessert.

Iced pudding moulds were made in various designs, some of them highly elaborate and detailed featuring birds and animals. The more elaborate they are, the better.

• **Look for** As with copper moulds, there is a good chance that pewter ice cream moulds may have been cleaned using chemicals. For this reason, you should always check before purchase if you intend to use your moulds.

• **Pewter** This metal used to contain lead, but lead pewter was banned from the late 1860s because of its poisonous nature. It is therefore important to avoid using these older pewter items for safety reasons.

• **Collectibility** This depends a great deal on the decorative appeal of the mould. The more elaborate the better. (See pp.186–188.)

• **Identification** Pewter moulds are usually marked, which can be a useful aid to identification. However, the patination is usually in itself a reliable guide to age and authenticity. The mould below was made in 1868 and is composed of three parts. The registration mark is dated 11th July 1868, which indicates that it is probably made from lead pewter. These are highly prized and can be expensive.

Jelly Moulds

Production of JELL-O, a gelatine dessert, started in 1897 in North America and was introduced to Britain in the 1900s. The marketing of this dessert was slick and included the slogan "There's always room for JELL-O". To promote the brand, aluminium jelly moulds were made from the 1920s to the 1930s and these were stamped with the maker's name on the base. JELL-O was sold as jelly crystals and an accompanying booklet offered a selection of recipe ideas (as in the picture below).

SHAPES AND SIZES

• **Variety** Copper jelly moulds come in various sizes. Small moulds would have been used to make individual servings and are especially popular with Japanese and American collectors.

• **Collectibility** Larger copper moulds can often realize two or three times the amount of smaller ones and interesting shapes also command higher prices, depending on their rarity, size, and condition.

• **Savoury dishes** These were made from moulds as well as sweet jelly; aspic is a savoury jelly made from meat or fish stock and was used with both meat and vegetable dishes. Moulds were often made in appropriate shapes, so a mould in the form of a cutlet or a ham is likely to have been intended for aspic. (See pp.189–192.)

MATERIALS

• **Copper** This was a popular material for jelly moulds, but some moulds were also made with a combination of copper and tin. English moulds are particularly prized because of the quality of their detail.

MANUFACTURERS

Grimwade is among the numerous makers of moulds, producing many fine ceramic examples.

• **Grimwade products** These include an attractively shaped example, 11in (28cm) wide and inscribed "The British Lion Blanc-Mange & Jelly Mould". Its attractive shape and the writing around the rim make a very appealing combination and it can be worth as much as 20% more than plainer examples.

PROMOTIONAL

Sometimes, jelly and blancmange moulds carried advertisements for food companies and/or recipes. Such moulds are generally more desirable than plain ones.

• **Brown & Poulson** Famous for their cornflour, this firm issued a particularly collectible version around the turn of the 20thC with a blancmange recipe on the side.

COLLECTIBILITY

• **Disney** Walt Disney's studios were quick to capitalize on the success of their characters such as Mickey Mouse and Donald Duck. Jelly moulds featuring the characters appeared in the 1930s and are very collectible because they appeal to the legions of Disney enthusiasts as well as to kitchenware collectors.

• **Plastic jelly moulds** These can sometimes be collectible if they are particularly interesting or unusual. Early plastics of any kind always have a good following.

• **Condition** Moulds in poor condition need not necessarily be rejected out of hand. They can sometimes be cleaned and restored, increasing their value.

Caution

Collectors must be aware that not all antique jelly moulds are suitable for use with food today. Copper examples were treated with a layer of tin to avoid contamination from the copper. They may need to be retinned, and lacquered moulds are unsuitable. They may also have been cleaned with chemicals, so it is best to check before purchase if you would like them for use rather than display.

MOULDS

Cookware

Pots & Pans

Boiling was the simplest and most widely-practised form of cooking for centuries, certainly until the 19thC. Large vessels known as cauldrons, kettles, boilers, and crocks were used and possibly the best-known type of pot was the legged cauldron, which was usually made of bell metal, an alloy of copper and tin. Cauldrons without feet were designed for hanging only.

Cauldrons were ideal for making soups and stews, but when smaller quantities were required, skillets were used. These were pots with three short legs and very long handles, which were placed over a fire.

The 18thC saw the introduction of the range (the first type of kitchen stove) and skillets and cauldrons were replaced by flat-bottomed saucepans, which rested on the hob, and pots that were placed inside the oven. In 1779, the first oval-bellied cast-iron pots that were tinned inside, making them both lighter and cleaner were made. Further technological advances led to the large scale production of pots and pans of all types during the 18thC and 19thC.

By the 20thC, mass production meant that pans were widely available, but some from this period are still nonetheless collectible. The 20thC saw the introduction of some unusual types of pans. These included a square saucepan, which was first made in the 1920s and was especially recommended for electric hotplates as a space saver.

MATERIALS
• **Cast Iron** By 1800, this was the most commonly used material and from 1840 onwards, pans were available with enamelled surfaces.
• **Aluminium** Pans were made in this from the 20thC, but it is best not to use them for cooking unless they were made after 1920.
• **Copper** Expensive to produce and to buy, and impractical for modern kitchens, copper pans largely disappeared from use during the early 20thC.

MAKERS
Well-known pan manufacturers include Judge Brand, Swan Brand, Daleware, Crown Merton, Siddons Ltd., and Jury.

IDENTIFICATION
On the left of the picture below is a Dutch milk pan in a mottled enamel that is often mistaken for American graniteware. The difference is that American enamel does not have any black in the mottling. This pan was made in the 1950s and has a sharp pouring lip.

The shaded orange enamel pan was made in France in the 1930s and is part of a larger range. Similar sets were produced in the 1950s, but these later ones have a bluish/grey interior.
• **Stewpans and saucepans** The important difference between these two types of pan is that the former are straight-sided, whereas the latter are rounded. Also, saucepans have "covers", but stewpans have tinned "lids".
• **Frying pans** Typically made from wrought iron, although cast iron and copper were used too.
• **Fish kettles** Fish kettles could be used for all kinds of fish, although some were designed with specific types in mind, such as mackerel or salmon. They included a perforated rack that was used to lift and drain out the fish intact. (See p.202.)
• **Salmon kettles** These were made for poaching a whole salmon. They were sometimes made from vitreous enamelled iron, but they were also available in tinned steel or copper and, by the 1920s, aluminium.
• **Shape** The shape of a fish kettle

can say a lot about the type of fish for which it was designed. Salmon kettles tend to be longer because they had to take a whole, large fish. Squarer-shaped fish kettles were made for poaching halibut, turbot, or carp.
• **Dating** Handles are a good guide to the dating of fish kettles. By the 1930s, handles were less heavy and made of tinned steel instead of iron. Earlier fish kettles, from before 1900, have flat lids whereas later ones, from the 1920s and 30s, have domed lids.

Collectibility
• **Graduating sets** The most desirable saucepans, then as now, were sets of heavy copper pans. A set would usually include at least one fish kettle, stewpans, and a bain-marie (for making sauces), and saucepans of varying sizes.
• **Materials** Pans made in cast iron, enamel, and wrought iron are less expensive, but still collectible.
• **Look for** Pans should be complete, with lids. Loose lids can be bought to fit to your matching pans.
• **Damage** The drainer on a fish kettle should not be damaged and its lifting rings should be intact.
• **Handles** Damage to a handle always devalues a pan.

PRESERVING PANS
Preserving pans are used for making jams or marmalade so they need to be strong and durable. Some have a bail-type hanging handle to hook the pan over the fire and some may also have a pouring lip. Some earlier ones do not have a pouring lip (see 19thC example below), which makes them less practical and more awkward to use. Preserving pans could also be used for boiling water, and by the 20thC were also known as maslin pans.

By the 20thC preserving pans were often made of aluminium. Aluminium pans are collectible, but Victorian brass ones such as the one shown below are much more desirable today, and this is reflected in their value. Enamel preserving pans were also made but older ones can be hard to track down. Surviving examples from the late 19thC, and in good condition are rare.

STEAMERS
19thC innovations included steamers, which allowed food to be cooked more gently, and double boilers, for cooking porridge. Cooking by steam was first practised in the 1840s, when double saucepans (made of iron) were introduced for making custards and sauces in wealthy homes. Steaming was not used on a large scale, however, until the 1870s with the development of the Captain Warren cooking pot. Named after its inventor, it was a large, oval tinned-steel pan with a tight-fitting lid, consisting of three interlocking compartments connected by a tube that allowed steam in to cook the food.
• **Heavy steamer saucepan** With a porcelain inner pan and a wooden handle attached to a collar around the inner pan's top, this was introduced in the 1870s and became very popular in the USA.
• **Porringers** Also known as double boilers, these were available by the late 19thC. Enamel versions were made by several manufacturers. They were often made in aluminium by the 1930s and pre-1950s ones have Bakelite handles.
• **Egg poacher** Another ingenious device, this was originally known in Britain as a steamer and in the USA as a poacher. The covered pan poacher was developed in Britain by the turn of the 20thC and has remained unchanged.

Trivets & Stands

Until the 19thC, trivets, for standing a kettle or pan on, were very simple affairs, made from wrought iron and twisted into shapes. Many kinds were made, including one with long legs that was placed in the fire and acted as a stand for the pot when cooking. In the 19thC the Pennsylvania Dutch produced iron trivets, often in decorative heart shapes.

With the advent of the kitchen range in the 18thC, trivets were made that hooked onto the front of the grate of a stove and were used to keep pots warm. Among the most elaborately designed trivets were "footmen", which were kept in the sitting room as a stand for a tea kettle or a plate of muffins or crumpets. Less decorative versions were used by the servants in the kitchen.

Brandreths were similar to trivets, and they were used to hold bakestones, griddles, and pans close to the fire for cooking. They were still widely used in remote areas of Scotland and Wales until the early 20thC.

- **Materials** Pot stands were made in various materials including iron, brass, and pottery.
- **Motifs** Earthenware pot stands of the 19thC reflect the decorative motifs of many earthenware items of the period. The Chinese influence is often apparent, and dragon designs were popular.
- **Wooden trivets** Not all trivets were elaborate. Below is an

example of the simple ones that were sometimes made, carved at home from a single piece of wood. It has simple wooden feet and a hole so that it could be hung close to the range. The patina of the wood, combined with scorching and soot marks only adds to the appeal of wooden trivets, which are rare.
- **Saucepan stands** These were first made for the kitchens of large 19thC households to store a column of pans. They were made in various types of metal and initially were very large, up to 14 tiers. By the early 20thC they had become much smaller, averaging only five to seven tiers. Stands with as few as three tiers do exist, but they are unusual.

- **Painted stands** Most saucepan stands were made from black japanned iron, but painted stands could be specially ordered if required. Small tins of paint were available so they could be painted at home as a cheaper alternative.
- **Makers** A name to look out for is Kenrick & Sons of West Bromwich, who made a variety of kitchenware including some very attractive fancy cast-iron stands, stamped with the firm's name.
- **Rare items** Chrome became very fashionable in the 1930s and so some chrome-plated stands were commissioned. It not only looks attractive, but this hard metal also protects against rust.

Waffle Irons & Toasters

Waffle irons originated in Europe in the 18thC. They developed from wafer irons, which date back to the 15thC and were originally used for making communion wafers. Wafer irons are much rarer and are very sought-after.

Waffle irons are round and smaller than wafer irons. Early versions were made of very heavy cast iron and ressembled a pair of tongs. At the end of two arms are hinged plates (round or square), patterned on the inside. Patterns varied from maker to maker, but the most common were grids of shapes such as squares, circles, and diamonds. By the late 19thC, waffle irons had developed into a rectangular or square shape in the form of a hinged iron box, with a raised pattern on the inside of the base and lid. (See p.208.)

By the 1930s, heavy chromium-plate waffle makers were being produced, similar to those we see manufactured today. Look for variations, such as fritter makers.

- **Original packaging** This is always a bonus and is desirable for many reasons, not least because it can help to date an item.
- **Decoration** If a waffle iron's plates are embossed on the outside it can be dated to after 1900, as before then they had flat tops.
- **Sandwich toasters** These developed from waffle irons and

work in the same way. They were made by several firms in the 1950s including Nutbrown and Made Rite, though Made Rite's were of lesser quality than Nutbrown's.
- **Toasting forks** These were already popular by the 18thC; American toasters of the late 18thC could be revolved so that both sides of the bread could be toasted.

European toasting forks were held with long handles. By the 20thC, toasting forks were noticeably different from other kinds of forks, such as those used for roasting meat, because they had blunt ends whereas forks for meat were sharp. Extending toasting forks can be a little stiff, but will become less so with use. Take care when using at first.

Utensils

The earliest of all utensils was probably the Stone Age flint knife. In more recent times, as cookery has become more sophisticated, so a whole host of utensils has appeared. Some utensils date back centuries, but they have been modified over the last century or so by commercial manufacturers. Others are relatively recent in origin and as technology advances and culinary tastes change, so new utensils are likely to appear in the future.

Many of the utensils we now take for granted were developed during the 19thC, and resulted from social change and industrial development. New and exotic foods were being imported into Europe, some of which required new utensils for eating and preparing them, while technology was increasingly brought into the kitchen in the form of labour-saving devices and handy gadgets. Even so, many of these new implements were only found in the kitchens of the well-off.

Bread Boards

Bread is one of our most ancient foods. Wooden kitchen utensils also have an ancient pedigree, and were traditionally made by local craftsmen or by householders themselves. Bread boards were made from various woods such as elm and sycamore and, as with most wooden items, bread boards can be difficult to date with any degree of accuracy. There are, however, useful clues to look out for. Early examples have a worn appearance after many years of use; patina is also a clue. Some bread boards came in a set with a matching knife and some were even made with a breadknife attached at the side. Bread knives can be collectible in themselves, especially those that were made in the 19thC and early 20thC and carved with the name of a bakery – Allinson, Hovis, and Turog are among the best known. Others were carved with the word "bread" and were made by ex-servicemen in the late 1940s; they received a percentage of the sales.

CARVING

Bread boards often bore carved decoration, which might feature the name of the bakery, or simply be an attractive design. However, the carving would often be added by the owner at home. The latter can give items a "folk art" quality that is appealing in itself. (See pp.217–219.)

- **Collectibility** Carved bread boards are always more interesting and the more elaborate they are the better.
- **Motifs** Typical and appropriate motifs might include ears or sheaves of wheat. Others had flowers or even quotations, often of a biblical nature, carved into them.
- **Style** The style of carving on bread boards varied over the years: fancy lettering was used in the 19thC, whereas from the 1920s onwards, lettering became plainer.
- **Identification** A board that has a deep, narrow trench around the edge is likely to have been originally used for cheese rather than bread. The trench would have fitted a glass, domed cover. Larger versions often were part of displays in shops.

EUROPE

In the Netherlands, wooden serving boards were traditionally made for use with sausages, to be passed round at the table. The board shown here is beautifully carved.

BEFORE YOU BUY

- **Shrinkage** Check for cracks caused by shrinkage in the wood.

- **Carving** Look for crisp, sharp carving on bread boards.
- **Woodworm** Check for signs of this, such as small holes.
- **Water** Avoid boards with a dry, white appearance. They are likely to have been immersed in water, which can lead to warping.

Carvers & Sharpeners

The very earliest knives were made from a piece of stone or bone, but by the Iron Age, developments in metalworking meant that iron was used. Knives were expensive and were made to last for a long time. By the 19thC, knives were also made of steel and from the 1920s, they were mass-produced in stainless steel. Until then, knives had always been hand-forged and were prone to rust.

Knife sharpening was traditionally carried out by itinerant knife grinders who would sharpen knives on a large stone. The first domestic sharpeners to be widely used date from the mid-19thC and are known as "steels". They are all of the same basic long, heavy shape, only differing in the type of handle used; some have horn handles and others, wooden ones.

Knife sharpeners as we know them date from the 20thC. Although they were produced in different shapes and sizes, they all work on the same principle.

Above are three different sharpeners. The "heart-shaped" one was made 1910–20. On the left is a Skyline knife sharpener from the late 1950s, first introduced in the 1930s and copied by many makers. The third is a c1930s slim version.

IDENTIFICATION
• **Domestic steels** These can be decorative, with handles of carved bone or stag's horn. This makes them very desirable to collectors.
• **Commercial steels** Butcher's shops' steels are larger.

CARVING SETS
Cased carving sets were produced for use at the table and are very collectible. A typical set comprises three pieces: a carving knife, fork, and sharpener. (See p.220.)
• **Materials** Some have horn, bone, or even ivory handles and may also have silver mounts.
• **Forks** Initially forks were aids to carving, and were not used for eating until the 18thC, but early forks were also used for roasting and toasting on an open fire. They were made from iron, brass, and by the 19thC, steel.
• **Flesh forks** Used to prepare meat, these have two prongs. (See p.219.)

CONDITION
Cases and their contents should be in good condition. Check the handles of knives, forks, and steels, to make sure that they are not loose.

Choppers & Slicers

The fall in demand for swords in the early 18thC led many swordsmiths to turn their hands to other items, including choppers. The blades were usually crescent-shaped and "pierced" with attractive designs.

The Industrial Revolution led to improvement in the design and manufacture of large tools, such as spades and hoes, and consequently of smaller items. By the 19thC, domestic chopping equipment was being made on a large scale in Britain in centres such as Sheffield in Yorkshire. In continental Europe and the USA however, tools such as choppers continued to be made by local craftsmen, so the pieces are often unmarked. Blades were originally made of iron, then fine steel in the 19thC, and stainless steel from the 1930s.

Flat metal herb and spice choppers are traditionally used on chopping boards, and curved blades on wooden bowls or mortars.

HANDLES

Several different styles of handles exist on herb choppers, see below. The earliest item shown is at the bottom of the picture and was made in the USA in the mid-19thC. The style of handle is known as a "tiller" handle. The feral (the part that joins the blade and handle) is made from brass.

On the left is an English chopper with a tee-shaped handle, stamped "Sheffield" on the blade. It was made in the early 1900s, although identical ones were still available in the 1930s. The one on the right was made in France in the 1950s and has a different style of handle again. It also has a "rocker-style" blade with the maker's name, Rival, stamped into it.

COLLECTIBILITY

• **Decoration** Those with decorative handles in the form of animals or attractive designs such as hearts or geometric patterns cut out of the blade itself are more appealing than plain examples.
• **Marks** As choppers were not always marked, a maker's name is not essential for it to be collectible.
• **Fruitwood** Choppers with turned fruitwood handles are occasionally found – even if unmarked, the presence of such an unusual handle will be enough to increase its value.

MEAT CLEAVERS

Meat cleavers or choppers consist of

a blade on a wooden handle, usually of beech, ash, sycamore, or fruitwood. They were used both for chopping meat and for disjointing bones. By the 19thC, most choppers were made in Sheffield and therefore are stamped on the blade.

IDENTIFICATION

• **Early 20thC herb choppers** Typical features of these include a decorative join between the handle and the blade. Triangular joins are also a common feature.
• **French meat cleavers** These have a distinctive shape – the blade turns up at the end.

CONDITION

• **Pitting** Choppers sometimes have substantial pitting on the surface of the blade. This should not affect value or deter collectors.
• **Packaging** Utensils are rarely found in their original packaging, so this increases value substantially.

SLICERS

• **Marmalade slicers** Among the most collectible types of slicers are marmalade cutters. First produced in the late 19thC, early marmalade cutters typically comprised a heavy iron mechanism that clamped onto a table and worked with a lever action. A typical example is the "Universal" marmalade cutter from 1900. By the 1920s, new designs had been introduced. These included a novel orange shredder

shaped like a patty pan. It was made of tinned steel and had cutting perforations. The orange was worked by hand around the shredder. Although ingenious, it was never as efficient as other slicers and few were produced.
• **Bean slicers** A special slicer was made for the purpose of preparing beans.
• **Cucumber slicers** These became popular in the 19thC; typical examples consisted of a wooden frame with a blade across it, which could be taken out for sharpening.
• **Sauerkraut slicers or graters** Used for shredding the cabbage for this traditional dish, these are similar in appearance to cucumber slicers, and easily mistaken for them. They have changed little in design over the years. They are very common in continental Europe. (See above.)
• **Multi-purpose** In the 1930s, the firm of Spong produced a marmalade slicer that was also promoted as a general purpose slicer for carrots, potatoes, and other vegetables, which increased its appeal to potential buyers. It was made in an acid-proof brown lacquer finish for durability.

MAKERS

Slicers were often marked with the maker's name, sometimes in raised lettering. Names to look out for include Spong and Rapid. Unmarked slicers can still be collectible, however.

Drainers & Strainers

Drainers and strainers have different functions. A drainer has larger perforations and is used to drain water away from food, whereas a strainer strains the food through a mesh to leave unwanted lumps behind.

Implements for draining food, for skimming fat from meat stews and soups, or for lifting food from boiling liquids have been known by a variety of names over the centuries. In the 17thC, a skimming tool, a ladle with crudely punched holes in the base to remove scum from soups, was known as a scummer. In the 18thC the name changed to skimmer. Tin skimmers were made in the late 19thC until the 1900s. Enamel was popular in the 20thC, as was aluminium. (See pp.225–227.)

COLANDERS

A colander is used to drain food cooked in liquid, but its name is derived from the Latin *colare*, to strain. Their basic design has not changed much, comprising a bowl with perforated holes in the base and side with two handles.

• **Bases** Colanders with a ring base, feet, or peg-legs are known as "foot-fast" while those without are commonly known as "foot-loose".

• **Materials** In the 18thC, colanders were often made from brass or even copper, but by the 19thC tin, earthenware, enamel, and copper were commonly used. They were sometimes made from brass and steel. Earthenware colanders can be very simple affairs, and sometimes resemble mixing bowls with holes in them.

• **Enamel** This has been a popular material for colanders since the 1900s in Britain, while in the USA it has been used since the 1880s.

• **Graniteware** This was popular in the United States and around 1900, some graniteware colanders were made in the form of a pan with a long handle, which even had a support for resting the pan. The enamel was applied onto iron, making it heavy, but durable.

• **Finland** There was a thriving enamel industry here until WWII, and its products are characterized by the unique use of an aqua-green colour. This is sometimes seen on the handles and rims of Finnish colanders and other implements.

• **1950s enamel colanders** These tend to be more lightly enamelled than later ones.

SALAD SHAKERS AND DRAINERS

These were both used to drain excess water away from lettuce, but shakers are made from flexible wire netting, while salad baskets are usually made of stronger wire. France is one of the main production centres for both types.

SLICES

Trowel-shaped draining slices are specifically for fish and their rounder blades distinguish them from egg slices. Slices are commonly found in both enamel and aluminium.

IDENTIFICATION & DATING

• **Salad shakers** Baskets for shaking salad bear a resemblance to egg baskets, but they have much smaller openings. Some have a piece of looped wire attached that can be folded over the opening when shaking the salad.

• **Earlier fish slices** These have a wider blade and more pronounced curve on the top of the blade.

• **Enamelware** Plain and simple designs were preferred in some countries, such as Britain,

Yugoslavia, and Poland. France, Germany, and Holland on the other hand, produced more imaginative and colourful pieces.

MAKERS

Colander makers include Crown Merton and Falconware; Diamond Brand were important makers of slices.

COLLECTIBILITY

• **Unusual and rare items** These include fish drainers such as below. Fish would be placed into these long drainers after preparation and washing to drain away excess water.

They are occasionally mistaken for plate drainers.

• **Pre-1960s enamelware** This is widely collected. Condition is important, but chips are acceptable as long as they do not come into contact with the food.

• **Wirework** Strainers and drainers were often made in wirework. It can be very attractive, so has many followers and is avidly collected in its own right.

Enamelling

Enamelling has been an art form since the Ancient Chinese first practised it in the Tang Dynasty (AD 618–906). However, the mid-19thC saw the first commercial use of enamelling on metals with the mass production of enamelled cookware, known as enamelware in Britain and graniteware in North America. Various metals have been successfully enamelled, especially iron and steel, and hard-wearing and attractive utensils were produced in a variety of colours and patterns. Appropriate names were quickly adopted for the different patterns, such as splatter, mottle, feathered, shaded, and chickwire.

Gadgets

The vast number and variety of kitchen utensils that has been made over the last century or so reflects the number of jobs carried out in the kitchen. The design of many items, such as nutcrackers or pepper-mills, has changed little over the years, an indication of their usefulness and durability. Others, such as tin openers, have changed as the early designs did not stand the test of time or were superseded. Gadgets to look out for include ice cream wafer holders and cheese testers, as well as the many specially-designed knives for opening oysters or segmenting grapefruit. Raisin seeders, cherry stoners, and apple peelers are also good examples of collectible gadgets.

OPENERS

While the first patent for the canning process was taken out in London in 1810, it was not until the 1870s that the first opener appeared. Until then, customers were advised to use a hammer and chisel! Credit for the first successful tin (or can as they are called in North America) depends on which side of the Atlantic you happen to be. In the USA, it is maintained that the first successful example was invented by Thomas Kensitt in 1813, while in Britain it is argued that it was first made in a cannery owned by Donkin & Hall of Bermondsey, London, in 1812.

One of the best-known early tin openers was launched in America in 1875 by J. A. Wilson of Chicago, who sold it with their newly-introduced tinned corned beef, known as bully beef.

• **Corkscrews** A very popular collecting field today, many designs were made and in large numbers, so condition is important. Some corkscrews come with a brush attached to the handle – this is for dusting cobwebs from bottles in a dusty cellar. Those of the "straight pull" variety are the simplest and are often among the most affordable.

• **Nutcrackers** These were made in large numbers and are collectible. They were made in various materials including wood, iron, brass, and even silver. One simple but effective design uses hinged jaws to crack the nut and many examples made in the 1920s were nickel-plated. This design is still being produced today, although rarely nickel plated.

• **Ballers** Used for making attractive spherical shapes of vegetables (for garnishing soups) or butter, these comprise a metal half-sphere attached to a handle.

Vegetable ballers appeared in the 19thC, with melon and butter ballers following in the 20thC.

• **Wooden honey sticks** The turned ridges at the end mean that when placed into a honey pot, turned and then lifted out, the honey holds between the ridges and can be dipped on to bread or toast.

• **Spurtles** Shown below, these are traditional Scottish kitchen utensils for stirring porridge to make a smooth texture and to stop it from sticking to the pan. A similar utensil, called a porridge stirrer, was used in

the north of England to a lesser extent, but these were simple plain-waisted sticks.

• **Pastry blenders** Those above are British, c1930–50s. They are used for blending the fat and flour together when making pastry. A similar blender was patented in the USA in 1929 and exported to

Britain, which suggests that Britain may have copied the idea.

IDENTIFICATION & DATING
• "Bull's head" tin openers (see below left) So-called because of their shape, these are among the simplest types and were produced by various firms betwen 1870 and the 1930s. Later ones have the blade fixed through the neck, but it could be unscrewed for sharpening.
• **Early spurtles** Plain and simple, these were waisted at the top end to form a grip with plain rounded ends. Later, the knobs developed into thistle tops.

COLLECTIBILITY
• **Palette knives and spreaders** Known as spatulas in the USA, these are collectible, but 19thC ones are especially sought after.
• **Unusual gadgets** Raisin seeders, for example, are fun to collect. Used to seed raisins – a tiring and

laborious task – they were first produced in the USA and later in Britain. In Britain they were known as raisin stoners. (See p.229.)

MAKERS
Names to look out for include the American firms of Lockey & Holland, Reading Hardware Co., and Hudson & Co., as well as Skyline, Nutbrown, and Fentons.

Condition
• With corkscrews, always check that the screw part, known as the "worm" is not damaged, as this can lower the value.
• If the paint has worn off on handles with use, value will be affected.
• Cast-iron gadgets should be inspected for signs of rust. Slight rust damage may be acceptable, but too much will devalue an object.

Graters & Grinders

Grinding and grating were tasks that were carried out by the same basic equipment, such as the mortar and pestle and the simple iron grater, for many centuries. The Great Exhibition of 1851 gave a showcase to British industries and encouraged makers to invent a whole new range of kitchen implements. After one such exhibition, in 1854, *The Times* described an "ingenious mincing machine"

exhibited by Nye & Company of Soho, London, which could make 8lbs (3.6kg) of minced meat in just four minutes. By the 1860s, industry had produced mincers, sausage-making machines, rotary graters, and a whole host of other clever labour-saving devices. Most were made from cast iron until the late 19thC when steel, and later stainless steel, became more common.

GRATERS
Punched iron graters have been used in cooking for centuries, mainly for grating hard cheese or for breadcrumbs from stale bread. In the 16thC, sheet brass graters were introduced to Britain when there was an influx of Dutch brass workers and brass graters were still popular in the 19thC.

• **Early 19thC graters** These were made from sheets of punched metal with rolled edges around an iron or wire frame. Later, the joins were machine-pressed or seamed.
• **Wooden box** Some graters incorporated a wooden box to catch the gratings. The box should be original; if it is not, this will reduce the value.

• **Bread rasp** This is another type of grater that was available in three sizes, whose purpose was to scrape the burnt bottoms of loaves.
• "Wonder shredders" Made in the USA, these came in sets of different sizes for fine or coarse shredding. The name is stamped into the metal.

PESTLES & MORTARS

The pestle and mortar has had a variety of uses, including pounding herbs and spices, crushing salt, and mashing vegetables. It was also used by apothecaries to make medicines from herbs and spices, in coffee shops to grind beans, and in tobacco shops, where the tobacco was crushed into snuff. The various shapes of the mortar – cylindrical, hexagonal, and octagonal – date back to the 17thC and they were made in all sizes, from a few inches/centimetres high to huge, ones up to 5ft (1.5m) high.

• **Floor standing mortars** These were usually made of stone or marble, while wood was used for smaller ones. Oak, elm, beech, and walnut were common, but the favourite was the hard, dark wood lignum vitae, partly because of its supposed medicinal properties.

MAKERS

• **Wedgwood** By the 19thC, this firm was the best known maker of earthenware mortars and pestles.
• **Kenrick** Best known for their coffee grinders (see the small one on the right), Kenrick made cast-iron pestles and mortars c1860–1900.
• **S. Maw & Son** Known for the manufacture of medical implements, they were leading manufacturers of mortars and pestles.

IDENTIFICATION

• **Kenrick** Their mortars were marked on the base.
• **"Made in England"** Mortars with this stamp date from after 1900.

COFFEE GRINDERS

Coffee had become a favourite drink with the middle and upper classes by the mid-18thC – these were the only people who could afford to drink it at the time. Coffee was ground by grocers in large cast-

iron mills, but it became fashionable to grind coffee at home, using small wooden coffee grinders.
• **France** Peugeot Frères was an important maker. (See p.233.)
• **Box-type** In 1815, the iron founder Archibald Kenrick patented this new type of cast-iron coffee grinder.
• **Copies** This design was copied by many other firms and iron founders such as Clark, Baldwin, and Siddons from the 19thC until WWI and they are highly collectible today.
• **Design** Box-type grinders were all similar in design. Two are shown below; the one on the left was made c1860 by Baldwin, iron founders based in Stourport in Worcs, while the smaller one is by Kenrick. They produced grinders in various sizes and the one that is shown is the "000" or smallest size, capable of producing enough coffee for a single cup. The largest, "No. 5", can grind approximately three to four cups' worth. The size of the grinder is determined by the amount of coffee the drawer can hold.

AMERICA

The major producer of coffee grinders in the USA from the 19thC onwards was the Enterprise Manufacturing Company of Philadelphia. Offered under the brand names American Coffee, Spice and Drug Mill, the company's grinders were originally intended for use by grocers and coffee dealers. Many were large in size and became a distinctive feature of many general stores.

COLLECTIBILITY

• **Cast iron wall-mounted grinders** These grinders are especially collectible.
• **Round coffee grinders** Much rarer than square ones, these are highly sought after.
• **Siddons** A large iron foundry in West Bromwich in the Midlands, this firm made round coffee grinders in the 1880s. They made far fewer grinders than Kenrick, so their products are particularly desirable today.
• **Kenrick** In the late 19thC, Kenrick made a cast-iron grinder/mincer that was modelled as York Minster. This highly unusual design is very collectible today.
• **Wood and brass** Coffee grinders made of these materials from the 1920s are worth around a quarter of the value of a comparable 19thC example.

Condition

• Always check that the bowl is in good condition; it is the weakest part of the coffee grinder and is prone to cracking or splitting.
• Some coffee grinders have a wooden base, which is painted. Others have a painted tin base. The paint should ideally be in good condition, although some collectors feel that a little wear adds to its character.

UTENSILS

IDENTIFICATION AND DATING

• **Early grinders** These had brass or copper bowls.
• **Kenrick** Their coffee grinders always have the company's name on the front on a thin oval brass plate.
• **Early Kenrick grinders** These are labelled Archibald Kenrick Iron Foundry, becoming Kenrick & Sons in the late 19thC.

NUTMEG GRATERS

Nutmeg was a very popular spice throughout Europe in the 18thC and 19thC and it was often ground up and sprinkled into drinks. Small nutmeg graters were often carried by travellers to add the spice to their ale at wayside inns. In the kitchen, it was widely used in baking and graters were made specifically for use when preparing nutmeg.
• **Late 19thC** The example below, made in the USA, stored the nutmeg inside the handle, fitting into the mechanism. It would be

ground by turning a handle. This model came complete with a wire brush for cleaning the grater.
• **Treen** Some nutmeg graters were made from treen. These were made in various shapes, but the acorn was a popular choice. Such graters might be made from the coquilla nut, or from carved sycamore or walnut. The nutmeg would be kept inside a decorative case, along with the grater. The metal grater inside can often be prone to rust, so beware.
• **Folding nutmeg graters** These were popular in the late 19thC. They were made to be carried around and used to grate nutmeg into milk, mulled wine, or hot chocolate. The grater folds in such a way that the sharp edges are covered, preventing damage to the pocket. Many of these examples were originally japanned, but the colour is prone to wear and may have worn off over the years. This will devalue the piece somewhat.

MINCERS

Mincers, which were known as grinders in the USA, first appeared in the 1870s for the grinding and mincing of meat and were generally made from tinned steel, cast iron, and enamelled iron or tin. Important makers of mincers in Britain included Spong, who produced a wide variety of machines for both domestic and professional catering use. In North America, mincers or grinders first appeared in large numbers from the 1890s. Well-known makers include the Enterprise Manufacturing Company.

COLLECTIBILITY

• **Treen** This is very collectible, so nutmeg graters with treen cases tend to be expensive.
• **Acme** This firm's products are always popular with collectors. The Acme range included tin graters, marked with the company name and a number. (See p.233.)

RARE ITEMS

Rare items include an ingenious coconut grater. It stood on a worktop and had a handle connected to circular blades with serrated edges that rotated when the handle was turned. It was made around the mid-19thC, possibly for use in British colonies. This very rare piece is highly sought after by collectors today.

Juicers & Funnels

Funnels were used for many different purposes in the kitchen such as funnelling lamp oil, jam, fruit juices, and drinks. Lamp and drink funnels were the earliest produced, dating from the early 19thC. By the late 19thC, funnels had more uses and the purpose of the funnel can be gauged by its size. Short, wide funnels were suitable for filling jars while long, thin ones were best used for bottles with similar-shaped necks. Some funnels have a fine mesh at the top of the tube, probably for filtering liquids.

Squeezers for citrus fruits were found in most homes in the 19thC. Fruit juices were not only important as ingredients in cooking, but also formed the basis of popular home-made drinks. These squeezers were made of glass and have remained unchanged ever since. Pottery squeezers were made, often in novelty shapes, in the 1920s and 30s and plastic ones started to appear in the late 1930s. Aluminium ones were also produced, many, but by no means all of them, in the USA. There are some differences in terminology for juicers and squeezers between the USA and the UK (see opposite).

• **Wall juicers** Some juicers, such as the American aluminium Speedo "Super Juicer", made in the 1930s, were designed to be attached to a wall. If the bracket is missing, a modern one can be substituted without affecting its value.

• **Pip guards** Useful features found on some squeezers. Labour-saving devices, they avoided the need to pour the juice through a strainer afterwards. Those with guards were more expensive than plain ones.

• **Lemon and lime squeezers** Some types had hinged arms and cups in which the fruit would be squeezed. The mid-19thC example above has hardwood arms and pottery cups, and the hinges were of brass so that they would not corrode. Cups were also made from enamel or glass. This type of squeezer was also made in cast iron from the late 1870s to the 1920s; galvanized to stop corrosion.

RARE ITEMS
One rare example is a large American squeezer that was made in the 1940s. It is marked "Ade-O-Matic-Pat-Pending-Patent Applied-Genuine Corsta Porcelain". It works on an armalian (spiral) mechanism and the dome can be easily removed for cleaning. Another rare item is an intricately-made mesh lemon squeezer that clips onto the top of a glass.

IDENTIFICATION
Squeezers were sometimes made from urea formaldehyde, a type of plastic that was used to make kitchenware, some in a mottled pattern. It is often mistaken for Bakelite, which also came in mottled patterns, but it is important to remember that Bakelite was only made in dark colours, such as brown, red, and green. Also, while Bakelite was widely used for handles, it was seldom used for items for food preparation because it tended to give off an unpleasant smell and taint food.

TYPES OF FUNNEL
The funnels shown on the right were made between the 1890s and the 1950s from a variety of materials. The oldest and rarest is on the far right, made in North America in the 1900s, specifically for stuffing a jam filling into Bismark cakes, a type of cake popular at the time but rarely made today. The most modern is the small white plastic salt funnel, offered as a promotional piece by the makers of Cerebos salt.

Ladles & Spoons

Ladles were traditionally made from many different materials including pewter, brass, and from the 19thC onwards, enamel. From this period, wooden handles were added. Look out for side-snipe ladles, which have a lip and were most suitable for pouring.

Ladles and spoons were traditionally hung up close at hand to the cooking area when not in use. By the 1850s, special racks had appeared, and by the late 19thC these had a trough at the bottom to catch any drips. Initially, they were made from wrought iron, then enamelled iron, and later from stamped sheet aluminium until the 1930s. Aluminium racks often featured embossed designs reflecting the style of where it was made.

The most colourful and collectible enamel racks were made in Belgium, Germany, and Holland in the early 20thC.

UTENSILS

from strong hardwoods such as beech, sycamore, ash, and olive and were versatile enough to tackle a variety of jobs. Mass production began in the 19thC both in Europe and North America.

TYPES OF SPOON

• **Wooden spoons** These were made in different forms according to their purpose. Spoons with holes can be used to add extra air to batter; long flat spoons are ideal for scraping bowls, while slotted ones can be used to serve and drain.

• **Metal spoons** A selection of metal spoons of different types can be seen below. At the top is a 1900s American stamped-tin tasting spoon with a suitably deep and curved bow. Below it is a Victorian tinned-steel basting spoon. The perforated spoon (second from bottom) was made in Belgium from the 1930s to

• **Racks** The red enamel utensil rack shown above was made in France and still has its original set of three matching utensils, a skimmer, a soup ladle, and a side-snipe ladle. The rack is a desirable piece as it has been beautifully designed and is in excellent condition.

• **Materials** Some ladles were made in brass and iron, the iron forming the handle, while the spoon was made of brass. They have a hole in the handle for hanging. Wooden spoons, like rolling pins, were originally carved by hand at home. They were made

Identification
• Until the 1920s, wooden spoons were available in only one shape, with the handle and bowl generally carved separately.
• From 1920 onwards, different designs were produced, based on the shapes of iron and steel spoons.
• The size and shape of a wooden spoon reveals its purpose. Early spoons often had a ball-end on the handle, which was used to settle fruit and vegetables in preserving jars and to help shape a cottage loaf in bread making.
• In Britain and North America, wooden spoons with thick scooped-out bowls are used to stir and beat.
• In France, flat rectangular spatulas are commonly used, as they fit the flat-bottomed mixing bowls used in a French kitchen.

the 1940s, while the slotted spoon (bottom) is a good example of an American cake mixer spoon.

Thermometers

The first thermometer was created in an experiment by Galileo in 1593. He discovered that liquid in a glass tube would rise and fall as the temperature changed. The modern thermometer dates back to the early 18thC when alcohol and mercury thermometers were invented by the German physicist Daniel Gabriel Fahrenheit (1686–1736), who gave his name to the Fahrenheit temperature scale. The Swedish astronomer Anders Celcius (1701–44) devised the scale that we also know as centigrade, based on water, with zero as

the freezing point of the liquid and 100 as its boiling point.

As recipes became more complicated and stoves more advanced and reliable, so the thermometer became a valuable cooking aid. It not only allowed the cook to keep an eye on the food to make sure it was perfectly cooked, but meat thermometers therefore made cooking safer, because it was possible to ensure that harmful bacteria had been destroyed. As you will see they were also used in the production of milk and cheese. (See p.242.)

• **Uses** Thermometers had many uses, including for jam- and preserve-making and bottling.

• **Dairy thermometers** These were essential aids to the production of butter or cheese. They would typically float on the surface of the milk and were made from glass. Some dairy thermometers have a wooden surround while others are ceramic.

• **Temperature advice** Some thermometers included advice on the appropriate temperatures required for various foods.

MAKERS

British makers of thermometers include Brooks & Walker of London, while Taylor is one of the best-known American makes. Another American maker is Buckeye of Ohio.

CONDITION

Thermometers should be complete and in good working order.

• **Scales** These should be complete and readable.

• **Discolouration** Some oven thermometers become discoloured through use – this may be acceptable

as long as it is not too serious.

• **Original boxes** Typically, these are always desirable.

COLLECTIBILITY

• **Advertising** Thermometers that feature advertising are particularly collectible. They can be subdivided into different themes according to the products advertised on them. Firms such as Pepsi and Coca Cola produced thermometers advertising their wares – collecting memorabilia relating to these products is a specialist field in itself.

Whisks & Beaters

Wire balloon whisks have been a favourite with cooks since the end of the 18thC, but it was the invention of the rotary egg beater in the early 20thC that had the most important impact on the development of kitchen utensils. It was capable of whisking food much faster and with greater efficiency than hand whisks. It was so successful that the

rotary mechanism was soon applied to a range of other cooking utensils, such as cake mixers, food blenders, and bread makers.

North America produced rotary egg beaters in large numbers and exported many of them to Europe in the 19thC. From the 20thC, European firms made their own, often copying American designs. (See pp.243–246.)

The whisks shown below include three "Archimedean" screw-type whisks, which work by pressing the knob up and down, thus curling or twisting the whisk part. The one with the green handle was made in the 1920s, while the version with the turned handle dates from the 1900s. This is more valuable as it has a particularly attractive wire arrangement. The red-handled one dates from the 1920s. Nutbrown made the spiral whisk at the bottom

from the 1930s to the 1950s.

• **Rotary whisks** When choosing a rotary whisk, always try it first but hold the beater upright whilst doing this otherwise the air will prevent it from turning smoothly.

• **Types** Other beaters and whisks that are now collectible include a special spoon, made in the late 1920s, that was capable of separating the white form the yolk of an egg and could also be used for beating eggs, stirring sauces, draining, and serving.

• **Egg beaters** These were produced in many different designs. One popular design comprised a ceramic jar with the metal beater inside. They would often have the name of the device on the jar, such as "The Speedy Egg Beater". Other names include the "Gourmet",

Terminology

In Britain, hand and rotary whisks have been called a various names, such as egg whisks, batter beaters, and egg beaters. In America, it is much simpler; rotary whisks (with handles) are called egg beaters, while those without handles are called whisks. Both countries produced a wide variety of each.

which was available in graduated sets. Beaters were also made with glass jars.

IDENTIFICATION AND DATING

• **Early whisks** These were generally made from twisted wire; they are desirable to collectors of wirework.

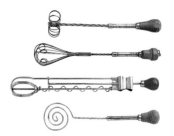

UTENSILS

Tableware

While much of the tableware we now take for granted was already established by the 19thC, the Victorian era saw the growth and development of formal dining as we understand it today. This encouraged the production of cutlery and tableware for very specific purposes and an emerging middle class was keen to acquire tableware that reflected its social status and aspirations.

Industry responded, producing a wealth of goods in a wide variety of patterns and designs. Companies competed fiercely to follow changing fashions and trends, so that the story of tableware reflects design history. The 1920s and 30s for example, saw the flourishing of Art Deco, a style that was manifested in colourful but practical and useful wares on countless breakfast tables.

Tableware is a rewarding field of collecting. with many individual collecting niches.

Butter & Cheese Dishes

Butter dishes were often made for storing butter in the pantry, and so many of these are of plain white earthenware. However, those used for bringing butter to the table were more decorative.

Butter dishes with carved wooden surrounds became popular in the 20thC. The surrounds, carved with the word "butter" and/or appropriate motifs, were often used with a blue or clear glass dish. They were also used with ceramic dishes. Being fragile, these glass or ceramic dishes were often broken and replacements were substituted.

Cheese was and is often served on wooden boards, rather like breadboards. Sycamore and elm were popular and, like breadboards, they are often decoratively carved. They sometimes simply feature the word "cheese" or they might have more complex designs and/or a motto.

ROYAL WINTON

Royal Winton is the trade name of Grimwade's Ltd., based at the Winton Pottery (est. 1885) in Stoke-on-Trent. The company made a wide range of tableware and, in the 1930s, became particularly well known for its chintzware (see p.253), a style that was also produced by other makers including Crown Ducal and Midwinter. This affordable tableware with its all-over floral patterns included butter and cheese dishes and was made in large quantities; it is increasingly sought after around the world.

• **Patterns** The first Royal Winton chintz pattern was "Marguerite", launched in 1928.

• **"Ascot" range** This was always popular and included the highly sought after "Julia" pattern which included a lidded butter dish. They were moulded, glazed, skilfully covered with the transfer-printed pattern, and then re-glazed.

The firm went on to produce more than 60 chintz patterns until the early 1960s when it was discontinued, although production of chintzware began again in the 1990s. New products are given a year stamp to avoid confusion with older pieces.

• **Condition** One drawback of the "double glazing" of the Ascot range is that it is particularly susceptible to crazing, which is a network of fine cracks. It will not normally detract from the value provided that the piece is otherwise in good condition, with no hairline cracks or hand-painted restoration.

COTTAGE WARE

In the 1920s and 30s, there was a nostalgic fashion for "Cottage Ware", featuring tableware in the form of an English country cottage complete with thatched roof. Teapots, milk jugs, sugar bowls, and butter and cheese dishes were made in this form by several factories including Royal Winton, SylvaC, Carlton Ware, and Beswick. The roof formed the lid of the dish with the butter or cheese inside the cottage. Cottage Ware was also made in Japan for export.

GLASS

Makers of glass cheese and butter dishes included Bagley's of Knottingley, Yorkshire, which became one of Britain's most successful glass manufacturers. The

firm opened in 1871 as a bottle works, but went on to become a major manufacturer of pressed glass from the 1920s. The firm produced tableware such as the cheese dish above as well as decorative items such as vanity sets for the dressing table and introduced its coloured "crystaltynt" glass in 1933, making objects in pastel green, pink, amber, and blue shades.

• **Popular patterns** These included the "honeycomb" and the "carnival" pattern. The latter is not, however, "Carnival Glass", which is a generic term for iridescent pressed glassware and is quite different.

NEW TYPES OF CHEESE
During the 19thC, different varieties

of cheese became more familiar at dinner tables. This was largely due to improving transport links, notably the railways. Some types of cheese, such as soft cheeses, did not previously travel well as they would have been spoilt during the journey. This made some varieties unknown outside the producing areas.

STILTON
One of the most famous regional cheeses is Stilton, which can only be given that name if it is made in one of the three English counties of Derbyshire, Leicestershire, and Nottinghamshire. There is a place called Stilton, but the cheese that bears its name has never been made there. The Victorians, in their fondness for specialist serving dishes for everything from sardines to oysters, served Stilton on special dishes.

• **Stands** Some Stilton dishes are in the form of stands. Many were made by the Staffordshire potteries and blue-and-white patterns were among the most popular.

• **Dudson** This Staffordshire firm made a variety of tableware including many cheese dishes, among them a Stilton dish in jasperware.

• **"Bells"** Covers on round cheese dishes are often referred to as "bells" because of their shape.

COASTERS
Cheese coasters were popular for serving cheese at the dinner table in the early 19thC. They were usually made of mahogany and in an undulating cradle form. They were ideal for passing cheese around from one guest to another and, when fitted with small brass castors, the task was made easier still. They are often of interest to collectors of treen and can be very valuable (see below).

Cruets

Cruets first appeared in the late 17thC, when oil and vinegar were introduced as condiments. Technically, a cruet set consists of a salt pot, a pepper pot, and a lidded mustard pot, but salt and pepper pots are often collected as pairs on their own. Cruet sets made by a particular pottery offer the chance to collect certain designs and patterns with a smaller outlay than would be required for larger items in the range.

Sometimes, sets were made which included egg cups or preserve pots. All the pieces should be present, although it may be possible to find a match for missing items.

NOVELTY AND FIGURAL SETS
Cruet sets are ideal as novelty items and have been used in this way for a long time.

• **Roger Giles** Staffordshire novelties of the early 19thC include an amusing pepper pot figure of Roger Giles in a stooping position (see right). It is said that the real-

life Roger Giles was a Devonshire man who advertised eggs for sale as "new laid by him each day", hence the inspiration. These pots are quite valuable today.

LAUREL AND HARDY
The popularity of the cinema saw many ceramic cruets inspired by

popular film or cartoon characters, in particular, Laurel and Hardy. An ingenious design by Beswick (est. 1840) featured the duo's heads on a separate base in the form of their collars and ties. The base is often missing and the complete set is rare.
• **Colour** The heads were painted in a variety of flesh tones; the deeper the tone the more desirable.
• **Collectibility** As individual pieces, "Hardy" is more popular than "Laurel".

OTHER SUBJECTS
• **Animals** Perennial favourites as many collectors have themed collections based on specific animals, so cruets in these forms will appeal to a wider group of collectors.
• **Japan** The Japanese made many inexpensive figural cruet sets. Subjects include birds, clowns, chickens, dogs, and pigs.
• **Sports** Sporting heroes have also been immortalized in cruet sets. Although not figural sets, the Staffordshire firm of Sandland (1944–68), made the salt and pepper pots below, with images of the famous cricketers Jack Hobbs and Maurice Tate in the 1950s.

CONDITION & COLLECTIBILITY
• **Damage** Good condition is essential for novelty ware. Very minor damage can be acceptable if it is a particularly unusual or rare piece, but it must be reflected in the price.
• **Check** Any protruding areas are particularly susceptible to damage and must be carefully checked for signs of chips and other damage.

PROMOTIONAL ITEMS
Cruet sets have proved ideal for promoting a variety of products. Bovril, the popular beef extract, spawned a variety of merchandise including the attractive pewter pepper pot on the right. Made in the early 20thC in the form of a castellated tower, rather like a chesss rook, it is a valuable collectible today.

JAPAN
In the first half of the 20thC, the Japanese exported vast quantities of tableware to suit Western tastes. They were inexpensive at the time and can still be affordable, but are increasingly popular with collectors.
• **Noritake** One of the most important Japanese companies to

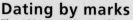

produce cruet sets and other tableware was the Noritake Co., established in Nagoya in 1904 by Icizaemon Morimura. Early products copied Rococo-style European wares decorated with flowers, fruit, foliage, and landscapes in pale pastel tones with gold relief highlights. During the 1920s, well known designers – including Frank Lloyd Wright – were commissioned to produced Deco-style designs.
• **Marks** Those used on many Noritake wares incorporate the letter "M" (for Morimura).

Cutlery

The typical modern day arrangement at the table of knife, fork, and spoon, evolved gradually. The knife was the earliest of the three, and people used to carry their own personal knives for eating. The spoon was known in Roman times and, like the knife, it was a treasured possession. Spoons were made from bronze, pewter, or if you were particularly wealthy, silver. During the middle ages and the Renaissance, things began to change. The fork was introduced as a table implement in its own right, rather than as a carving aid. The Italians are believed to have been the first to use forks in this way, instead of using the fingers to pick up food. Italian fashions were much admired all over Europe and so the habit spread. Even

so, forks were only used for sweetmeats or desserts until the 16thC in continental Europe and the late 17thC in Britain. It was not until the 18thC that matching sets of spoons, forks, and knives were produced, probably because of the fashion for dinner services with matching ornament. Thereafter, they were made on a large scale and in an extensive range of patterns.

The 19thC brought new technology and production methods that brought down the cost of cutlery. The Birmingham firm of Elkington & Co. took out the first patent for the first effective process of electroplating, which led to the mass production of affordable cutlery with the appearance of silver.

THE VICTORIANS

The Victorian passion for formal dining gave rise to many new forms of cutlery, designed to be used with a specific course or type of food. A complete table service would normally comprise 12 each of tablespoons, table forks, dessert spoons, and dessert forks; nine teaspoons; and a pair of basting spoons. However, many services were augmented during the Victorian period with, among other items, fish and dessert knives and forks (below are fruit knives and forks). It would therefore not be unusual to find some pieces of a later date than the rest of the service.

MANUFACTURERS

In Britain, Birmingham and London boasted many cutlery makers, but by far the most important centre of manufacture was Sheffield, where cutlery has been made since the end of the 13thC. Names to look out for include Viners, Mappin & Webb, Atkin Bros., Cooper Bros., Henry Wilkinson & Co., and James Dixon & Sons.

PATTERNS

• **Hanoverian** This was the first pattern for matching flatware. It features a flat, rounded end turned upward and a ridge across the front of the handle. Coats of arms or crests were engraved on the back of the stem, as flatware was laid face down, in the French manner.
• **Old English** Available from the 1760s, with a plain, rounded end but turned down instead of up (on spoons), according to the new fashion of placing cutlery face up on the table. In the same period, forks were made with four instead of three tines, or prongs.

• **Other popular styles** By the late 18th and 19thC these included the "fiddle" (with the end of the handle in a fiddle shape), and the more ornate "King's" and "Queen's" pattern. Flatware of this date was often supplied with a fitted case.
• **"Beaded"** Flatware edged with a row of small beads was popular in the Victorian period.
• **Plated wares** These followed the patterns of their silver counterparts.

COLLECTIBILITY

Cutlery is known as flatware and remains among the most popular antique silver today.
• **Sets** Complete and original sets of silver flatware, even from the 20thC, are rare because individual pieces were often very heavily used and then replaced.
• **Look for** Check patterns for small variations in design. However, old services will have been hand forged, so there may be slight variations in size.
• **Electroplated flatware** This is generally less collectible than silver,

unless it is by Elkington's, who first developed the technique.

CONDITION

• **Sets** The most collectible sets are those with an equal amount of wear on each piece.

• **Look for** Beware of forks that have been trimmed off (this is hard to detect) and for spoons whose bowls have been reshaped to disguise wear.

• **Knives made before 1800** These are quite common, but very few have survived in good condition. Reproduction knives of the same pattern are commonly offered to accompany an antique service of this age and this is quite acceptable.

• **Handles** Always check bone or wooden handles to make sure they are firm and have not worked loose. Solder on old silver-handled knives

is prone to crumbling.

• **Arms** Silver flatware from the 18th and 19thC was often engraved with the owner's coat of arms. The arms may have been subsequently removed when a service was sold on. This is not a problem so long as it has been properly done and the surface is flat, with no sign of indentations where the removal has been carried out.

• **Patina** Silver acquires a unique patina over the years, which can be destroyed by excessive polishing and this will adversely affect the value.

IDENTIFICATION AND FAKES

• **Hallmarking** This was introduced in England in 1300.

• **Electroplating** This was initially carried out using copper, but nickel was later used. The initials EPNS on flatware, stands for Electroplated Nickel Silver).

• **Early forks** These are rare and much sought after. Some fakes have been converted from spoons, but they can be identified because the proportions are wrong and the tines are too thin. Early forks were usually thick and heavy (see above).

Honey Pots

Honey has always been highly prized since Ancient times. Until the arrival of sugar from the West Indies in the 18thC, honey was the only widely available form of sweetener.

Although it was largely supplanted by sugar as far as everyday sweetening was concerned, honey continued to be popular at the table.

CLARICE CLIFF

Clarice Cliff produced honey pots in her "Bizarre" range of pottery.

• **Autumn Crocus** This is among the most popular of her honey pots. It was made in two sizes, with a bee on the lid. Made in large quantities from the late 1920s to 1939, it is widely found and so affordable.

• **Colours** By 1934, it was available in different colour schemes, "Spring" with pastel pink, blue, and green flowers as well as "Autumn" with blue, purple, and orange flowers; "Sungleam" with orange and yellow flowers; and the more rare "Blue" and "Purple" (with blue and purple flowers respectively).

SHAPES

• **Various** Hives or skeps (portable hives often made of straw) are popular forms for honey pots, but other popular choices include bears and bees. Honey pots are mostly round, but a great many square honey pots were made by various firms such as Poole Pottery, Shorter & Son, and Carlton Ware.

• **Winnie the Pooh honey pots** These were made in large numbers under licence from Walt Disney, so are likely to attract Disney collectors.

MAKERS

Most of the major potteries have included honey pots in their

repertoire; the following are just a few of those worth looking out for.

• **Crown Devon** This is the trade name used by the family firm of S. Fielding & Co., founded in Stoke-on-Trent in 1873.

• **Belleek** Founded in 1857, this Irish pottery initially produced earthenware. It went on to produce highly acclaimed quality tableware in fine parian china.

• **Wemyss Ware** This highly collectible Scottish pottery, which has risen considerably in value in recent years, is best known for figures of cats and pigs, although it also produced a large range of tableware. In 1930 the rights to produce Wemyss were bought by the Bovey Tracey pottery in Devon, which continued its production. Since the 1980s, Wemyss Ware returned to Fife, at the Griselda Hill pottery, which owns the name. Below is an early piece, dating to c1900.

• **Mellona** The best-known producer of honey in Holland is the firm of Mellona, who promoted its honey by selling it in attractive ceramic pots of various designs.

• **Goebel** Founded by Wilhelm Goebel in 1871, this is one of the best known German potteries and is still in business today. It is known for its Hummel figurines, but also produced many functional

items for the home including cruet sets and honey pots.

MARKS

• **Crown Devon** These wares are marked with the name of the firm and an elaborate crown. Some also feature the mark of the artist.

• **Belleek** Marks incorporate the company name, an Irish wolfhound, a tower, and a harp. The marks appeared in slightly different versions over time, but the colour is an important clue to dating Belleek. Marks were in black until 1946, when the colour was changed to green. Gold was used from 1981, blue from 1993, black again from 2000, and green from 2001.

Condition

• Lids may not be original, but do not assume that a slight difference in colour and glaze necessarily means that the lid does not match, as some variation does occur naturally.

• Inspect any moulded bees carefully and look for signs of damage on the wings, which are particularly vulnerable and may have been repaired.

• **Goebel** This pottery used a mark in the form of a bee inside a letter V. The bee was dropped in 1979, but re-introduced in 1991.

COLLECTIBILITY

• **Bees** This is a popular subject for themed collections, so honey pot collectors as can find themselves in competition with bee enthusiasts.

• **Potteries** Collectors of specific potteries can drive up the price of honey pots from a specific factory.

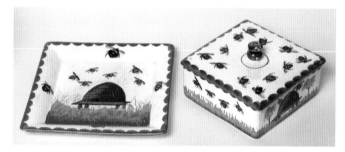

Jugs & Boats

Sauceboats were first introduced in the early 18thC for serving gravy or the rich, thick sauces that accompanied meat and fish dishes. Silver boats were often made in pairs and sometimes in sets of four or six for larger services. Ceramic boats tended to follow the forms of silver boats.

Unlike tableware such as honey pots, or teapots, there are comparatively few dedicated collectors specializing specifically in jugs and boats. Most collectors in this field are interested in tableware in general or, more likely, in the products of specific factories.

MOCHAWARE

Named after the mocha stone, a type of chalcedony said to have come from Mocha in Arabia. Mochaware was made by many factories between the late 18thC and the first half of the 20thC. It is a form of glazed earthenware decorated with bands and often

with tree-like patterns (see right).

• **Typical colours** Base colours include greens and browns.

• **Availability** Jugs and mugs are the most commonly found pieces.

MAKERS

All of the major potteries have included boats and jugs in their

production at some point. These are just a few worth looking out for.

• **Burgess & Leigh** This firm (est. 1851) manufactured Burleigh Ware. From the late 1880s the company produced a wide range of earthenware designs including cottage ware and novelties. Their hand-painted jugs in quirky designs with handles in the form of animals were extremely popular when launched in the 1930s and are sought after today.

• **Gray's** Originally founded in 1907, Gray's products include a range of "globe jugs" made in different sizes and decorated in the bold, colourful patterns that typify Gray's pottery. These jugs are globular in form, though some were made with narrower bodies. They were decorated in floral designs in various colour schemes including autumnal hues of red, orange, and yellow; blues; lilacs; pinks and greens; and yellows.

• **Midwinter** Established in 1910, this is one of the most collectible names in pottery of the mid-20thC. Midwinter ranges launched in the 1950s included Stylecraft (1953) and Fashion (1954), modernist forms that required patterns to match. Resident designer Jessie Tait (b.1928) devised many essentially abstract designs to suit, and many other artists and designers were also commissioned.

• **Myott, Son & Co.** By the 1920s, this company had a thriving home and export market for moulded tableware. In the 20s and 30s, Myott developed an exciting Art Deco range alongside more traditional wares; jugs are among the firm's most popular products. Wares from the 1930s include a conical earthenware jug with an attractive, stylized geometric spout and handle, decorated in bright

colours. In general, densely painted patterns are the most popular.

• **T. G. Green** Although known for their blue-and-white banded Cornish Ware, this firm produced all kinds of kitchen ware, from spice jars to teapots to cream jugs and gravy boats. The firm's products included attractive tableware in the Domino pattern, such as the sauceboat above. This effective design featured white spots on a blue background. Jugs in the Delft pattern, c1900–10, are much less common than the popular Cornish Ware range, but they still appeal to collectors because of their quality and attractive pattern.

COLLECTIBILITY

• **Mochaware** This can be hard to find today, possibly because it was common and heavily used. It is increasingly collectible today and prices have risen sharply recently.

• **Burleigh Ware** Among the most sought after Burleigh Ware are jugs in the "Sporting" range. They have handles in the form of sporting characters, such as golfers and are quite rare and consequently valuable. A golfer with checked trousers is more valuable than one with plain trousers. Rarity is not, however, the prime concern in the case of animal jugs. Certain animals, such as rabbits, squirrels, parrots, and kingfishers are not particularly rare, but are very popular with collectors who often concentrate

on collecting different versions of one animal.

MARKS

• **Burleigh Ware** This is marked with a backstamp featuring the name of the firm and is often accompanied by an artist's or designer's mark.

• **Gray's** These pieces are marked in varying ways, but most marks are brightly coloured and feature either a galleon, a liner, or a clipper.

• **Midwinter** This company's backstamps sometimes include the name of both the pattern and the designer.

• **Myott** Myott wares of the Deco era usually feature the name of the firm together with a crown. Sometimes, a painter's mark is also found.

Condition

• Spouts and handles are vulnerable and prone to chips and cracks. It is best to avoid picking up boats and jugs by the handle.

• If a jug or boat has suffered damage, it is best dealt with by a professional restorer. A poorly-executed repair can seriously affect the value and may not be reversible.

• A minor chip, especially if it is not immediately visible, is acceptable, but hairline cracks are not and should be reflected in the price.

Preserve Pots

The exact origin of preserves is not known, but jams, jellies, and preserves are centuries old. Marmalade was known as far back as the 15thC. Preserves had already been enjoyed at the table for a long time and pots had been made for storing them, but with the popularity and wider availability of tea in the 19thC and of marmalade, the modern breakfast was taking shape. In the 19th and 20thC, potteries produced a wide range of pots to contain these treats. The development of afternoon tea as a ritual provided a further impetus. Most preserve pots are ceramic, but pots in other materials, such as glass, are also found. As with honey pots, there are collectors who specialize in preserve pots, designed for jams and marmalades. They are often colourful, with imaginative designs and forms, and make an ideal focus for a collection.

MAKERS

• **Clarice Cliff** (See above.) This collectible name can be very expensive. One way of building a collection for a more modest sum is to concentrate on small pieces, such as preserve pots. Patterns include "Crocus", "Celtic Harvest", "Berries", "Rhodanthe", and "Secrets".

• **Wemyss Ware** Known for its floral and fruit decoration. Roses, so often featured on other items from this pottery, also appeared on preserve pots. Fruits, such as plums and oranges are also found.

• **William Moorcroft** Moorcroft founded his own pottery in 1913. Although usually associated with decorative items such as vases, the pottery produced many equally decorative but practical household wares, including preserve pots. The Pomegranate pattern, introduced in 1910 and produced until around 1938, is one of the most popular.

Although it was produced in large numbers, it is still very collectible and particularly good examples can fetch large sums.

• **Royal Winton** This firm made a wide range of tableware and was especially known for its Chintzware (see p.253). However, in the 1930s, the firm also made the unusual jam pot in the form of a Pekingese dog, decorated in a dark grey-purple, shown below.

• **Mintons (est. 1793)** Makers of a vast range of tableware. In the 1920s, they introduced a collectible range of novelty jam pots in the form of apples, oranges, and grapes. These pots display the typical high quality hand-painting but they are easily damaged. The "stalk" handles are particularly vulnerable. The printed mark of the firm appears on the base.

• **Carlton Ware** In the 1930s they produced relief-moulded earthenware in large quantities. Patterns included "Apple Blossom",

which sold in large numbers and the less successful and therefore rarer, "Cherries". As well as cheese dishes, teapots and toast racks, the repertoire included an attractive jam dish with a matching ceramic spoon. These spoons are often damaged or missing altogether. This tableware often came in a presentation box, so a dish and spoon complete in its box, is particularly sought after. The base of the box was always marked with the details of the contents, including shape and pattern.

CRANBERRY GLASS

There are many preserve pots and dishes in Cranberry glass, which is a collecting field in itself. Very popular around the turn of the 20thC, it is a delicate pink colour and was first produced in Bohemia in the 18thC. It was later produced in many countries, especially Britain and the USA, where the name was coined.

Condition

Lids are particularly vulnerable and have often suffered some damage, so inspect them carefully. They must be present as this can make a great difference to a pot's value.

Sugar Sifters

Although sugar was known in Europe as far back as the Middle Ages, it was an expensive luxury. It was not until the 18thC with the arrival of sugar from the West Indies that it became an important cooking ingredient. Even so, it was heavily taxed until the 1870s, after which it became much more popular.

Sugar sifters, sifter spoons, shakers, or casters are used to shake sugar over desserts, strawberries, or pastries. Collecting sugar shakers is a very popular niche, largely because they come in so many different patterns and shapes and can be of interest to ceramics, glass, or silver enthusiasts.

MAKERS

Many factories made sugar sifters or shakers, including Minton, Crown Devon, Portmeirion, Royal Winton, and Parrott & Co. The latter made a particularly appealing range known as Coronet, which included shakers with chrome tops, although silver plate was also used.

• **Clarice Cliff** The 1930s saw the production of attractive sugar sifters by Clarice Cliff, including conical pieces as shown here (in "Crocus"), which rank among the most desirable of all her shapes. However, the conical shape is fragile, so check for damage to the tip and also to the holes, which may have been restored. Certain shapes and patterns are rare and a combination of a rare shape and a rare pattern can be worth thousands. Well-known Clarice Cliff ranges include "Fantasque" and "Appliqué", the latter being especially desirable.

• **Portmeirion** In the 1960s, the pottery acquired the original copper plates of Kirkham's, a company that produced pot lids and containers for patent medicines. The plates were used on china to create a range that reflected Pop Art fashion and the revival of interest in Victoriana. Sugar shakers were included in this range, which has become collectible.

• **Carlton Ware** Their range of sugar shakers included one in the "Fruit Basket" range of inexpensive tableware. The base colours were a strong green and a chrome yellow, contrasting with the bright colours used on its moulded decoration. They are popular with collectors and are still relatively affordable.

MARKS

Clarice Cliff sugar shakers are marked with the name of the range, Bizarre being perhaps the best known. Initially they were applied with a rubber stamp, resulting in a mark that is less crisp than those on later products, where the mark was transfer-printed.

CONDITION

• **Stoppers** Sugar shakers are often found without their stoppers, which were usually of cork. Some sugar shakers have replacement plastic plugs to the base. This is acceptable, although damage or restoration to the pouring holes is not.

• **Clarice Cliff** Original stoppers on Clarice Cliff sifters are cork bungs covered with a reddish-coloured enamelled tin.

• **Liners** In common with certain other tableware, such as mustard pots, many silver casters have blue glass liners. If they have been cracked or otherwise damaged or are missing, replacement liners are available from specialist firms.

• **Holes** The holes in some sugar shakers seem rather large by today's standards, but they were made this way to prevent clogging.

Identifying fakes

Clarice Cliff's designs have proved easy to copy and there are reproductions of many items, including the popular sugar shakers, that can fool the unwary.

• Originals are crisply potted with careful control of the painted colours, which is lacking in reproductions.

• Glazes on fakes tend to be thin and pale compared with the richer, honey-coloured glazes of the originals.

• Recent copies have improved greatly in terms of colour and design, so it is important to familiarize yourself with the real thing before buying.

• Note that there are also legitimate reproductions. These are mostly made by Wedgwood, and are clearly marked accordingly.

Tea & Coffee Pots

The origins of tea drinking dates back many centuries to the Far East. Tea was introduced to Europe in the 17thC. It was initially expensive and was heavily taxed, but during the 19thC it became affordable to everyone. In Britain, tea drinking reached its peak of popularity in the 1930s.

Coffee was discovered by the Arabs and, like tea, reached Europe in the 17thC; it has remained popular ever since. Tea and coffee pots make an excellent collection; they are not difficult to find, come in a range of styles, and include some interesting novelty items. Teapots in particular are very popular with collectors and form a niche in their own right.

MAKERS

• **Susie Cooper** Along with Clarice Cliff, Susie Cooper (1902–95) is among the most sought after designers of the Deco era. She joined Gray's pottery, where she designed geometric and floral patterns in enamel colours and lustre for hand-painted tableware. One of her most successful designs was "Kestrel", a range that included a coffee pot that was originally made as part of a set but is still desirable on its own.

• **James Sadler & Sons** This firm produced many teapots although only a relatively small range of novelty teapots. However, they are known for their novelty pieces in the 1930s. These include a collectible racing car teapot (with the jokey OKT42 number plate) in various colours.

• **Poole Pottery** This firm was known as Carter, Stabler, & Adams, and although early wares are known as Poole Pottery, this did not become the official name until 1963. Poole Pottery is a collecting niche in itself and has its own collectors' club. In the 1920s, Poole Pottery made a number of small coffee and tea-sets, most of which were made for presentation purposes. Less densely patterned than many of the wares of the period, they are now rare and sought after.

• **Portmeirion** Founded in the 1950s, when Susan Williams-Ellis began designing ceramics for her gift shop in Portmeirion. Her designs proved so popular that she and her husband, Euan, took over Gray's pottery in 1960. Portmeirion pottery became very fashionable and its tall, cylindrical coffee pots captured the style of the 60s. Wares of the 1960s, especially the more Pop Art styles, are much sought after.

DESIGNS

• **Cube teapot** This was patented by Robert Johnson in 1916 as a safety teapot and was used by the Cunard shipping line on its cruise liners; easy to stack it would not tip over on stormy seas. Made in earthenware, metal, and bone china, they were purchased in large numbers by cafes, restaurants, and railway companies. They were made in various colours and patterns, under licence by many firms including T. G. Green and George Clews & Co. (est.1906).

COLLECTIBILITY

• **Royal Winton's Chintzware** Teapots in these all-over floral patterns are very collectible. There are more than 50 to choose from and those with a black ground were produced in relatively small numbers, so are more sought after today.

• **Sadler's racing car teapots** These are most commonly found in green, yellow, and cream. The rarer glazes include black, blue, grey, pink, and maroon. Until 1939, they were finished in a platinum lustre. After WWII, chrome plating was abandoned in favour of a cheaper, sponged, mottled glaze and the number plate was no longer applied. Production ended in 1952.

• **Poole Pottery** The most collectible wares are those with floral patterns in pastel colours on a matt ivory ground.

• **Portmeirion's "Totem" pattern** Launched in 1963, with its raised, abstracted designs, this pattern was an immediate success. Amber brown was a very popular colour, but it was also produced in blue, green, grey, and white – the latter is especially desirable today.

• **T. G. Green** Collectible teapots include one decorated with hunting scenes in the "Tally Ho" pattern, made briefly in the 1950s for the Canadian market.

• **Susie Cooper's "Patricia Rose"** This floral pattern, in the "Kestrel" range, came in four colour schemes and is the most popular of Cooper's transfer-printed patterns.

Toast Racks

Toast racks make an interesting focus for a collection. They are also highly sought after to make up breakfast sets. They come in a variety of sizes and designs, including three-bar and pierced styles and take up relatively little space. Ceramic toast racks have been made by most well known factories and can be a relatively inexpensive way of collecting popular patterns and styles. Many ceramic toast racks from the 1930s featured small dips at each end – these were intended for butter and jam (see p.286).

MAKERS

These are just a few of the many factories that produced toast racks.
• **S. Hancock & Sons (1857–1937)** This company is particularly known for its hand-painted tableware, and they produced some appealing toast racks. The "Ivory Ware" range is perhaps the best known.
• **Shelley (1872–1966)** A wide range of high quality fashionable tableware was made by this firm in the 1920s and 30s, featuring the latest geometric styles. Original packaging is always a bonus; boxes were usually plain and marked only with the company name.
• **Crown Ducal (est.1915)** This company is particularly known for its attractive tableware of the 1920s and 30s, especially the Orange Tree pattern, which is very collectible today (see below). It is also known for its association with

designer Charlotte Rhead, who produced many designs for the firm during the 1930s.

PROMOTIONAL ITEMS

Toast racks have proved ideal for promoting breakfast-related products. Among the products that have been promoted in this way are Lurpak Danish butter and Robertson's Marmalade, whose trademark Golly figure appeared on toast racks in the 1980s (see below right). Of the four different versions issued, only one was actually a direct promotion by Robertson's; the others were made under licence. The character was becoming controversial at the time because of alleged political incorrectness. That said, Gollies are very collectible in their own right and have many followers today.

COLLECTIBILITY

• **Export** Shelley made some patterns and colour schemes for export only; special order teaware may be found with interiors in a solid colour or gold. On more standard shapes, patterns in typical Deco colour combinations such as green, black, and silver, or red,

orange, and yellow (sometimes black) are very popular.
• **Chintzware** This, made by Shelley, Royal Winton, Crown Ducal, and many others, is sought after both by collectors interested in a specific factory or specializing in Chintz. Applying a transfer pattern to such an irregular shape would have been tricky and on some Chintz racks, the bars are left plain.

CONDITION

• **Damage** Ceramic racks are vulnerable and should be checked carefully for signs of damage and/or restoration.
• **Bleach** Hairline cracks are sometimes "cleaned up" using bleach, so watch for the characteristic smell.

Scullery

As the centre of activity in households, the kitchen was a place of hard work and uncomfortable conditions. The scullery was a room or area in the kitchen where the tasks such as scrubbing, washing dishes, and cleaning were carried out.

In the 18th and early 19thC, the kitchen sink was usually made from stone or hard wood, with a pipe to discharge the dirty water outside the house. Because there were no drains, the waste often soaked away into the ground. Sewage systems were not developed until the mid-19thC.

Items relating to the scullery are interesting from the point of view of social history and prices are still very reasonable.

Brushes

The oldest brush was almost certainly the besom, a bundle of twigs tied around a wooden handle. In the mid-19thC, brush making was something of a cottage industry with home-workers being paid on a piece basis. Most brushes are not very valuable, such as this cleaning brush, but this of course makes them affordable and it is not difficult to build up an interesting and varied collection for a small outlay.

MANUFACTURERS
• **Hamilton Acorn** Founded in the 18thC, this British firm is still in business. It made all kinds of brushes and won a huge contract in WWI to supply shaving brushes to the troops.
• **The Fuller Brush Company** This is perhaps America's best known brush maker. Founded in 1906, Fuller was disappointed with the quality of many brushes on offer at the time, so he began making and selling his own. The company went on to make much general purpose and specialist brushes, including one designed for cleaning hats, sold by door-to-door salesmen. After 15 years, Fuller was selling millions of dollars' worth of brushes each year.

USAGE
Brushes were specifically made for many tasks in the 19thC home.
• **Black lead brushes** These featured a wooden handle on top of the brush and were used to black lead the kitchen range. Black lead was a kind of graphite-based polish that was used to give fire grates and ranges a black metallic sheen.
• **Banister brushes** These are quite slim and have a long wooden handle, like this 1930s one below, making them ideal for cleaning between the banisters on staircases.
• **Special brushes** were made for cleaning the chimneys on oil or paraffin lamps. They are long and slim and resemble bottle brushes.

FIGURAL BRUSHES
• **Hearth brushes** In the 1930s, a range of hearth brushes with brass sheaths became very popular in Britain. The brush was pushed out from its sheath for sweeping away ashes and could be popped back in to stand decoratively in the hearth when not in use. The tops of the brushes would often be decorated with figural forms such as heads of famous people or ships, giving them added decorative appeal.

COLLECTIBILITY
Very few people collect brushes in their own right, but they can be attractive to display and are an important component of a collection of scullery items.

CONDITION
• **Wooden-handled scrubbing brushes** The slightly bleached look that often comes from water is not such a problem as it is with breadboards, since collectors expect them to have been used.
• **Missing bristles** This often happens through wear. While this is acceptable, brushes with most bristles badly worn or missing will inevitably be less valuable.

Cleaning Equipment

By the 18th and 19thC, in wealthy homes the washing up took place in the scullery in a large stone sink, while poorer homes used a large metal bowl. Few specialist implements for the task were available until the 20thC.

Sweeping the floor was a daily task, which was ultimately made easier by inventions such as the carpet sweeper and the vacuum. It was not until the 20thC that practical vacuum cleaners were produced, however.

SWEEPERS

The sweeper was an improvement on brushes and dustpans because it stored the sweepings inside the device to be emptied later. Although the brushes on most sweepers cannot penetrate the deep pile of a carpet as effectively as a vacuum cleaner, consumers found them less heavy and awkward to use. They were a feature of most households well into the 1950s and 60s.

• **Bissell** The carpet sweeper was invented by American Melville Bissell in 1876. The first Bissell factory was built in 1883 and the Bissell company makes sweepers to this day. A particularly interesting early design is the "crystal sweeper", which was made with a glass top, allowing the contents to be seen.

• **Ewbank (est.1880)** This British firm also made carpet sweepers. Since then, the firm has made a wide range of sweepers, many of which are of interest to the collector. (See p.289.)

WIREWORK

• **Dishcloth holders** Also known as dishtowel holders in the USA, these wirework implements such as those shown (top p.77) are often mistaken for whisks. In spite of their mundane use, they were often elaborately designed.

• **Wall racks** Wirework was also used to make racks to hang either dishcloths or utensils. Such racks are easy to differentiate from racks

BOWLS

Washing up bowls were made of enamelled iron and steel and came in various sizes and shapes. They were made in the USA from c1870 and in Britain from c1890s onwards. They would be placed inside a large stone sink.

• **Shape** Shallow washing up bowls in an oval shape with handles at the side were commonly used in continental Europe, such as the red Dutch bowl above, while round ones were favoured in Britain and North America, such as the round cream bowl.

• **Use** Some enamelled metal bowls were used for both washing up and as small laundry bowls. They came in various colours; ivory with blue relief, ivory with scarlet relief, silvery green with black relief, and white with blue relief.

SODA CRYSTALS

Sodium carbonate decahydrate was first used in the home more than 150 years ago. In the 19thC the crystals were an important part of domestic cleaning products. Very effective at cutting through grease, they had many uses.

• **Storage** Special containers were made for storing soda crystals; a very popular range of household utensils made in France in red enamelled metal included a soda crystals container. Made for the domestic market, it was labelled "Soda" (they use the same word). An example is shown below along with a French *allumette* (match) container, which was made from 1900 to the 1920s; similar versions were available in Britain and the USA. It would have been kept near the cooking area. Early versions often incorporated a striking strip on the top or inside the lid.

COLLECTIBILITY

Match containers in the orange and white colour shown are rare, and the "feather" pattern is much sought after. Other rare colours include aqua and white, and blue and white.

for coats, as they are not as sturdy. They were available in various sizes; some had as many as ten hooks, while others had just a single hook.

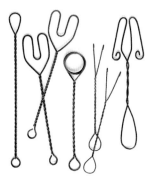

• **Sink tidies** Also called sink baskets, and used in all European countries, these were first produced in the 1900s in enamelled iron or steel. They are triangular in shape so that they can fit neatly in the corner of a traditional glazed earthenware sink, and are used to scrape waste into before washing the dishes. This waste would then have been burnt on the kitchen fire as inexpensive fuel at one time.

• **Materials** Sink tidies are made from enamelled iron or steel, although aluminium ones were also produced.

CONDITION

• **Washing up bowls** These can vary in condition. Feel inside the bowl, as years of using soda can take the sheen off, but they can be found in good condition.

• **Soda boxes** Few of these exist today, because many of them have been destroyed by the soda, which corrodes the metal.

• **French enamel soap dishes** These are collectible, and popular versions were made in a choice of blue or white. It is important for a dish to have its drainer, as it is less valuable without it.

Kettles

Before the electric kettle, most homes used stove kettles to boil water – the term kettle originally referred to a type of large, general-purpose cooking pan. It later became known as a tea kettle, since it was gradually used only for boiling water for tea. The earliest kettles were made of iron, but copper was commonly used by the 19thC. Copper's advantages included its excellent heat conducting properties, but its disadvantages included the fact that it needed regular cleaning to keep its attractive appearance; it would be blackened and discoloured each time it was used.

• **Marks** Copper kettles are not always marked, but many are. Marks to look out for include the "orb and cross" symbol, which was used by Benham & Froud, one of the better-known makers of copper wares.

• **Engraving** Copper kettles are usually plain, but occasionally you will find one that has been engraved with a motto, which adds novelty value.

• **Enamel** An increasingly popular and collectible material, and French enamelling is very highly regarded. French enamel kettles of the 19thC are often very attractive, sometimes featuring hand painted floral designs that make them ideal for display purposes. The 1930s Swedish enamelled iron kettle pictured here was widely exported so examples can be found in many countries today and in various sizes up to 20 pints (12 litres).

• **Ceramic kettles** During WWII, it became important to conserve metal for the war effort, so many kettles were made with ceramic bodies at this time. They continued in production after the war.

• **Electric** Some kettle designs combine the visual appeal of the old copper kettles with the functionality of modern electric models. One example of this was made by the Birmingham firm of Bulpitt & Sons in 1921, who made kettles for Swan Brand. It was made from copper, with a bakelite handle. Although it was traditional in appearance, it was innovative in that it was the first kettle to use a totally immersed heating element. The first electric kettles dated back to the 1890s, but the element was housed in a separate compartment, which wasted heat. As a result, it took much longer to boil.

• **Materials** Early electric kettles continued to use copper, but a fashion for chrome in the 1930s saw the introduction of chrome-plated examples. Chrome remained the most popular look for kettles until the 1970s.

MANUFACTURERS

Look out for electric-kettle makers Ediswan, General Electric, Premier, Bulpitt & Sons (made for Swan Brand), Hotpoint, and HMV.

CONDITION

Condition is important, but some minor signs of wear, and small holes may be acceptable if they are not visible and if the kettle is intended for display purposes only.

COLLECTIBILITY

• **Copper** This the most desirable

material. Cast-iron kettles, however, are also popular. Electric kettles are not yet as sought after. Kettles of the 1950s have a certain retro appeal, largely linked to their design. If they are typical of the era, then they are more likely to appeal, but kettles generally need to be in perfect condition.

• **60s and 70s kettles** These can also be attractive, and they were often made with typical "flower power" decoration. They appeal to those interested in the design of the period rather than in

kitchenware for its own sake.

• **Bakelite handle** This makes a kettle more collectible as Bakelite is sought after in its own right.

Laundry

Doing the weekly laundry was a major chore. In the absence of modern detergents, soap or soap flakes were all that was available to help with getting clothes clean.

During the 20thC, washing clothes was revolutionized, relegating many objects to the history books. Mangles, washboards, and dolly tubs are now quaint curiosities, while few people today would know the use of a goffering iron (see p.292). These changes have only served to make laundry-related items even more interesting to the collector.

IRONS

Irons are among the most collectible of laundry items, partly because there are so many different types.

• **Flat iron** Also known as "sad" iron, the name being a corruption of "solid", these have been used in Europe from as early as the 1600s and were made in various different weights (see above). They often came in pairs, so that one could be warmed at the fire while the other was in use.

• **Box and "ember" irons** Developed in the 18thC, a box iron's hollow body held a heated slug of metal; and "ember irons" contained burning charcoal.

• **Iron stoves** Small stoves were made in cast iron specifically to heat irons. They are very collectible today.

• **Electric iron** Invented in 1882, the first commercially-produced example was by Hotpoint in the 1890s. Early electric irons were heavy and took a while to catch on – many homes still did not have electricity. They were much improved, and lighter, by the 30s. The 50s were boom years for many household appliances, made in space age designs. Most electric irons are more interesting than valuable.

WASHBOARDS

Washboards were an important part of laundry equipment They were

used to get the dirt out of clothes by rubbing them on the board.

• **Materials** Washboards were made from a combination of wood (such as sycamore), and tin (see opposite). Some were also made from wood and brass, wood only, or wood and glass. Although glass had been used in washboards before, the use of glass came into its own during WWII when metal shortages forced manufacturers to look to alternatives for the rubbing surface.

• **USA** Here the best known washboard firm is the National Washboard Co., some of whose designs have lettering advising users to "let the board do the work". Others were specifically designed for delicate items, such as lingerie.

WASHING MACHINES

Patents for washing machines were taken out in the 19thC, while the

tub was a popular model at this time, because it combined the washer and spin dryer in a single cabinet. Values of washng machines can be difficult to determine. It is important for a machine to be in good condition.

MANGLES

• Mangles are very popular with collectors and as individual display pieces so can be expensive. They usually bear the name of their maker and a number. The c1860 mangle on the right is Irish.

first electric washing machine was produced in the early 20thC. Many different manufacturers were producing them as early as the 1920s but they remained expensive until well into the 1950s. The twin

COLLECTIBILITY

• **Laundry items** These are very collectible, especially if they are in good condition.

• **Small irons** These are more popular with collectors than full-size examples.

Packaging

After WWII, packaging became more of an important part of commercial competition than ever before. Manufacturers vied with each other to produce the most appealing packaging. Soap powder makers were at the forefront of this competition and companies advertised their products heavily in women's magazines. Packaging relating to the scullery, such as soap products and polishes, has been at the forefront of the revival of interest in advertising memorabilia. Such packaging is collected for its own sake, but it is also used in interior design schemes to create a nostalgic feel.

• **Soap** In common with many products, soap was once sold without packaging. In the mid-19thC, recognized brands of soap began to appear, and packaging bearing the company name became important as a way of promoting the product. Well known names include Fairy, Palmolive, Lifebuoy, and Pears all of which began in the 19thC .

• **Ammonia** Stronger than soap, ammonia was a popular cleaning agent in the 19thC. The bottle pictured here, the most commonly found of the stoneware ammonia bottles, was made for Plynine Household Ammonia, in Edinburgh

c1900. Stoneware bottles and jars were used widely in 19thC homes and they are very collectible today, especially printed rather than plain.

• **Look for** Packaging that relates to products that are no longer widely used is particularly interesting. At the same time, packaging for well-known products that have almost iconic status is also collected. The red, white, and blue design of Brasso metal polish tins has remained largely unchanged for generations, with only slight differences to the typeface and graphics. Even tins from as recently as the 1960s are collected.

• **Wellington Knife Polish** This

was a particularly successful polish of the 19thC. The packaging is of interest for its typical Victorian style.

• **Kewpie Klenser** This product was made in Australia from the 1920s. The Kewpie character

(illustrated on the tin on p.294) was the creation of American artist Rosie O'Neill. Kewpie dolls have a large following among collectors in their own right.
• **Look for** You can find 1950s washing powder and starch

packets that are un-opened and still contain their original contents, with designs typical of their time.

CONDITION
• **Old tins** These are vulnerable to rust, which can appear in the form

of specks. If not too severe, this can be acceptable at a lower price. The same is true of small dents.

COLLECTIBILITY
• **Contents** Items with their original contents are more desirable.

Trugs & Baskets

Basketry is one of the oldest known crafts due to the availability of materials. Willow (as in the basket below) is particularly useful. Planted in the spring and harvested in the summer, willow gave seasonal employment to whole families who cut, stripped, and prepared it. This pattern of growing and weaving remained the same from the 15thC until the eve of WWI, resulting in a wide range of baskets for household use.

customers included Queen Victoria. They are based on the "trog", a wooden Anglo-Saxon vessel.
• **Knife basket** Also called a cutlery basket, or tray in the USA, this was made in France in the 1920s (below right). It was used to carry cutlery from the kitchen to the dining room and for storing it when not in use. The attractive "blue" was achieved by painting the basket with enamel paint. This collectible basket is in good condition overall, and even has its original lining, adding to its value.
• **Wicker bottle baskets** These were made for carrying bottles to and from the wine cellar, and were commonly made to take a dozen bottles. (See p.296.)
• **Picnic baskets** Traditional wicker versions complete with leather straps are popular, but there are many reproductions around, mostly from China. The patina acquired by a genuinely old basket is a good guide.

COLLECTIBILITY
• **Later baskets** Those from the 1920s onwards are less collectible.
• **Wirework** This is collectible in

its own right; deep baskets made in the 19thC for hanging eggs in the larder, which were sometimes painted, are particularly interesting.
• **Wicker** This is a collecting niche, so may also be of interest to wicker as well as kitchenware collectors (see p.297).

CONDITION AND CARE
• **Antique wicker baskets** These are hard to find in good condition.
• **Patina** Old baskets are likely to have acquired a patina over the years, or signs of wear and tear. Some wear is to be expected.
• **Repair** This is common and will reduce the value, although it often adds appeal.
• **Cleaning** This can be done with warm water, drying naturally.
• **Storage** Avoid damp conditions, which can lead to mould and mildew, or rust on wirework. Extremely dry conditions can also make wickerwork brittle.

• **Trugs** These are shallow baskets traditionally used for tasks such as collecting eggs, flowers, or vegetables from the garden. They are often made of wood, but can also be wicker, wirework, or metal.
• **Sussex trug** This (below) is traditionally made from chestnut and willow and was popularized by Thomas Smith of Sussex, whose

Books

A good collection of books can offer a fascinating insight into the development of cooking and complements any collection of kitchenware. During the 19thC cookbooks and books on household management enjoyed a boom and they were published in large numbers; all but the rarest of books are still reasonably priced.

The same rules for collecting all kinds of books also apply to cookery books and books on household management. There is a premium for a fine-jacketed copy as opposed to a worn one, and many collectors prefer the addition of contemporary notes. At the bottom end of the range, recent cookery books written by less well-known cooks are fun to collect and can often be found for little money.

General Recipe Books

The oldest known book of recipes in English is *The Forme of Cury*, written by the Master Cooks of King Richard II and compiled around 1390. It is written on vellum and describes over 200 recipes, but it is by no means the oldest cookery book of all. Much of our knowledge of what the Romans ate and drank comes from writers such as Apicius, who wrote a cookery book almost 2,000 years ago.

General cookery books can be interesting for many reasons, not least because they can tell us about the content and preparation of dishes that are not made today.

AUTHORS
• **Elizabeth David (1912–92)** This author of cookery books is one of the most collectible. For many people Elizabeth David helped to radically change the whole nature of cooking, and her books often form a strong starting point for a collector. Her books often feature an attractive dust jacket, "decorated" as he called it, by John Minton.
• **Jane Grigson** Books by this author are comparatively recent, but they are already classics in their own right.
• **Maria Parloa (1843–1909)** Maria was one of the most popular authors of cookery books in the 19thC. She was popular in her native USA, and in Britain and France, where she gave lecture tours. Parloa's books, which are collectible today, not only included recipes but also discussed the chemistry of food and the

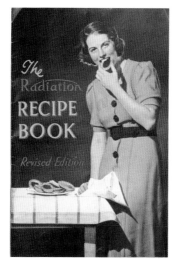

digestive system, giving them a hard scientific edge.

THE 1930S AND 40S
• *A Country Kitchen* Published in 1936, this is a cookery book with a difference. It is a semi-

autobiographical work based on the early life of its American author, Della Thompson Lutes, in late 19thC rural Michigan. Alongside stories of the country people she knew, there are traditional recipes. This book has been reprinted many times since with updated recipes suitable for the modern cook. A sequel, *Home Grown*, followed in 1937; both books are collectible.
• **Promotional** Manufacturers of cookers and other equipment saw recipe books as an ideal way to promote their products. *The Radiation Recipe Book* shown here was published in the 1930s and 40s and was intended to promote the New World gas cookers by Radiation Ltd. of London. These cookers had been fitted with the first commercial thermostat for domestic ovens, the Regulo, in 1923, which revolutionized cooking by allowing cooks to set precise

temperatures. Cookers of this era, up until the late 1940s, were very well built and easy to use; the basic design of gas cookers has changed relatively little since. *The Radiation Recipe Book* is packed with recipes and is keen to emphasize the modern nature of the cookers.

POST-WWII
• *The Cartoonist Cookbook* Edited by Theodora Illenberger and Avonne Eyre Keller, this book (shown above) was published in 1966. It is a curious mix of cartoons and cookery. Forty-

five of America's greatest cartoonists, including *Peanuts* creator Charles Schultz, contributed anecdotes, cartoons, and their favourite recipes. This book has a strong "cross-over" appeal, as it will be of interest to cookery book collectors and followers of cartoon art.
• *Cook Now, Dine Later* This book by Catherine Althaus and Peter ffrench-Hodges was one of the most popular cookery books of the late 1960s and early 1970s. The design of the cover was typical of the period and adds to its appeal.
• **Characters** In the 1970s and 80s, many fictional characters from novels were brought to life through the medium of television. At the same time, cookery programmes were very popular, so combining the two seemed to make sound commercial sense. *The Lord Peter Wimsey Cookbook* by Elizabeth Bond Ryan and William J. Eakins, is based on the tales of the aristocratic sleuth written by Dorothy L. Sayers, which had been turned into a highly successful TV series. Published in 1981, the book takes the many descriptions of meals included in the

Sayers books and gives recipes for the various dishes. It also suggests wine accompaniments. (See p.300.)

CONDITION AND CARE
• **Jackets** If the book originally had a dust jacket, then it should be present to achieve maximum value. The difference in price between a book with and without its jacket can be considerable.
• **Spines** Many people remove a book from a shelf by hooking a finger into the top of the spine. This can cause damage to the spine and you should never remove books from their shelves in this way.
• **Storage** Never pack books too tightly on the shelves. Leave enough room for them to be removed and replaced without forcing them.

COLLECTIBILITY
In addition to such famous writers as Mrs Beeton (see below), collectible names of the 19thC include Eliza Acton (1799–1869) who published *Modern Cookery for Private Families* in 1845. Jane Grigson and Elizabeth David are the most collectible 20thC authors.

Home Management

Books on home management, almost by definition, reflect the social changes that have taken place like no others can. In the 19thC, a newly-emerging middle class could not afford to have servants, but aspired towards a better and more genteel lifestyle. There was no shortage of advice on how to improve oneself and one's home. Women's magazine articles

discussed the latest trends in the home and gave advice.
It was not unusual for middle class homes to employ servants, although households often had just one maid, or a maid and a cook. Not all young housewives were used to dealing with staff, so such books would include relevant advice.

• **Mrs Beeton** The best-known book on home management is *Mrs Beeton's Book of Household Management* as shown opposite.

Mrs Beeton (1836–1865) was born Isabella Mayson and in 1856, she married Samuel Orchard Beeton, a publisher. This book made her a

household name, and was published in several parts from 1859 to 1860 in a successful women's magazine founded by her

husband called *The Englishwoman's Domestic Magazine*, which covered cookery and other branches of domestic science. Leather bound first editions of Mrs Beeton's famous book, first published in 1861, are much sought after and expensive, but numerous reprints are available for much less. It was a huge success from its first publication and was originally aimed at young middle-class 19thC wives who did not employ many servants. Her recipes always included the cost, cooking time, and number of servings.

• *Good things Made, Said and Done for Every Home and Household* This is the long-winded title of a book published in the 1880s by the makers of Goodall's Baking Powder. It includes recipes but also features advice on health matters. The collectible appeal of this book lies partly in its attractive green (later red) cloth cover with an embossed design, but also in its content. It is a charming, even quaint book, with pieces of homespun philosophy on each page, such as "without economy, none can be rich". The book is also interesting for its numerous advertisements for products from a bygone era.

• *Meal Planning and Table Service* Shown on the left, this book by Beth Bailey was aimed specifically at homes that had no servants at all. Published in the 1920s, it was widely used in college courses and six editions were published, the final one in 1964. It is not a recipe book, but a textbook for menu planning, place settings, food service in the home, and preparations for weddings. It also includes etiquette and advice on the correct way to eat soup.

• *Mother James' Key to Good Cooking* This volume by Virginia E. James is one of the more sought after American books written on household management. Published in the late 19thC, it is fairly comprehensive, including both household management advice and recipes. (See p.301.)

• **Unusual publications** These include *New Dinners for All Occasions*, which has both recipes and advice on the correct way to set a table for formal and informal dining. Made in the form of a calendar with decorative tassels, it was intended to be hung on the kitchen wall for easy reference. It originally came in a gold coloured box, which should be present to achieve maximum value.

• **Books on home decorating** These include *My Home, Why Not Yours?* This book was published in 1915 in the USA (see p.301). It was written by Margaret Greenleaf and Helen R. Churchill and was published by Pratt & Lambert, important makers of paints and varnishes. This company is still in business today. The book is particularly interesting for its photographs and illustrations of contemporary interiors, including kitchens.

Speciality Recipe Books

General cookbooks were practical, but many books devoted to specialist areas of cookery were also published. These books are of great culinary interest as they describe foods that are no longer eaten, techniques that are no longer used, or recipes that have been all but lost. Speciality cookbooks reflect food trends. In the 1970s for example, books on baking bread became more popular in Britain as people began to seek something more satisfying than factory-produced bread, and were prepared to make it themselves.

• *Treatise on Confectionery in all its Branches* This book by Joseph Bell (above) is one of the most sought after cookery books. It was privately published in 1817 and has a section on making different ice creams.
• *War Time Recipes for use in the West Indies* (below) This is a fascinating selection of recipes by Mrs St. John Hodson, reflecting social attitudes at the time.
• *Mediterranean and French Country Food* (below right) By

Elizabeth David and published in 1951, this introduced the flavour, colour, and smell of the Mediterranean to a British public still experiencing rationing. The attractive cover was designed by John Minton.

THE 1970S
• "Wholefood cookery" In the 1970s this was an important trend. Books include Ursula M. Cavanagh's *The Wholefood Cookery Book*.
• **Delia Smith** Britain's answer to America's popular Martha Stewart, Delia devoted a whole chapter to wholefood cookery in her book *Family Fare*, named after her BBC television series. Books that accompanied her shows are classic collectibles, although they are not worth a great deal at the moment.
• **Ena Baxter's recipes** First published by Johnston & Bacon in 1974, these spread the word about Scottish healthy eating on both sides of the Atlantic and millions of Americans watched her TV cookery demonstrations in the USA.
• **Crock-pot cookery** In the1970s this was aimed at the busy housewife who relished her independence, or the part-time worker who needed to plan ahead. Just pop fried meat and onions into the cooker and leave it to itself. The food would be cooked slowly during the day, using "as much electricity as a lightbulb". Books of

crock-pot cookery were published and are increasingly treasured.

PROMOTIONAL BOOKS
Many companies produced literature to promote their wares. They make interesting collectibles even though worth relatively little.
• **Tala** This firm produced *All About Icing* in the 1920s, giving advice on using the firm's products for icing cakes. (See p.303.)
• *The McDougall's Cookery Book* Issued by the manufacturers of McDougall's self-raising flour, this has become a classic.
• *250 Recipes for use with Borwick's Baking Powder* A booklet by Elizabeth Craig (see p.304).
• **Chocolate manufacturers** Cadbury's in Britain and Hershey in the USA both produced many collectible publications with chocolate recipes.

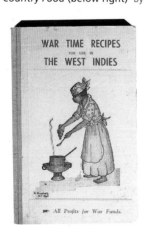

WAR TIME RECIPES
FOR USE IN
THE WEST INDIES

All Profits for War Funds.

Mediterranean and French COUNTRY FOOD by Elizabeth David

what to to pay

Storage

A wrought-iron game hanger, 18thC,
10in (25.5cm) high.
£130–145 / €195–220
$240–270 ⊞ TOP

Two glazed redware storage jars, American, c1800,
larger jar 11¼in (28.5cm) high.
£185–210 / €280–320
$340–380 ♪ COBB

A wrought-iron game crown, early 19thC,
12in (30.5cm) high.
£400–450 / €600–670
$730–820 ⊞ WeA

**◀ A stoneware
crock,** decorated
with a bird on a
branch, incised
mark, 1865–75,
13in (33cm) high.
**£300–360
€450–540
$550–660
♪ COBB**

Two stoneware jugs, the larger decorated with an underlined
'2', the smaller incised 'Charlestown', American, 19thC, larger jug
13in (33cm) high.
£60–70 / €90–105
$110–130 ♪ COBB

A pottery yeast pot, American, 1870–1900,
6¼in (16cm) high.
£30–35 / €45–50
$55–65 ⊞ MSB

A pine pot rack, Romanian, c1880, 60in (152.5cm) wide.
£125–140
€190–210
$230–260 ⊞ HRQ

◄ **A tin lunch pail,** American, 1875–1900, 11½in (29cm) high.
£30–35 / €45–50
$55–65 ⊞ MSB

A wooden miniature ice chest, lined with metal, the two doors with glass panels, early 1900s, 13in (33cm) wide.
£170–190 / €260–290
$310–350 ⊞ MSB

A grocer's ceramic crock, inscribed 'S. & J. Melross, Pollokshields', c1900, 6in (15cm) high.
£140–160 / €210–240
$260–290 ⊞ WeA

► **A stoneware jar,** inscribed 'Army & Navy, Westminster, S.W.', c1920, 4½in (11.5cm) high.
£35–40 / €50–60
$65–75 ⊞ AL

A tin food safe, c1930, 19in (48.5cm) wide.
£60–70 / €90–105
$110–130 ⊞ DaM

An enamel match box, inscribed 'Allumettes', French, c1930, 7½in (19cm) high.
£70–80 / €105–120
$130–145 ⊞ AL

An enamel and tin food safe, c1930, 17in (43cm) wide.
£35–40 / €50–60
$65–75 ⊞ AL

Biscuit Barrels

A glass biscuit barrel, with hand-painted decoration, c1890, 9in (23cm) high.
£65–75 / € 100–110
$120–135 ⊞ GLAS

A Doulton ceramic biscuit barrel, c1890, 5in (12.5cm) diam.
£130–145 / € 195–220
$240–270 ⊞ SAT

An opaline glass biscuit barrel, with silver-plated mounts, decorated with two storks and flowering plants, 19thC, 7in (18cm) high.
£100–120 / € 150–180
$185–220 ➢ SWO

▶ An enamelled glass biscuit barrel, probably by Moser, with silver-plated mounts and cover, c1895, 11in (28cm) high.
£310–350 / €470–530
$570–650 ⊞ GRI

A Bretby ceramic biscuit barrel, c1915, 4in (10cm) high.
£70–80 / € 105–120
$130–145 ⊞ DSG

Further reading
Miller's Twentieth-Century Ceramics, Miller's Publications, 1999

◀ A wooden biscuit barrel, with metal mounts, 1920s, 11in (28cm) high.
£10–15 / € 15–22
$19–28 ⊞ BET

An enamel biscuit barrel, c1920, 15in (38cm) high.
£65–75 / € 100–115
$120–135 ⊞ AL

A Belleek ceramic biscuit barrel, Third Period, 1926–46, 7in (18cm) diam.
£310–350 / € 470–530
$570–650 ⊞ MLa

A T. G. Green ceramic Streamline biscuit barrel, 1930, 8in (20.5cm) high.
£180–200 / € 270–300
$330–370 ⊞ CAL

A Barker Brothers ceramic Chintz ware biscuit barrel, c1930, 6in (15cm) high.
£90–100 / € 135–150
$165–185 ⊞ BD

A Clarice Cliff ceramic biscuit barrel, decorated with Gardenia pattern, 1930s, 5in (12.5cm) high.
£900–1,000 / € 1,350–1,500
$1,650–1,850 ⊞ BD

▶ **A Carlton Ware ceramic Blackberry biscuit barrel,** 1930s, 6in (15cm) high.
£135–150
€ 200–230
$240–270
⊞ HarC

LOCATE THE SOURCE
The source of each illustration in Miller's can be found by checking the code letters below each caption with the Key to Illustrations, pages 313–315.

▶ **A Meredith & Drew glass biscuit barrel,** with a metal lid, 1930s, 7in (18cm) high.
£60–70 / € 90–105
$110–130 ⊞ JWK

A T. F. & Sons ceramic biscuit barrel, 1930s, 6in (15cm) high.
£50–60 / € 75–90
$95–110 ⊞ BAC

A pressed glass biscuit barrel,
1930s, 7in (18cm) high.
£8–12 / €12–18
$15–22 ⊞ BAC

**A T. G. Green ceramic
Blue Domino biscuit
barrel,** 1930–50,
5in (12.5cm) high.
£400–450 / €600–670
$730–820 ⊞ CAL

**A T. G. Green ceramic Cornish Ware
biscuit barrel,** 1930s–50s, 5in (12.5cm) high.
£400–450 / €600–670
$730–820 ⊞ CAL

A plastic and chrome biscuit barrel, 1950s,
7in (18cm) high.
£30–35 / €45–50
$55–65 ⊞ AL

**A Stelton stainless steel Cylinda Line biscuit
barrel,** by Arne Jacobsen, Danish, Denmark, c1967,
8in (20.5cm) high.
£105–120 / €160–180
$195–220 ⊞ MARK

◄ **A Marks & Spencer ceramic biscuit barrel,**
decorated with Harvest pattern, c1979, 8in (20.5cm) high.
£25–30 / €40–45
$45–55 ⊞ CHI

Bread Bins

A salt-glazed bread crock, Scottish, c1880,
20in (51cm) wide.
£220–250 / €330–380
$400–460 ⊞ B&R

A ceramic bread crock, inscribed 'Mrs Wilson',
Scottish, dated 1899, 10in (25.5cm) high.
£80–90 / €120–135
$145–165 ⊞ B&R

▶ An enamel bread bin, 1900–20, 14½in (37cm) high.
£40–45 / €60–70
$70–80 ⊞ CHAC

An enamel bread bin, c1930, 12in (30.5cm) high.
£35–40 / €50–60
$65–75 ⊞ CHAC

▶ An enamel bread bin, 1930, 11in (28cm) wide.
£50–60 / €75–90
$95–110 ⊞ AL

Canisters & Jars

A Wemyss ceramic storage jar, decorated with Beehives, c1900, 6¼in (16cm) high.
£670–750 / € 1,000–1,150
$1,200–1,350 ⊞ GLB

▶ **Three Maling ceramic storage jars,** inscribed 'Tapioca', 'Salt', and 'Currants', c1910, 6in (15cm) high.
£65–75 / € 100–115
$120–135 each ⊞ SMI

Four Grimwade ceramic storage jars, inscribed 'Sugar', 'Raisins', 'Arrowroot' and 'Sago', c1910, 6in (15cm) high.
£135–150 / € 200–230
$250–280 each ⊞ SMI

A set of three enamel storage canisters, inscribed 'Sucre', 'Café' and 'Chicorée', c1920, 6½in (16.5cm) high.
£125–140 / € 190–210
$230–260 ⊞ AL

Two Maling ceramic storage jars, decorated with Cobblestone pattern, c1920.
£70–80 / € 105–120
$130–145 ⊞ SMI

◀ **A set of four ceramic storage jars,** with wooden lids, one inscribed 'Pepper' and another 'Cloves', c1920, 4in (10cm) high.
£90–100 / € 135–150
$165–185 ⊞ AL

◀ **A set of six enamel storage canisters,** inscribed 'Sucre', 'Farine', 'Café', 'Poivre', 'Chicorée' and 'Pâtes', c1920, largest 6½in (16.5cm) high.
£210–240 / €330–360
$400–440 ⊞ AL

A set of five graduated enamel storage canisters, inscribed 'Flour', 'Sugar', 'Rice', 'Tea' and 'Coffee', c1920, largest 7in (18cm) high.
£135–150 / €200–230
$240–270 ⊞ B&R

A set of five ceramic storage jars, with wooden lids, inscribed 'Currants', 'Sago', 'Sugar' and 'Tapioca', c1920, 6½in (16.5cm) high.
£180–200 / €270–300
$330–370 ⊞ AL

Two enamel storage canisters, inscribed 'Peas' and 'Currants', 1920s, 7in (18cm) high.
£35–40 / €50–60
$65–75 ⊞ B&R

A set of three enamel storage canisters, inscribed 'Biscuits', 'Sugar' and 'Currants', 1920s, 9in (23cm) high.
£35–40 / €50–60
$65–75 each ⊞ B&R

▶ **A set of four fruitwood graduated storage boxes,** c1930, largest 8in (20.5cm) high.
£85–95 / €130–145
$155–175 ⊞ MLL

A set of six enamel storage canisters, inscribed
'Café', 'Farine', 'Sucre', 'Poivre', 'Chicorée' and 'Pâtes',
French, c1930, largest 8in (20.5cm) high.
£240–270 / €360–410
$440–490 ⊞ AL

A set of six enamel storage canisters, inscribed
'Sucre', 'Café', 'Farine', 'Poivre', 'Epices' and 'Thé',
French, c1930, largest 7½in (19cm) high.
£290–320 / €450–500
$530–600 ⊞ AL

A set of four enamel storage canisters, inscribed
'Pâtes', 'Chicorée', 'Café' and 'Sucre', French, c1930,
7in (18cm) high.
£120–135 / €180–200
$220–250 ⊞ AL

A set of five enamel storage canisters, inscribed
'Sucre', 'Café', 'Farine', 'Pâtes' and 'Chicorée', French,
c1930, largest 5in (12.5cm) diam.
£105–120 / €160–180
$195–220 ⊞ B&R

◀ **A set of six enamel
graduated storage
canisters,** inscribed
'Sucre', 'Farine', 'Café',
'Pâtes', 'Thé' and 'Poivre',
French, c1930, largest
5in (12.5cm) diam.
£105–120 / €160–180
$195–220 ⊞ B&R

Five T. G. Green ceramic Cornish Ware storage jars, inscribed 'Castor Sugar', 'Lump Sugar', 'Granulated Sugar',
'Brown Sugar' and 'Flour', 1930s, largest 8in (20.5cm) high.
£320–380 / €480–570
$590–700 ⚒ G(L)

A T. G. Green ceramic Cornish Ware storage jar, 1930s, 6in (15cm) high.
£35–40 / €50–60
$65–75 ⊞ CAL

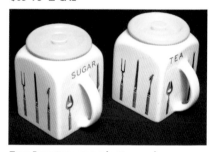

Two Pountney ceramic storage jars, decorated with Longline pattern, c1950, 6in (15cm) high.
£35–40 / €50–60
$65–75 ⊞ B&R

Twelve T. G. Green ceramic Cornish Ware storage jars, inscribed 'Rosemary', 'Saffron', 'Mixed Herbs', 'Thyme', 'Bay Leaves', 'Mace', 'Spice', 'Cloves', 'Sage', 'Tarragon', 'Pepper-corns' and 'Nutmegs', marked, three lids missing, one damaged, 1930s, largest 12in (30.5cm) high.
£1,600–1,900 / €2,400–2,850
$2,950–3,500 ✗ RTo

A set of seven Sandland Ware ceramic storage jars, with wooden lids, c1950, 4½in (11.5cm) high.
£120–135 / €180–200
$220–250 ⊞ AL

A set of four aluminium graduated storage canisters, American, 1950s, largest 8in (20.5cm) high.
£15–20 / €22–30
$25–35 ⊞ FLD

◀ **A T. G. Green ceramic storage jar,** 1950s, 5½in (14cm) high.
£25–30 / €40–45
$45–55 ⊞ CAL

A T. G. Green ceramic storage jar,
lid damaged, Gresley mark, 1950s,
2½in (6.5cm) high.
£25–30 / €40–45
$45–55 ⊞ CAL

A Pountney ceramic storage jar,
decorated with Longline pattern,
1950s, 7in (18cm) high.
£45–50 / €70–80
$80–95 ⊞ CHI

A T. G. Green ceramic Cornish Ware
storage jar, 1960, 6in (15cm) high.
£35–40 / €50–60
$65–75 ⊞ CAL

**A T. G. Green ceramic Cornish
Ware storage jar,** 1960,
5in (12.5cm) high.
£90–100 / €135–150
$165–185 ⊞ CAL

**A Portmeirion ceramic storage
jar,** decorated with Talisman
pattern, c1962, 8in (20.5cm) diam.
£150–165 / €220–250
$270–300 ⊞ CHI

**A Portmeirion ceramic storage
jar,** decorated with Malachite
pattern, 1960s, 5in (12.5cm) high.
£165–185 / €250–280
$300–340 ⊞ CHI

**A Portmeirion ceramic storage
jar,** decorated with Greek Key
pattern, c1963, 8in (20.5cm) high.
£90–100 / €135–150
$165–185 ⊞ CHI

Two Portmeirion ceramic storage jars, decorated with Greek Key pattern,
inscribed 'Salt' and 'Rice', c1963, 6in (15cm) high.
£60–70 / €90–105
$110–130 ⊞ CHI

A Portmeirion ceramic storage jar, decorated with Samarkand pattern, c1964, 4in (10cm) high.
£60–70 / €90–105
$110–130 ⊞ CHI

Two Portmeirion ceramic storage jars, decorated with Tivoli pattern, c1964, 6in (15cm) high.
£65–75 / €100–115
$120–135 ⊞ CHI

A Portmeirion ceramic storage jar, decorated with Stoke pattern, c1964, 7in (18cm) high.
£85–95 / €130–145
$155–175 ⊞ CHI

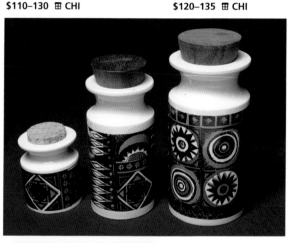

◄ Three Portmeirion ceramic storage jars, c1964, largest 8in (20.5cm) high.
£65–75
€100–115
$120–135 ⊞ CHI

A T. G. Green ceramic Channel Isles storage jar, designed by Judith Onions, 1968, 5½in (14cm) high.
£15–20 / €22–30
$25–35 ⊞ CAL

Items in the Storage section have been arranged in date order within each sub-section.

A T. G. Green ceramic Channel Isles storage jar, designed by Judith Onions, 1968, 5½in (14cm) high.
£35–40 / €50–60
$65–75 ⊞ CAL

A set of three T. G. Green ceramic Granville storage jars, inscribed 'Tea', 'Coffee' and 'Sugar', 1970–80, 5in (12.5cm) high.
£35–40 / €50–60
$65–75 ⊞ CAL

Oils, Herbs & Spices

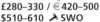

A boxwood spice tower, with four sections, inscribed 'Mace', 'Cloves', 'Cinnamon' and 'Nutmeg', 19thC, 7in (18cm) high.
£280–330 / €420–500
$510–610 ⚒ SWO

A wooden spice cabinet, the nine drawers with bun handles, 19thC, 9in (23cm) high.
£360–430 / €540–630
$660–790 ⚒ SWO

A japanned tin spice box, c1800, 9in (23cm) wide.
£135–150 / €200–230
$240–270 ⊞ SMI

A fruitwood spice tower, with five sections, c1810, 9in (23cm) high.
£360–400 / €540–600
$660–730 ⊞ F&F

A boxwood spice tower, with three sections, inscribed 'Cloves', 'Nutmegs' and 'Caraway', c1810, 6in (15cm) high.
£270–300 / €410–450
$490–550 ⊞ F&F

A boxwood spice tower, with three sections, inscribed 'Cloves', 'Mace' and 'Nutmeg', c1810, 6in (15cm) high.
£260–290 / €390–440
$480–530 ⊞ F&F

A tin spice rack, with original paint, c1880, 9in (23cm) high.
£85–95 / €130–145
$155–175 ⊞ SMI

A sycamore spice cabinet, two knobs missing, c1880, 8in (20.5cm) high.
£150–165
€220–250
$270–300
⊞ NEW

► **A metal spice tin,** c1890, 7in (18cm) diam.
£50–55
€75–85
$90–100 ⊞ AL

A Bryant & May metal spice box, c1890, 4½in (11.5cm) diam.
£50–55 / €75–85
$90–100 ⊞ AL

► **A wooden spice cabinet,** c1900, 8in (20.5cm) wide.
£170–190
€260–290
$310–350
⊞ WeA

A T. G. Green ceramic Streamline storage jar, inscribed 'Mixed-Herbs', 1930, 4in (10cm) high.
£65–75 / €100–115
$120–135 ⊞ CAL

A Cottage Green ceramic spice jar, inscribed 'Nutmegs', c1930, 3½in (9cm) high.
£45–50 / €70–80
$80–90 ⊞ Cot

A wooden spice cabinet, c1910, 19in (48.5cm) high.
£270–300 / €400–450
$490–550 ⊞ SMI

▶ **A T. G. Green ceramic spice jar,** 1930s, 4in (10cm) high.
£60–70 / €90–105
$110–130 ⊞ SCH

A T. G. Green ceramic Cornish Ware pepper shaker, 1960, 5½in (14cm) high.
£90–100 / €135–150
$165–185 ⊞ CAL

LOCATE THE SOURCE

The source of each illustration in Miller's can be found by checking the code letters below each caption with the Key to Illustrations, pages 313–315.

A Sadler ceramic Kleen Ware spice jar, inscribed 'Cloves', 1940s, 3½in (9cm) high.
£45–50 / €70–80
$80–90 ⊞ SCH

◀ **A T. G. Green ceramic Cornish Ware oil jug,** 1960s, 7½in (19cm) high.
£100–110 / €150–165
$185–200 ⊞ CAL

Packaging

A waxed paper sliced bread wrapper, early 20thC, 20 x 15in (51 x 38cm).
£4–8 / €6–12
$8–15 ⊞ MSB

A Junket Rennet Powder container, American, early 20thC, 2½ x 3in (6.5 x 7.5cm).
£6–10 / €9–15
$10–20 ⊞ MSB

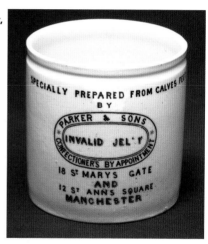

▶ **A Parker & Sons ceramic jar,** inscribed 'Invalid Jelly', 1920s, 3in (7.5cm) diam.
£40–45 / €60–70
$70–80 ⊞ BS

A paper sugar bag, early 20thC, 9½in (24cm) high.
£1–5 / €2–7
$3–9 ⊞ MSB

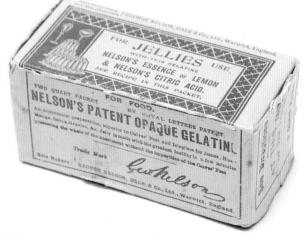

A Nelson's Patent Opaque Gelatine box, 1920s–30s, 4½in (11.5cm) long.
£4–8 / €6–12
$8–15 ⊞ RTT

A Sawyer Biscuit Co biscuit box, American, 1920s–1930s, 9in (23cm) wide.
£50–55 / €75–85
$90–100 ⊞ MSB

An Armour's Cloverbloom wooden cheese box, 1920–40, 11½in (29cm) wide.
£7–11 / €11–17
$13–20 ⊞ MSB

A Clark Coconut box, American, 1930s, 10½in (26.5cm) wide.
£40–45 / €75–90
$90–110 ⊞ MSB

◀ **A Lyle's Golden Syrup free sample tin,** 1930, 2in (5cm) high.
£35–40 / €50–60
$65–75 ⊞ HUX

A Bottomley's Ice Cream cardboard container, American, 1930s.
£15–19 / €22–28
$30–35 ⊞ MSB

◀ **A Wellcome Soda-Mint bottle,** 1930s, 2in (5cm) high.
£1–5 / €2–7
$3–9 ⊞ HUX

A Favarger Cacao packet,
1930s, 4½in (11.5cm) high.
£10–15 / €15–22
$20–25 ⊞ Do

A Sto-Mike coffee tin, c1930,
5in (12.5cm) high.
£25–30 / €40–45
$45–55 ⊞ HUX

A Verifine Ice Cream container, 1930s–40s,
7½in (19cm) high.
£15–19 / €22–28
$30–35 ⊞ MSB

◀ **A bottle of Camp Coffee,** with contents,
c1940, 9in (23cm) high, with box.
£45–50 / €70–80
$80–95 ⊞ MRW

Insurance values
Always insure your valuable antiques for the cost of replacing them with similar items, regardless of the original price paid. Both dealers and auctioneers can provide a valuation service for a fee.

A Cox's Instant Powdered Gelatine packet,
with contents, 1940s, 4in (10cm) high.
£1–5 / €2–7
$3–9 ⊞ NFR

◀ **A National Household Dried Milk can,**
American, 1950s, 5in (12.5cm) high.
£4–8 / €6–12
$8–15 ⊞ TWI

A Lyle's Golden Syrup can, c1950,
12in (30.5cm) high.
£6–10 / €9–15
$12–19 ⊞ AL

Plastic

A plastic storage jar, 1940s,
5in (12.5cm) high.
£20–25 / €30–35
$35–45 ⊞ TWI

A set of four plastic storage tubs, inscribed 'Tea', 'Coffee',
'Sugar' and 'Flour', American, 1950s, largest 6¾in (17cm) high.
£45–50 / €70–80
$80–90 ⊞ TWI

A set of five plastic storage tubs, inscribed 'R', 'T', 'F', 'S', and
'C', Australian, 1950s–60s, largest 9¾in (25cm) high.
£60–70 / €90–105
$110–130 ⊞ TWI

**An Arthur Douglas plastic Caddy-Matic
Junior tea dispenser,** with wall bracket,
early 1960s, 8in (20.5cm) high, boxed.
£10–15 / €15–22
$20–25 ⊞ TWI

Three Tupperware plastic containers, 1960, 5in (12.5cm) diam.
£4–8 / €6–12
$8–15 each ⊞ Mo

◀ **A Tupperware plastic container,** 1960s, 5in (12.5cm) wide.
£1–5 / €2–7
$3–9 ⊞ Mo

A plastic spice rack,
1960s, 9½in (24cm) wide.
£20–25 / €30–35
$35–45 ⊞ JWK

▶ **Two Tupperware**
plastic storage tubs, 1962,
largest 8in (20.5cm) diam.
£20–25 / € 30–35
$35–45 ⊞ Mo

Two Tupperware plastic beakers, with snap tops,
left made in UK, right made in Belgium, 1960s,
9in (23cm) high.
£4–8 / €6–12
$8–15 ⊞ Mo

For further information on
Oils, Herbs & Spices see pages 98–100

A set of seven Tupperware plastic spice storage
jars, 1970s, 2¼in (5.5cm) high.
£8–12 / € 12–18
$15–20 ⊞ TWI

Preserves & Ingredients

► **A pottery salt pot,** decorated with slip-trailing, inscribed 'W. M. Wilson, Higher Aigden, Yorkshire', 19thC, 12¼in (31cm) high.
£350–420
€ **530–630**
$640–770
⚒ **TEN**

A fruitwood salt box, late 18thC, 13in (33cm) high.
£200–230 / € **300–350**
$360–420 ⊞ **F&F**

A fruitwood and birchwood salt box, c1840, 13in (33cm) high.
£100–110 / € **150–165**
$180–200 ⊞ **F&F**

A wooden flour barrel, 19thC, 5¾in (14.5cm) high.
£200–220 / € **300–330**
$360–400 ⊞ **WeA**

► **Two stoneware jars,** inscribed 'Meal' and 'Barley', Scottish, c1850, 10in (25.5cm) high.
£180–200 / € **270–300**
$330–370 ⊞ **SMI**

Three stoneware storage jars, inscribed 'Barley', 'Tapioca' and 'Cornflower', Scottish, c1880, largest 10in (25.5cm) high.
£90–100 / €135–150
$165–185 each ⊞ SMI

An oak flour barrel, c1880, 10in (25.5cm) high.
£120–135 / €180–200
$220–250 ⊞ Cot

◀ **Two stoneware storage jars,** inscribed 'Barley' and 'Sago', Scottish, c1880, larger 10in (25.5cm) high.
£105–120 / €160–180
$195–220 each ⊞ SMI

A stoneware storage jar, inscribed 'Meal', Scottish, c1890, 11in (28cm) high.
£70–80 / €105–120
$130–150 ⊞ B&R

A tin flour bin, c1890, 9in (23cm) high.
£50–55 / €75–85
$95–105 ⊞ AL

◀ **A stoneware storage jar,** inscribed 'Barley', Scottish, c1890, 12in (30.5cm) high.
£105–120 / €160–180
$195–220 ⊞ B&R

A stoneware storage jar,
inscribed 'Rice', Scottish, c1890,
8½in (21.5cm) high.
£50–60 / €75–90
$95–110 ⊞ B&R

A wooden flour barrel,
1890–1920, 11¾in (29cm) high.
£65–75 / €100–115
$120–140 ⊞ CHAC

A ceramic salt box, c1900,
9in (23cm) high.
£50–55 / €75–85
$95–105 ⊞ CHAC

◄ **A Denby ceramic storage jar,**
inscribed 'Barley', c1910,
14in (35.5cm) high.
£105–120 / €160–180
$195–220 ⊞ SMI

A Bretby ceramic storage jar,
inscribed 'Cream of Tartar', c1900,
4in (10cm) high.
£30–35 / €45–50
$55–65 ⊞ B&R

**A Grimwade ceramic storage
jar,** inscribed 'Rice', c1910,
6in (15cm) high.
£35–40 / €50–60
$65–75 ⊞ AL

◄ **Two Grimwade ceramic
storage jars,** inscribed 'Sago'
and 'Lump Sugar', c1910,
largest 9in (23cm) high.
£135–150 / €200–230
$250–280 each ⊞ SMI

An enamel flour bin, c1910,
9½in (24cm) high.
£25–30 / €40–45
$45–55 ⊞ **CHAC**

Two Grimwade ceramic storage jars, inscribed for 'Sago' and
'Meal', c1910, largest 8in (20.5cm) high.
£55–65 / €85–100
$100–120 ⊞ **SMI**

A toleware treacle dispenser, c1920,
10in (25.5cm) wide.
£220–250 / €350–390
$400–460 ⊞ **B&R**

A painted tin flour bin, with original
paint, c1920, 9in (23cm) high.
£90–100 / €135–150
$165–185 ⊞ **SMI**

A boxwood salt box,
with a hinged cover,
c1920, 8in (20.5cm) high.
£45–50 / €70–80
$80–90 ⊞ **Cot**

◀ **A painted tin flour bin,**
c1920, 21in (53.5cm) high.
£115–130 / €175–195
$210–240 ⊞ **SMI**

▶ **A painted tin flour
bin,** with original paint,
c1920, 24in (61cm) high.
£220–250 / €350–390
$400–460 ⊞ **SMI**

An enamel storage jar, inscribed 'Salt', c1920, 6in (15cm) high.
£25–30 / €40–45
$45–55 ⊞ AL

A ceramic storage jar, inscribed 'Sugar', c1920, 13in (33cm) high.
£250–280 / €380–420
$460–510 ⊞ SMI

A T. G. Green ceramic Cornish Ware storage jar, inscribed 'Table Salt', 1920s, 5in (12.5cm) high.
£220–250 / €350–390
$400–460 ⊞ SMI

An enamel flour bin, 1920s, 13in (33cm) high.
£35–40 / €50–60
$65–75 ⊞ JWK

Two T. G. Green ceramic Cornish Ware storage jars, inscribed 'Baking Powder' and 'Mustard', 1920s, 3½in (9cm) high.
£100–110 / €150–165
$180–200 ⊞ CHI

A Sadler ceramic Kleen Ware storage jar, inscribed 'Rice', 1920s, 5in (12.5cm) high.
£25–30 / €40–45
$45–55 ⊞ B&R

▶ **A ceramic storage jar,** inscribed 'Rice', c1930, 5½in (14cm) high.
£45–50 / €70–80
$80–90 ⊞ AL

A T. G. Green ceramic Streamline storage jar, inscribed 'Currants', 1930, 5½in (14cm) high.
£60–70 / €90–105
$110–130 ⊞ CAL

A T. G. Green ceramic Cornish
Ware storage jar, inscribed 'Pearl
Barley', c1930, 4½in (11.5cm) high.
£90–100 / €135–150
$165–185 ⊞ AL

◀ An enamel salt box, inscribed
'Sel', French, c1930, 9¾in (25cm) high.
£70–80 / €105–120
$130–145 ⊞ AL

An enamel flour bin, c1935,
9in (23cm) wide.
£40–45 / €60–70
$70–80 ⊞ B&R

A T. G. Green ceramic Cornish
Ware storage jar, inscribed
'Raisins', 1930s, 7in (18cm) high.
£55–65 / €85–100
$100–120 ⊞ CAL

A ceramic storage jar, inscribed
'Tapioca', 1930s, 6in (15cm) high.
£45–50 / €70–80
$80–90 ⊞ YT

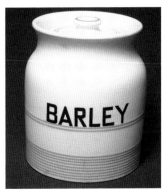

A Sadler ceramic Kleen Ware
storage jar, inscribed 'Barley',
1940s, 5in (12.5cm) high.
£40–45 / €60–70
$70–80 ⊞ SCH

A T. G. Green storage jar,
inscribed 'Marmalade', 1950s,
4in (10cm) high.
£70–80 / €105–120
$130–145 ⊞ HSt

A Portmeirion ceramic storage
jar, decorated with Dolphins
pattern, inscribed 'Dried Fruit',
c1965, 7½in (19cm) high.
£165–185 / €250–280
$300–340 ⊞ CHI

A T. G. Green ceramic Cornish
Ware marmalade jar, designed by
Judith Onions, 1966, 4in (10cm) high.
£45–50 / €70–80
$80–90 ⊞ CAL

Tea, Coffee & Sugar

A painted tin coffee dispenser, with a máhogany lid, c1809, 24in (61cm) wide.
£760–850 / €1,150–1,300
$1,400–1,550 ⊞ SMI

A burr-elm-veneered campaign tea caddy, c1840, 4in (10cm) wide.
£200–220 / €300–330
$360–400 ⊞ MRW

◀ **A tin coffee canister,** with original paint, c1880, 13in (33cm) wide.
£580–650 / €880–980
$1,050–1,200 ⊞ SMI

A ceramic sugar jar, Scottish, late 19thC, 10in (25.5cm) high.
£90–100 / €135–150
$165–185 ⊞ B&R

◀ **A Dalu Kola tea canister,** 1895, 7in (18cm) wide.
£500–550 / €750–830
$900–1,000 ⊞ HUX

A Mazawattee tea canister, decorated with scenes from *Alice in Wonderland*, 1895, 8½in (21.5cm) high.
£220–250 / €340–380
$420–480 ⊞ HUX

A copper tea caddy, embossed to resemble crocodile skin, c1900, 7in (18cm) high.
£120–135 / €180–200
$220–250 ⊞ BS

A Lipton's Tea canister, 1915, 9in (23cm) high.
£135–150 / €200–230
$250–280 ⊞ HUX

LOCATE THE SOURCE

The source of each illustration in Miller's can be found by checking the code letters below each caption with the Key to Illustrations, pages 313–315.

A ceramic yellow ware sugar storage jar, early 20thC, 5½in (14cm) high.
£95–105 / €145–160
$170–190 ⊞ MSB

A Mazawattee tea canister, 1920s, 8½in (21.5cm) wide.
£30–35 / €45–50
$55–65 ⊞ RTT

A T. G. Green ceramic Streamline sugar storage jar,
1930, 7in (18cm) high.
£50–60 / €75–90
$95–110 ⊞ CAL

◀ **A pair of tea canisters,** c1930, 6½in (16.5cm) high.
£8–12 / €12–18
$18–22 ⊞ AL

A T. G. Green ceramic sugar storage jar, c1930,
5in (12.5cm) high.
£90–100 / €135–150
$165–185 ⊞ AL

A Cornish Ware ceramic tea storage jar, 1930s,
6in (15cm) high.
£35–40 / €50–60
$65–75 ⊞ CAL

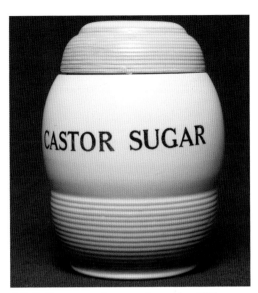

A T. G. Green ceramic sugar storage jar, 1930s, 6in (15cm) high.
£60–70 / €90–105
$115–130 ⊞ SCH

A T. G. Green ceramic lump sugar storage jar, c1935, 5in (12.5cm) high.
£90–100 / €135–150
$165–185 ⊞ AL

A Té Sol tea tin, 1930s–40s, 6½in (16.5cm) wide.
£20–25/ €30–35
$35–45 ⊞ RTT

A tin wall-mounted tea dispenser, 1950s, 8in (20.5cm) wide.
£30–35 / €45–50
$55–65 ⊞ DaM

◄ **A Hornsea ceramic coffee storage jar,** with a wooden lid, decorated with Heirloom pattern, 1960s, 4in (10cm) high.
£6–10 / €9–15
$10–20 ⊞ CHI

◀ **A Hornsea ceramic coffee storage jar,** decorated with Heirloom pattern, 1960s, 6in (15cm) high.
£8–12 / €12–18
$18–22 ⊞ CHI

A Portmeirion ceramic tea storage jar, decorated with Dolphins pattern, c1965, 4in (10cm) high.
£135–150 / €200–230
$240–270 ⊞ CHI

A Portmeirion ceramic coffee storage jar, decorated with Dolphins pattern, c1965, 7in (18cm) high.
£70–80 / €105–120
$130–145 ⊞ CHI

Two T. G. Green ceramic Spectrum storage jars, inscribed 'Coffee' and 'Tea', Gresley mark, 1970s, 6in (15cm) high.
£6–10 / €9–15
$10–20 each ⊞ CAL

◀ **A T. G. Green ceramic Cornish Ware tea storage jar,** 1980s, 6in (15cm) high.
£60–70 / €90–105
$110–130 ⊞ TAC

▶ **A T. G. Green ceramic Cornish Ware sugar storage jar,** 1996–2000, 5in (12.5cm) high.
£25–30 / €40–45
$45–55 ⊞ CAL

Tins

A Victorian Murray & Co Superfine Cocoanut tin,
9in (23cm) wide.
£35–40 / €50–60
$65–75 ⊞ AL

A Huntley & Palmer's biscuit tin, in the form
of a marble pedestal, c1890, 7½in (19cm) high.
£105–120 / €160–180
$195–220 ⊞ HUM

Three Huntley & Palmer's biscuit tins, Floral, Ivory and Mosaic,
1899–1901, 8¼in (21cm) wide.
£80–90 / €120–135
$145–165 each ⊞ HUX

**A Huntley & Palmer's Fire Brigade biscuit
tin,** c1892, 6in (15cm) high.
£580–650 / €890–980
$1,050–1,200 ⊞ HUX

A biscuit tin, modelled as a ship, 1900, 26½in (67.5cm) long.
£1,050–1,200 / €1,600–1,800
$1,900–2,200 ⊞ HUX

◄ **A metal biscuit tin,** in the form of a casket decorated with
medieval scenes, marked G. B. & Co, 20thC, 16½in (42cm) wide.
£95–110 / €140–165
$175–200 ⚒ SWO

A Baker's Cocoa tin, American, c1900.
£60–70 / €90–105
$110–125 ⊞ MSB

A Mackenzie & Mackenzie biscuit tin, c1900,
10in (25.5cm) wide.
£310–350 / €470–530
$570–640 ⊞ HUX
When the tin had been emptied, the lid could be
used as a wall-mounted letter rack.

**A Huntley & Palmer's Literature
biscuit tin,** in the form of eight
embossed books with marbled
edges, c1901, 3½in (9cm) wide.
£100–120 / €150–180
$185–220 ↗ DN

A Le Fevre-Utile biscuit tin, in the form of a trunk,
French, 1905, 8½in (21.5cm) wide.
£270–300 / €400–450
$490–550 ⊞ HUX

▶ **A biscuit tin,** in the form of a
railway carriage, Spanish, 1905,
6½in (16.5cm) wide.
£760–850 / €1,150–1,300
$1,400–1,550 ⊞ HUX

A Little Folk Pudding Powder tin, c1905,
7½in (19cm) square.
£250–280 / €380–420
$450–500 ⊞ MSB

A biscuit tin, German, 1910–20, 4¾in (12cm) high.
£10–15 / €15–22
$20–25 ⊞ RTT

A Huntley & Palmer's Easel biscuit tin, c1914,
7in (18cm) high.
£680–750 / €1,050–1,150
$1,250–1,350 ⊞ HUX

▶ **A Gaufrettes Hemosine biscuit tin,** French, 1915,
7in (18cm) wide.
£35–40 / €50–60
$65–75 ⊞ HUX

A Whitman's Instantaneous Sweet Chocolate tin,
American, 1900–25, 6in (15cm) high.
£70–80 / €105–120
$130–150 ⊞ MSB

A George V coronation biscuit tin, c1911,
7in (18cm) high.
£60–70 / €90–105
$110–125 ⊞ MSB

A Satin Finish Butter Scotch Waffles tin, American, 1900–25,
3¾in (9.5cm) wide.
£30–35 / €45–50
$55–65 ⊞ MSB

**A Huntley & Palmer's Caucasian biscuit
tin,** lithographed with a Russian rural scene,
1920, 8in (20.5cm) wide.
£60–70 / €90–105
$110–130 ✎ G(L)

A Cremona Dairy Cream Brazils sweet tin, c1920,
5¾in (14.5cm) wide.
£40–45 / €60–70
$75–85 ⊞ MSB

An enamel cake tin, c1920, 11in (28cm) diam.
£45–50 / €70–80
$80–90 ⊞ SMI

An enamel cake tin, 1920s, 10in (25.5cm) diam.
£105–120 / €160–180
$195–220 ⊞ JWK

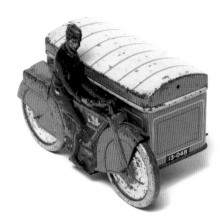

A CWS biscuit tin, in the form of a motorcyclist and sidecar, 1925, 7in (18cm) long.
£2,700–3,000 / €4,100–4,550
$4,950–5,500 ⊞ HUX

A Brazil Dainty Dinah Toffee tin,
1920s–30s, 8in (20.5cm) high.
£80–90 / €120–135
$145–165 ⊞ MSB

A Crawford's biscuit tin, in the form of a tractor, c1925, 7in (18cm) long.
£1,350–1,500 / €2,000–2,250
$2,450–2,750 ⊞ HUX

A Crawford's biscuit tin, in the form of an aeroplane, 1925, 16½in (42cm) long.
£1,800–2,000 / €2,700–3,000
$3,300–3,650 ⊞ HUX

A Mackintosh's Christmas Carnival Assortment biscuit tin, c1925, 10in (25.5cm) diam.
£60–70 / €90–105
$110–130 ⊞ HUX

A cake tin, c1930, 8in (20.5cm) diam.
£15–20 / €22–30
$28–38 ⊞ AL

A cake tin, c1930, 10in (25.5cm) diam.
£70–80 / €105–120
$130–145 ⊞ AL

A storage tin, in the form of a house, c1930,
5½in (14cm) wide.
£8–12 / €12–18
$15–20 ⊞ AL

An enamel cake tin, c1930, 10in (25.5cm) wide.
£45–50 / €70–80
$85–95 ⊞ B&R

Four Huntley & Palmer's sample biscuit tins, 1930s, 2¼in (5.5cm) high.
£40–45 / €60–70
$70–80 each ⊞ HUX

▶ **A Flavour Black Walnut Flakes tin,** American, 1930s, 6in (15cm) high.
£45–50 / €70–80
$80–90 ⊞ MSB

A biscuit tin, depicting SS *Normandie*, French, 1935, 7in (18cm) wide.
£35–40 / €50–60
$65–75 ⊞ HUX

A McVitie & Price's sample biscuit tin, 1930s, 3¼in (8.5cm) diam.
£12–16 / €18–24
$20–25 ⊞ Do

A biscuit tin, in the form of an inlaid tea caddy, c1936, 6in (15cm) wide.
£60–70 / €90–105
$110–130 ⊞ F&F

An Atlantic & Pacific Tea Company allspice tin, 1930s–50s, 3in (7.5cm) high.
£6–10 / €9–15
$15–20 ⊞ MSB

▶ A Carr's biscuit tin, in the form of a bus, 1950, 10in (25.5cm) long.
£360–400 / €540–600
$660–730 ⊞ HUX

A Cerebos Table Salt tin, c1950, 10in (25.5cm) high.
£15–20 / €22–30
$28–38 ⊞ AL

A Weston's Bleu Cheese Biscuits tin, c1950, 8in (20.5cm) high.
£4–8 / €6–12
$8–15 ⊞ AL

A Huntley & Palmer's Horse Guards biscuit tin, 1950s, 10in (25.5cm) wide.
£10–15 / €15–22
$19–28 ⊞ RGa

A Bahlsen Express sample tin, German, 1950s, 1½in (4cm) high.
£15–20 / €22–30
$28–38 ⊞ HUX

A Gourmets Delight biscuit tin, in the form of a book, 1950s–60s, 10in (25.5cm) high.
£15–20 / €22–30
$28–38 ⊞ DaM

A Blue Bird Toffee tin, 1950s–60s, 13in (33cm) wide.
£15–20 / €22–30
$28–38 ⊞ DaM

A Huntley & Palmer's Cocktail Biscuits tin, 1960s, 8in (20.5cm) diam.
£6–10 / €9–15
$12–19 ⊞ DaM

A Huntley & Palmer's Black and White Minstrels biscuit tin, 1963, 9in (23cm) square.
£30–35 / €45–50
$55–65 ⊞ HUX

Wirework

A wire basket, 1875–1925, 8in (20.5cm) diam.
£15–20/ €22–30
$25–35 ⊞ MSB

A wire oyster basket, with a wooden handle, 1900,
16in (40.5cm) wide.
£65–75 / €100–115
$120–135 ⊞ MLL

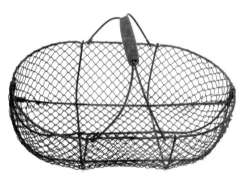

◀ **A wire vegetable basket,** with a wooden handle,
1900, 18in (45.5cm) wide.
£60–70 / €90–105
$110–130 ⊞ MLL

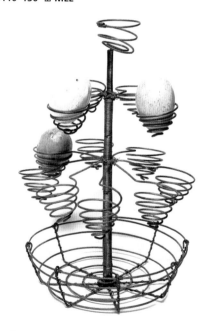

A wire egg stand, c1920, 12in (30.5cm) high.
£55–65 / €85–100
$100–120 ⊞ Cot

◀ **A wire two-tier egg basket,** American, early 20thC,
8in (20.5cm) high.
£80–90 / €120–135
$145–165 ⊞ MSB

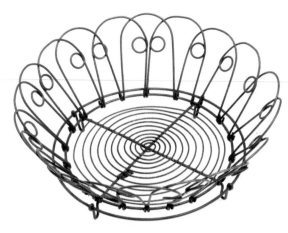

A wire steamer basket/cake tray, c1920, 12in (30.5cm) diam.
£10–15 / €15–22
$20–25 ⊞ **AL**

A wire egg basket, American, early 20thC,
7¼in (18.5cm) high.
£35–40 / €50–60
$65–75 ⊞ **MSB**

◄ **A wire bottle holder,** French, 1920s,
16in (40.5cm) wide.
£6–10 / €9–15
$12–19 ⊞ **AL**

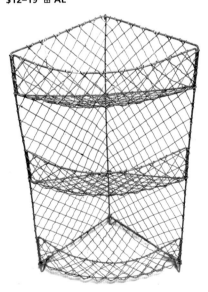

◄ **A wire egg
basket,** French,
c1930, 12in
(30.5cm) diam.
£25–30
€40–45
$45–55 ⊞ **AL**

A wire vegetable rack, 1930s,
26in (66cm) high.
£40–45 / €60–70
$70–80 ⊞ **JWK**

Dairy
Butter & Cheese

A sycamore butter scoop, Welsh, c1860, 8½in (21.5cm) long.
£60–70 / €90–105
$110–130 ⊞ MFB

A wooden butter stamp, with a carved design, c1870, 2in (5cm) diam.
£50–60 / €75–90
$95–110 ⊞ WeA

A sycamore butter churn, Welsh, c1840, 24in (61cm) high.
£440–490 / €660–740
$810–900 ⊞ MFB

A brass butter iron, with a wooden handle, c1860, 15in (38cm) long.
£160–180 / €240–270
$290–330 ⊞ WeA

Two wooden butter stamps, carved with acorns, c1870, larger 3½in (9cm) diam.
£60–70 / €90–105
$110–130 ⊞ AL

▶ **A wooden butter stamp,** c1870, 3¾in (9.5cm) diam.
£75–85
€115–130
$140–160
⊞ WeA

A sycamore butter stamp, carved with fruit, c1870, 3½in (9cm) diam.
£60–70 / €90–105
$110–130 ⊞ AL

A late Victorian sycamore butter wheel, 6½in (16.5cm) long.
£70–80 / € 105–120
$130–150 ⊞ SDA

**A sycamore two-piece butter mould and
stamp,** late 19thC, 10½in (26.5cm) wide.
£330–370 / € 500–560
$600–680 ⊞ BS

Three sycamore butter stamps, carved with leaves and flowers,
c1880, largest 4in (10cm) diam.
£110–125 / € 165–190
$200–230 ⊞ MFB

A sycamore butter stamp, with a carved
design, Welsh, c1880, 8in (20.5cm) wide.
£200–220 / € 300–330
$360–400 ⊞ MFB

A sycamore butter skimmer, late 19thC, 8in (20.5cm) diam.
£20–25 / € 30–35
$35–45 ⊞ MFB

◄ **A wooden
butter stamp,**
c1890, 1¼in
(3cm) diam.
£20–25
€ 30–35
$35–45 ⊞ WeA

A sycamore butter stamp, carved with a
swan, c1880, 4in (10cm) long.
£130–145 / € 195–220
$240–270 ⊞ MFB

A sycamore butter stamp,
late 19thC, 4in (10cm) diam.
£250–280 / €380–420
$460–510 ⊞ SEA

A wooden butter stamp,
late 19thC, 2in (5cm) diam.
£30–35 / €45–50
$55–65 ⊞ WeA

A wooden butter stamp, in a
case, late 19thC, 1¾in (4.5cm) diam.
£50–55 / €75–85
$95–105 ⊞ WeA

**An oak pump-action
butter churn,** with iron
binding, late 19thC,
38in (96.5cm) high.
£110–125 / €165–190
$200–230 ⊞ CHAC

An oak butter churn, with cast-iron fittings,
on a stand, marked 'R. A. Lister & Co',
late 19thC, 48in (122cm) high.
£120–140 / €180–210
$220–260 ➤ SJH

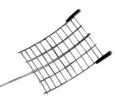

A wooden butter scoop,
American, 1880–1910,
9¼in (23.5cm) long.
£30–35 / €45–50
$55–65 ⊞ MSB

A metal curd cutter, with a wooden handle, late 19thC, 59in (150cm) long.
£180–200 / €270–300
$330–370 ⊞ WeA

A wooden butter stamp, early 20thC, 3½in (9cm) diam.
£60–70 / €90–105
$110–125 ⊞ MSB

Two sycamore butter stamps, carved with a swan and a thistle, c1900, larger 5in (12.5cm) diam.
£70–80 / €105–120
$130–150 ⊞ SMI

A porcelain cheese/butter display stand, inscribed 'Danish', Scottish, Glasgow, c1900, 16in (40.5cm) wide.
£145–165 / €220–250
$270–300 ⊞ MSB

A glass butter churn, early 20thC, 10¾in (27.5cm) high.
£100–110 / €150–165
$180–200 ⊞ MSB

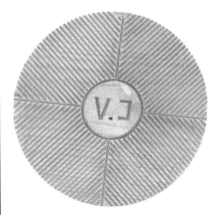

A wooden butter stamp, early 20thC, 7½in (19cm) diam.
£75–85 / €115–130
$135–150 ⊞ MSB

▶ **Three sycamore butter stamps,** carved with birds, c1900, largest 5in (12.5cm) diam.
£70–80 / €105–120
$130–150 each ⊞ SMI

A sycamore butter curler, c1900, 5½in (14cm) long.
£15–20 / €22–30
$28–38 ⊞ AL

DAIRY

A wooden butter stamp, carved with a thistle and a rose, c1900, 3½in (9cm) wide.
£45–50 / €70–80
$85–95 ⊞ CHAC

Three wooden butter stamps, carved with a thistle, a rose and a pineapple, c1900, largest 2¾in (7cm) diam.
£45–50 / €70–80
$85–95 each ⊞ JWK

A wooden butter roller, c1900, 6½in (16.5cm) long.
£60–70 / €90–105
$110–130 ⊞ WeA

A wooden butter stamp, with a carved design, c1900, 3½in (9cm) diam.
£45–50 / €70–80
$85–95 ⊞ CHAC

A wooden butter stamp, carved with a cow, c1900, 4in (10cm) diam.
£50–55 / €75–85
$95–105 ⊞ JWK

A wooden butter stamp, carved with a swan, c1900, 2½in (6.5cm) diam.
£45–50 / €70–80
$85–95 ⊞ JWK

▶ **An S. Banfield ceramic butter slab,** inscribed 'Brighton, Hastings & Horsham', c1900, 12½in (32cm) diam.
£160–180 / €240–270
$290–330 ⊞ JWK

A **butter knife,** with a wooden handle, carved 'butter', c1900, 7in (18cm) long.
£15–20 / €22–30
$28–38 ⊞ JWK

▶ **A butter crock,** inscribed 'Wm Millar's Stores Dundee', Scottish, c1900, 8in (20.5cm) diam.
£110–125
€165–190
$200–230
⊞ Cot

◀ **A butter crock,** inscribed 'Wm Farmer & Sons, Hillhead and Bearsden', c1900, 10in (25.5cm) diam.
£110–125
€165–190
$200–230
⊞ Cot

A **ceramic butter jar,** c1900, 9in (23cm) high.
£35–40 / €50–60
$65–75 ⊞ AL

A **Lipton butter crock,** 1900–20, 8in (20.5cm) diam.
£90–100 / €135–150
$170–190 ⊞ Cot

A **tin butter/cream churn,** 1900s, 9½in (24cm) wide.
£70–80 / €105–120
$130–145 ⊞ MSB

DAIRY

A Buttercup Dairy Co stoneware butter pot, c1910, 6in (15cm) high.
£270–300 / €400–450
$490–550 ⊞ AL

A wooden butter stamp, 1900–25, 3in (7.5cm) wide.
£35–40 / €50–60
$65–75 ⊞ MSB

▶ A Wm Low & Co stoneware butter pot, c1910, 5½in (14cm) high.
£240–270 / €360–410
$440–490 ⊞ AL

A wooden butter stamp, c1920, 5in (12.5cm) diam.
£155–175 / €230–260
$280–320 ⊞ SMI

A metal butter curler, with a wooden handle, c1920, 8½in (21.5cm) long.
£7–11 / €11–17
$13–20 ⊞ AL

A pair of wooden butter hands, c1920, 14in (35.5cm) long.
£15–20 / €22–30
$28–38 ⊞ AL

A sycamore butter smoother, c1920, 6in (15cm) diam.
£8–12 / €12–18
$15–22 ⊞ AL

A wooden butter hand, c1920, 14in (35.5cm) long.
£15–20 / €22–30
$28–38 ⊞ AL

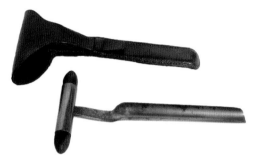

◄ **A steel and brass cheese taster,** c1920, 8in (20.5cm) long, with a leather case,
£50–60
€75–90
$95–110 ⊞ AL

A Harrods stoneware Stilton jar, c1920, 4in (10cm) high.
£35–40 / €50–60
$65–75 ⊞ AL

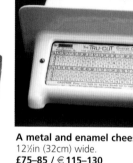

A metal and enamel cheese slicer, c1920, 12½in (32cm) wide.
£75–85 / €115–130
$135–150 ⊞ MSB

A Dairy Supply Co Ice Berg butter box, 1920, 7½in (19cm) wide.
£165–185 / €250–280
$300–340 ⊞ B&R

A pine Ice Berg butter box, 1920s, 14in (35.5cm) wide.
£130–145 / €195–220
$240–270 ⊞ B&R

A cast-iron and glass butter churn, with metal paddles, American, 1930s, 12¾in (32.5cm) high.
£35–40 / €50–60
$65–75 ⊞ MSB

A glass butter churn, 1948, 14in (35.5cm) high.
£55–65 / €85–100
$100–120 ⊞ BS

Cream & Milk

◀ **A brass cream skimmer,** with an iron handle, c1760, 23in (58.5cm) long.
£170–190
€260–290
$310–350
⊞ **F&F**

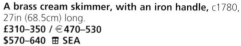

A brass cream skimmer, c1780, 18in (45.5cm) long.
£85–95 / €130–145
$160–180 ⊞ **F&F**

A brass cream skimmer, with an iron handle, c1780, 27in (68.5cm) long.
£310–350 / €470–530
$570–640 ⊞ **SEA**

A brass cream skimmer, with a wrought-iron handle, c1790, 20in (51cm) long.
£250–280 / €380–420
$460–510 ⊞ **SEA**

◀ **An elm dairy bowl,** 19thC, 9in (23cm) diam.
£310–350 / €470–530
$570–640 ⊞ **SEA**

An elm dairy bowl, 19thC, 12in (30.5cm) diam.
£250–280 / €380–420
$460–510 ⊞ **SEA**

A ceramic two-handled milk pail, with printed and hand-painted enamel decoration, repaired, 19thC, 12½in (32cm) diam.
£800–960 / €1,200–1,450
$1,450–1,700 ✗ **SWO**

A brass cream skimmer, with a steel handle, early 19thC, 21½in (54.5cm) long.
£190–220 / €290–330
$350–400 ⊞ WeA

▶ **A brass counter display milk churn,** c1860, 22in (56cm) high.
£1,800–2,000 / €2,700–3,000
$3,300–3,650 ⊞ SMI

A porcelain counter display milk churn, c1860, 18in (45.5cm) high.
£1,250–2,500 / €3,400–3,800
$4,100–4,600 ⊞ SMI

A sycamore dairy bailer, c1870, 3½in (9cm) diam.
£25–30 / €40–45
$50–55 ⊞ AL

Three ceramic Kent's Patent milk savers, c1860, largest 6in (15cm) high.
£180–200 / €270–300
$330–370 each ⊞ SMI

A sycamore dairy bailer, damaged, c1870, 6½in (16.5cm) diam.
£35–40 / €50–60
$65–75 ⊞ AL

▶ **A brass and copper dairy can,** c1880, 12in (30.5cm) high.
£125–140 / €190–210
$230–260 ⊞ NEW

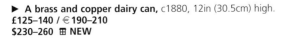

A milk pail, with a brass cover, c1880,
16in (40.5cm) high.
£1,800–2,000 / €2,700–3,000
$3,300–3,650 ⊞ SMI

A sycamore dairy bowl, c1880, 17in (43cm) diam.
£270–300 / €400–450
$490–550 ⊞ SMI

A ceramic milk pan, 1880–1900, 10½in (26.5cm) diam.
£80–90 / €120–135
$110–125 ⊞ MSB

A Royal Doulton ceramic milk pan, inscribed 'Pure
Milk', c1890, 10in (25.5cm) high.
£1,800–2,000 / €2,700–3,000
$3,300–3,650 ⊞ SMI

A wooden cream skimmer, late 19thC, 9½in (24cm) long.
£30–35 / €45–50
$55–65 ⊞ B&R

◀ A metal skimmer, 1890–1920, 26½in (67.5cm) long.
£40–45 / €60–70
$75–85 ⊞ MSB

DAIRY

A Danish Dairy Co crock, late 19thC, 5in (12.5cm) high.
£220–250 / €330–380
$400–460 ⊞ WeA

A steel and brass cream can, inscribed 'Run for the Cream Tom', Scottish, late 19thC, 6in (15cm) high.
£135–150 / €200–230
$250–280 ⊞ WeA

A C. Hull steel dairy can, early 20thC, 20in (51cm) high.
£270–300 / €400–450
$490–550 ⊞ B&R

A W. James Ford Farm dairy can, with a brass plate, 20thC, 18in (45.5cm) high.
£250–280 / €370–420
$460–520 ⊞ B&R

A brass and tin milk can, c1900.
£180–200 / €270–300
$330–370 ⊞ SMI

A steel and brass cream can, Scottish, c1900, 6in (15cm) high.
£180–200 / €270–300
$330–370 ⊞ SMI

Items in the Dairy section have been arranged in date order within each sub-section.

A steel and brass cream can, Scottish, c1900, 5in (12.5cm) high.
£135–150 / €200–230
$250–270 ⊞ SMI

◄ **A John Tyler & Sons steel and brass milk strainer,** c1900, 16½in (42cm) wide.
£70–80 / €105–120
$130–150 ⊞ B&R

DAIRY

◄ A steel and brass milk can, c1900, 10in (25.5cm) high.
£70–80 / €105–120 $130–150 ⊞ SMI

A copper milk delivery jug, with brass fittings, 1900, 8½in (21.5cm) high.
£170–190 / €260–290 $310–350 ⊞ WeA

► **A Grimwade ceramic Patent Safety Milk Bowl,** c1910, 9in (23cm) wide.
£50–60 / €75–90 $95–110 ⊞ SMI

A Gourmet & Co ceramic Eddystone Milk Boiler, c1910, 7in (18cm) high.
£180–200 / €270–300 $330–370 ⊞ SMI

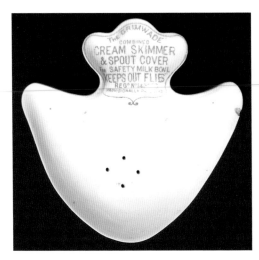

◀ **A Grimwade ceramic cream skimmer,** c1910, 6in (15cm) wide.
£135–150 / €200–230
$250–280 ⊞ SMI

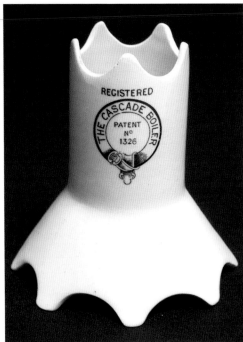

A ceramic Cascade Boiler, c1910, 4½in (11.5cm) high.
£70–80 / €105–120
$130–150 ⊞ SMI

◀ **A steel and brass milk bucket,** c1910, 13in (33cm) high.
£360–400 / €540–600
$660–730 ⊞ SMI

Further reading

Miller's Collectables Price Guide, Miller's Publications, 2004

▶ **A ceramic Hobson's milk boiler,** c1910, 5in (12.5cm) high.
£70–80 / €105–120
$130–150 ⊞ SMI

A ceramic milk pail, c1920, 9½in (24cm) high.
£540–600 / €820–910
$990–1,100 ⊞ SMI

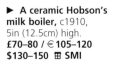

A steel and brass milk can, with three measures, c1920, 9in (23cm) high.
£270–300 / €400–450
$490–550 ⊞ **AL**

A steel and brass milk can, c1920, 4in (10cm) high.
£105–120 / €160–180
$190–220 ⊞ **SMI**

A steel and brass milk can, c1920,
5in (12.5cm) high.
£105–120 / €160–180
$190–220 ⊞ **SMI**

A steel and brass dairy can,
c1920, 19in (48.5cm) high.
£220–250 / €330–380
$400–460 ⊞ **SMI**

◀ **A steel and brass cream can,**
c1920, 5in (12.5cm) high.
£105–120 / €160–180
$190–220 ⊞ **SMI**

▶ **Two Borden's Malted Milk
ceramic beakers,** c1920,
4in (10cm) high.
£30–35 / €45–50
$55–65 ⊞ **SMI**

A ceramic milk barrel, c1920,
10in (25.5cm) high.
£180–200 / €270–300
$330–370 ⊞ **SMI**

A ceramic milk cooler, c1920, 8in (20.5cm) diam.
£115–130 / €175–195
$210–240 ⊞ **SMI**

Two ceramic milk beakers, c1920, 4in (10cm) high.
£45–50 / €70–80
$85–95 ⊞ **SMI**

An enamel milk can, c1930,
16in (40.5cm) high.
£35–40 / €50–60
$65–75 ⊞ **AL**

A metal milk churn, 1920s,
18½in (47cm) high.
£55–60 / €85–100
$100–120 ⊞ **AL**

A child's wooden dairy cart,
c1930, 17in (43cm) high.
£220–250 / €330–380
$400–460 ⊞ **SMI**

A Bel Bakelite cream maker, 1950–60, boxed, 12in (30.5cm) high.
£45–50 / €70–80
$85–95 ⊞ **DaM**

A Bel Bakelite cream maker,
1950s, 7½in (19cm) high, with box.
£15–20 / €22–30
$28–38 ⊞ **JWK**

Eggs

A Spode ceramic egg stand, transfer-printed with sarcophagi and sepulchres at the head of Cacamo harbour, from the Caramanian series, 1810, 7¼in (18.5cm) diam.
£490–550 / €740–830
$900–1,000 ⊞ GRe

▶ **A Spode ceramic egg stand,** transfer-printed with Gothic Castle pattern, 1815–20, 7¼in (18.5cm) diam.
£190–210
€290–320
$350–390
⊞ GRe

A Spode ceramic egg stand, decorated with Chinese flowers, c1820, 7½in (19cm) diam.
£90–100 / €135–150
$170–190 ⊞ SCO

A Parnall ceramic bowl, inscribed 'New Laid Eggs', c1850, 10in (25.5cm) diam.
£450–500 / €680–760
$820–920 ⊞ SMI

A ceramic egg crock, c1910, 12in (30.5cm) high.
£50–60 / €75–90
$95–110 ⊞ B&R

A wooden egg box, c1920, 14in (35.5cm) wide.
£70–80 / €105–120
$130–150 ⊞ SMI

A metal egg scoop,
c1920, 7in (18cm) high.
£7–11 / €11–17
$13–20 ⊞ AL

A wire egg basket, c1920,
12in (30.5cm) high.
£25–30 / €40–45
$50–55 ⊞ AL

A wooden egg stand, c1920,
37in (94cm) high.
£310–350 / €470–540
$570–640 ⊞ B&R
**This egg stand may have been
used in a shop or in a large
household.**

▶ **A pine egg
box,** c1920,
13in (33cm) wide.
£115–130
€175–195
$210–240
⊞ B&R

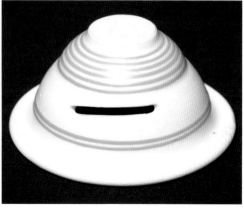

A pine egg box, 1920–30,
14in (35.5cm) wide.
£105–120 / €160–180
$190–220 ⊞ B&R

A wire egg basket,
French, c1930,
12in (30.5cm) high.
£25–30 / €40–45
$50–55 ⊞ AL

**A T. G. Green Cornish
Ware double egg cup,**
1930–50, 4in (10cm) high.
£90–100 / €135–150
$170–190 ⊞ CAL

A T. G. Green egg separator 1930s, 4in (10cm) wide.
£105–120 / €160–180
$190–220 ⊞ SCH

DAIRY

A Shelley ceramic egg cup set, 1930s, 4½in (11.5cm) high.
£100–110 / €150–165
$180–200 田 TAC

A set of Bakelite egg cups, in a stand, 1940s, 8in (20.5cm) wide.
£25–30 / €40–45
$55–65 田 JWK

A Bakelite egg stand, 1940s, 6in (15cm) wide.
£15–20 / €22–30
$28–38 田 JWK

A Bakelite egg separator, 1940s, 4in (10cm) high.
£10–15 / €15–22
$18–28 田 JWK

A set of felt egg cosies,
1950s, 3½in (9cm) high.
£10–15 / €15–22
$18–28 田 JWK

▶ **A Tala Egg Wedger,**
1950s, 5in (12.5cm) high.
£6–10 / €9–15
$11–18 田 JWK

A Worcester ceramic egg coddler,
decorated with June Garland
pattern, 1960s, 2in (5cm) high.
£15–20 / €22–30
$28–38 田 CHI

Ice Cream

Two ice cream spatulas, late 19thC, 22in (56cm) long.
£65–75 / €100–115
$120–140 each ⊞ BS

A glass ice cream lick, c1840,
3in (7.5cm) high.
£75–85 / €115–130
$140–160 ⊞ JAS

A metal ice cream scoop, with a wooden handle, American, early 20thC,
10¼in (26cm) long.
£20–25 / €30–35
$35–45 ⊞ MSB

A metal ice cream wafer maker, with a wooden
handle, American, early 20thC, 12in (30.5cm) long.
£90–105 / €135–160
$160–190 ⊞ MSB

▶ **A Royal Doulton
stoneware ice cream
drum,** the inner
compartment with
a wooden cover,
impressed mark, c1910,
10½in (26.5cm) high.
£110–130 / €165–195
$200–240 ⋏ SWO

A Bonton mechanical tin ice cream maker,
1930–40, 10in (25.5cm) wide.
£55–65 / €85–100
$100–120 ⊞ DaM

**An Iceland wood
and metal ice cream
freezer,** 1920s–30s,
7½in (19cm) high.
£70–80 / €105–120
$130–150 ⊞ MSB

**A Crawford's Biscuits
metal ice cream wafer
maker,** 1940s,
5in (12.5cm) high.
£35–40 / €50–60
$65–75 ⊞ HUX

Baking

A wire cooling rack, late 19thC, 16in (40.5cm) wide.
£40–45 / €60–70
$75–85 ⊞ WeA

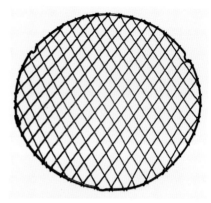

A wire cooling rack, 1880,
12¾in (32.5cm) wide.
£45–50 / €70–80
$85–95 ⊞ WeA

A metal cookie press, with a wooden ram, American,
late 19thC, 15¼in (38.5cm) long.
£80–90 / €120–135
$150–170 ⊞ MSB

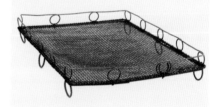

A wire cooling rack, American, 1890–1910,
13½in (34.5cm) wide.
£80–90 / €120–135
$145–165 ⊞ MSB

**A hand-made
iron cooling
rack,** American,
early 20thC,
9½in (24cm) diam.
£20–25 / €30–35
$40–45 ⊞ MSB

▶ **A Roe's
ceramic pie
funnel,** early
20thC, 3in
(7.5cm) high.
£50–60 / €75–90
$95–110 ⊞ B&R

A Gourmet Pie Cup ceramic pie funnel,
1900s, 3½in (9cm) high.
£40–45 / €60–70
$75–85 ⊞ JWK

A set of three Grimwade ceramic pie dividers, c1910, largest 5in (12.5) wide.
£270–300 / €410–450
$500–560 ⊞ SMI

A child's baking set, comprising a tin tray and cutters, three rolling pins, a wooden board and Boston Cooking School recipes, 1920s–30s, in a cardboard box, 8¾ x 12¼in (22 x 31cm).
£60–70 / €90–105
$110–125 ⊞ MSB

◀ A set of Tala tin meringue tubes, 1950s, with box, 4in (10cm) high.
£15–20
€22–30
$28–38 ⊞ DaM

A wire cooling rack, 1910, 10¾in (27.5cm) diam.
£50–60 / €75–90
$95–110 ⊞ WeA

Three ceramic pie funnels, in the form of blackbirds, 1930–40, smallest 3in (7.5cm) high.
£40–45 / €60–70
$75–85 ⊞ JWK

◀ **Five ceramic pie funnels,** c1930s, largest 3in (7.5cm) high.
£1–5 / €2–7
$3–9 each ⊞ AL

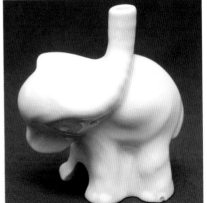

A Nutbrown ceramic pie funnel, slight damage, 1950, 3½in (9cm) high.
£35–40 / €45–50
$55–65 ⊞ BS

Bowls & Basins

A hand-carved pine bowl, 19thC, 22in (56cm) wide.
£20–25 / €30–35
$35–45 ⊞ HRQ

A glazed terracotta mixing bowl, c1880,
13in (33cm) diam.
£50–55 / €75–85
$90–100 ⊞ AL

A Mrs Olive's ceramic plum pudding mould,
c1880, 7in (18cm) diam.
£135–150 / €200–230
$250–280 ⊞ SMI

▶ **A yellow ware batter bowl,** with a
pouring spout, 1890–1910, 15¾in (40cm) diam.
£170–190 / €260–290
$310–350 ⊞ MSB

An Albany ceramic mixing bowl,
1880–1900, 9½in (24cm) high.
£50–55 / €75–85
$90–100 ⊞ MSB

A Grimwade ceramic Quick Cooker, slight
damage, 1890–1920, 7½in (19cm) diam.
£50–60 / €75–90
$95–110 ⊞ CHAC

▶ **A sponge-
ware mixing
bowl,** c1900s,
9½in (24cm) wide.
£70–80
€105–120
$135–150 ⊞ MSB

BAKING

A Dorchester Pottery mixing bowl, early 1900s,
10¼in (26cm) high.
£100–110 / €150–165
$180–200 ⊞ MSB

A Doulton ceramic bread pan, c1910,
15in (38cm) diam.
£105–120 / €160–180
$195–220 ⊞ Cot

A ceramic Aulsebrooks christmas pudding bowl,
c1910, 7in (18cm) diam.
£90–100 / €135–150
$165–185 ⊞ SMI

A Grimwade ceramic Quick Cooker, c1910,
5in (12.5cm) diam.
£135–150 / €200–230
$250–280 ⊞ SMI

> Items in the Baking section have been arranged in
> date order.

A Clarke's ceramic 'Rigid' icing bowl, c1920,
9in (23cm) diam.
£140–160 / €210–240
$260–290 ⊞ SMI

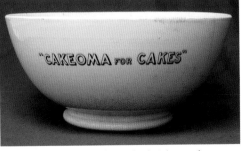

A ceramic mixing bowl, inscribed 'Cakeoma for
Cakes', c1920, 12in (30.5cm) diam.
£70–80 / €105–120
$130–145 ⊞ B&R

A Lovatts ceramic mixing bowl, with lip, c1930,
7in (18cm) diam.
£25–30 / €30–35
$35–45 ⊞ AL

A Fortnum & Mason ceramic mixing bowl, c1930,
5in (12.5cm) diam.
£10–15 / €15–22
$18–28 ⊞ AL

A ceramic mixing bowl, 1930s, 10¼in (26cm) diam.
£20–25 / €30–35
$35–40 ⊞ MSB

A copper bowl, 1940s, 11¼in (28.5cm) diam.
£40–45 / €60–70
$70–80 ⊞ MSB

A ceramic mixing bowl, c1940, 9in (23cm) diam.
£15–20 / €22–30
$28–38 ⊞ JWK

A ceramic mixing bowl, c1940, 10in (25.5cm) diam.
£20–25 / €30–35
$35–45 ⊞ JWK

BAKING

An enamel pie dish, 1940s, 9½in (24cm) wide.
£5–10 / €8–13
$10–15 ⊞ **JWK**

An enamel pie dish, 1940s, 8in (20.5cm) wide.
£5–10 / €8–13
$10–15 ⊞ **JWK**

A T. G. Green Cornish Ware mixing bowl,
1940s, 10in (25.5cm) diam.
£40–45 / €60–70
$75–85 ⊞ **HSt**

An enamel pie dish, 1940s, 10in (25.5cm) wide.
£5–10 / €8–13
$10–15 ⊞ **JWK**

A Pyrex mixing bowl, c1950, 10in (25.5cm) diam.
£20–25 / €30–35
$35–45 ⊞ **JWK**

An enamel bowl, c1960, 6in (15cm) diam.
£6–10 / €9–15
$11–18 ⊞ **AL**

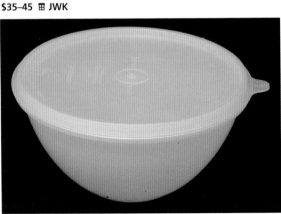

Condition

The condition is absolutely vital when assessing the value of an antique. Damaged pieces on the whole appreciate much less than perfect examples. However, a rare desirable piece may command a high price even when damaged.

◄ **A Tupperware Wonderlier pudding bowl,** with a cover for steaming, 1960, 7½in (19cm) diam.
£10–15 / €15–22
$19–28 ⊞ **Mo**

Cake Decorating

A tin icing table, early 20thC, 8½in (21.5cm) diam.
£90–100 / €135–150
$165–185 ⊞ MSB

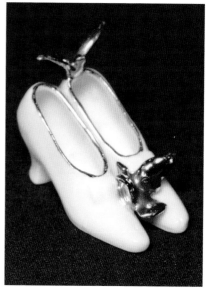

A bisque cake decoration, in the form of a pair of shoes, decorated with doves, German, 1910, 2in (5cm) wide.
£25–30 / €40–45
$50–55 ⊞ CCs

A bisque wedding cake decoration, in the form of a good luck figure, German, 1910–20, 2½in (6.5cm) high.
£65–75 / €100–115
$120–140 ⊞ CCs

A porcelain wedding cake decoration, in the form of a pair of bridal slippers, decorated with a dove, c1920, 1½in (4cm) high.
£15–20 / €22–30
$28–38⊞ FMN

▶ **A porcelain wedding cake decoration,** c1920, 5in (12.5cm) wide.
£20–25 / €30–35
$35–45 ⊞ FMN

◀ **A plaster Christmas cake decoration,** in the form of a robin, damaged, c1925, 1in (2.5cm) wide.
£1–5 / €2–7
$3–9 ⊞ YC

A tin cake icer, 1920s, 7in (18cm) long.
£50–60 / €75–90
$95–110 ⊞ BS

A porcelain wedding cake decoration, in the form of a horseshoe, decorated with a dove, 1920–40, 1in (2.5cm) wide.
£10–15 / €15–22
$18–28 ⊞ FMN

A porcelain birthday cake decoration, in the form of a key, decorated with a dove, 1920–40, 2in (5cm) long.
£10–15 / €15–22
$18–28 ⊞ FMN

A porcelain wedding cake decoration, in the form of a horseshoe, decorated with doves, 1920–40, 2in (5cm) wide.
£15–20 / €22–30
$28–38 ⊞ FMN

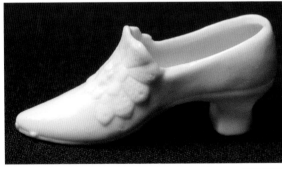

◄ **A porcelain cake decoration,** in the form of a slipper, 1920–40, 2in (5cm) long.
£20–25 / €30–35
$35–45 ⊞ FMN

► **A porcelain 21st-birthday cake decoration,** in the form of a key, 1920–40, 3in (7.5cm) wide.
£15–20 / €22–30
$28–38 ⊞ FMN

A bisque Christmas cake decoration, in the form of Father Christmas on his sleigh, c1930, 2½in (6.5cm) high.
£35–40 / €50–60
$65–75 ⊞ YC

A bisque cake decoration, in the form of a musician, 1930, 2½in (6.5cm) high.
£50–60 / €75–90
$95–110 ⊞ YC

A bisque cake decoration, in the form of a man eating a melon, 1930, 1½in (4cm) high.
£50–60 / €75–90
$95–110 ⊞ YC

A set of three bisque cake decorations, each in the form of a pixie, c1930, 3in (7.5cm) high.
£70–80 / €105–120
$135–150 ⊞ YC

A bisque cake decoration, in the form of a horse jumping over a heart, c1930, 2in (5cm) high.
£60–70 / €90–105
$110–130 ⊞ YC

Three bisque and plaster Christmas decorations, each in the form of Father Christmas, c1935, largest 2in (5cm) high.
£50–60 / €75–90
$95–110 ⊞ YC

A pack of 36 birthday cake candles, 1930–40, in original box, 2½in (6.5cm) square.
£1–5 / €2–7
$3–9 ⊞ RTT

A Tala icing set, late 1940s, boxed, 8½in (21.5cm) square.
£15–20 / €22–30
$28–38 ⊞ JWK

A Tala icing syringe, 1950s, 6in (15cm) long, with box.
£10–15 / €15–22
$19–38 ⊞ JWK

◀ **A Tala icing set,** c1950, with box, 4½ x 6¼in
(11.5 x 16cm).
£4–8 / €6–12
$8–15 ⊞ AL

An icing table, c1950, 7in (18cm) high.
£35–40 / €50–60
$65–75 ⊞ AL

◀ **A set of Tala meringue tubes,** 1950s, boxed,
4¼in (11cm) high.
£1–5 / €2–7
$3–9 ⊞ JWK

► **A Tala tin icing kit,** 1950s–60s, with box.
£30–35 / €45–50
$55–65 ⊞ DaM

A **Tala tin icing syringe,** 1950s, 6in (15cm) long, with box.
£25–30 / €40–45
$50–55 ⊞ DaM

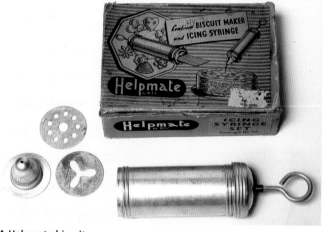

A Helpmate biscuit maker and icing syringe, 1950s–60s, 6in (15cm) long, with box.
£25–30 / €40–45
$50–55 ⊞ DaM

◄ **A Tala icing set,** 1950s–60s, syringe 6in (15cm) long, with box.
£25–30 / €40–45
$50–55 ⊞ DaM

► **A Nutbrown icing outfit,** 1960s, boxed, 14in (35.5cm) wide.
£30–35 / €45–50
$55–65 ⊞ DaM

BAKING

Cutters

A steel and brass pastry jigger, c1820, 6in (15cm) long.
£310–350 / €470–530
$570–640 ⊞ NEW

A hand-carved wooden springerle rolling pin, American, late
19thC, 18in (45.5cm) long.
£120–140 / €180–210
$220–250 ⊞ MSB

Three brass pastry cutters and crimpers,
late 19thC, largest 5in (12.5cm) long.
£30–35 / €45–50
$55–65 ⊞ BS

◄ **A brass pastry cutter,** with a wooden
handle, c1858, 11in (28cm) long.
£160–180 / €240–270
$290–330 ⊞ WeA

A tin cookie cutter, in the form of a woman,
1875–1900, 3½in (9cm) high.
£30–35 / €45–50
$55–65 ⊞ MSB

◄ **A tin cookie cutter,** in the form of a
horse, 1875–1900, 4½in (11.5cm) wide.
£40–45 / €60–70
$75–85 ⊞ MSB

A wooden pastry cutter, 1875–1900, 5½in (14cm) wide.
£25–30 / €40–45
$45–50 ⊞ MSB

A hand-made tin cookie cutter, in the form of an anchor, 1890–1910, 4½in (11.5cm) wide.
£70–80 / €105–120
$135–150 ⊞ MSB

A set of tin graduated cookie cutters, in the form of hearts, c1900, largest 6in (15cm) long.
£60–70 / €90–105
$110–125 ⊞ MSB

A tin cookie cutter, in the form of an angel, American, c1900, 5¾in (14.5cm) wide.
£140–155 / €200–230
$250–280 ⊞ MSB

A tin cookie cutter, American, c1900, 12¾in (32.5cm) long.
£50–55 / €75–85
$90–100 ⊞ MSB

A tin biscuit pricker, c1900, 3in (7.5cm) diam.
£40–45 / €60–70
$75–85 ⊞ BS

A sycamore biscuit roller, c1900, Scottish, 5in (12.5cm) wide.
£70–80 / €105–120
$120–150 ⊞ SMI

BAKING

A set of three tin pastry cutters, c1900, largest 3in (7.5cm) diam.
£10–15 / €15–22
$18–38 ⊞ Cot

A wood and bone pastry cutter, c1900,
5½in (14cm) long.
£10–15 / €15–22
$18–38 ⊞ AL

A set of tin pastry cutters, c1900, largest 7in (18cm) diam.
£15–20 / €22–30
$28–38 ⊞ AL

A set of wooden pastry cutters, c1900,
largest 5in (12.5cm) diam.
£10–15 / €15–22
$18–38 ⊞ SDA

▶ A tin tart cutter, early 20thC,
6¾in (17cm) diam.
£20–25 / €30–35
$40–45 ⊞ MSB

A tin cookie cutter, in the form of a pig,
American, early 20thC, 6½in (16.5cm) wide.
£85–95 / €130–145
$155–175 ⊞ **MSB**

Further reading
Miller's Antiques Price Guide, Miller's Publications, 2004

A carved wood pastry cutter,
1900s, 6in (15cm) long.
£30–35 / €45–50
$55–65 ⊞ **MSB**

BAKING

A steel biscuit pricker, c1900, largest
3in (7.5cm) diam.
£40–45 / €60–70
$75–85 ⊞ **BS**

A set of five tin ridged pastry cutters, with case, 1900–25,
largest 4¾in (12cm) wide.
£40–45 / €60–70
$75–85 ⊞ **MSB**

A tin cookie cutter, in the form of a goose,
1915–30, 2¾in (7cm) high.
£45–50 / €65–75
$80–90 ⊞ **MSB**

A set of tin pastry cutters, in a case, c1920, 4in (10cm) diam.
£15–20 / €22–30
$28–38 ⊞ **AL**

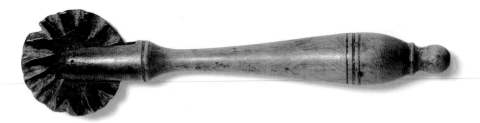

A wooden pastry cutter, c1920,
5½in (14cm) long.
£7–11 / €11–17
$13–20 ⊞ AL

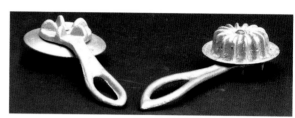

Two cast-metal pastry cutters, 1925–50, 5in (12.5cm) long.
£4–8 / €6–12
$8–15 each ⊞ MSB

A tin cookie cutter, with 12 different shapes,
1920s–30s, 6½in (14cm) diam.
£55–65 / €85–100
$100–115 ⊞ MSB

A set of four Davis Baking Powder tin cookie cutters,
1925–50, 3¾in (9.5cm) wide.
£10–14 / €15–20
$20–25 ⊞ MSB

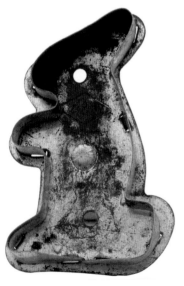

A tin cookie cutter, in the form of a rabbit,
with a handle, 1925–50, 2½in (6.5cm) high.
£4–8 / €6–12
$8–15 ⊞ MSB

A tin cookie cutter, in the form of an elephant, with a wooden
handle, 1930s, 2¾in (7cm) wide.
£10–15 / €15–20
$20–25 ⊞ MSB

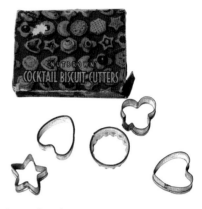

A set of Tala tin pastry cutters, with tin, 1940s, 4in (10cm) high.
£15–20 / €22–30
$28–38 ⊞ JWK

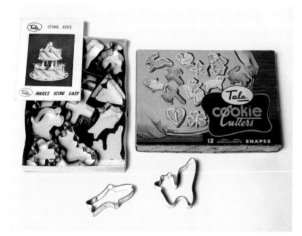

A set of Nutbrown tin cocktail biscuit cutters, 1950s, with box, 4in (10cm) wide.
£30–35 / €45–50
$55–65 ⊞ DaM

A set of 12 Tala tin cookie cutters, 1950–60, boxed, 8in (20.5cm) wide.
£25–30 / €40–45
$50–55 ⊞ DaM

A set of Tala tin aspic and hors d'oeuvres cutters, 1950s, 4¾in (12cm) diam.
£15–20 / €22–30
$28–38 ⊞ JWK

Dredgers & Shakers

A Bretby Pottery flour shaker, c1900, 5in (12.5cm) high.
£30–35 / €45–50
$55–65 ⊞ B&R

A tin flour dredger, c1900, 5in (12.5cm) high.
£60–70 / €90–105
$110–130 ⊞ BS

▶ **A silver-plated sugar shaker,** c1910, 5½in (14cm) high.
£50–60 / €75–90
$95–110 ⊞ AL

A Maling flour shaker, decorated with Cobblestone pattern, c1920, 5in (12.5cm) high.
£70–80 / €105–120
$130–150 ⊞ SMI

Two glass and metal sifters, c1930, 4¼in (10.5cm) high.
£20–25 / €30–35
$35–40 ⊞ MSB

A T. G. Green Cornish Ware flour shaker, c1930, 5½in (14cm) high.
£75–85 / €115–130
$140–160 ⊞ AL

A ceramic sugar shaker, c1930, 5½in (14cm) high.
£25–30 / €40–45
$50–55 ⊞ AL

A T. G. Green Cornish Ware flour shaker, 1930s–50s, with a handle, 5½in (14cm) high.
£140–160 / €210–240
$260–290 ⊞ CAL

◀ **A T. G. Green Cornish Ware sugar shaker,** 1950, 7in (18cm) high.
£900–1,000
€1,350–1,500
$1,650–1,850 ⊞ CAL

▶ **A T. G. Green Cornish Ware sugar shaker,** 1960s, 5½in (14cm) high.
£25–30 / €40–45
$50–55 ⊞ CAL

Rolling Pins

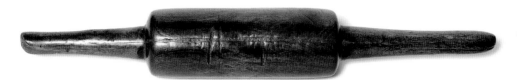

A wooden rolling pin, c1800, 12in (30.5cm) long.
£60–70 / €90–105
$110–130 ⊞ SDA

A Victorian oak rolling pin, 24in (61cm) long.
£20–25 / €30–35
$35–45 ⊞ Cot

A wooden pie crust rolling pin, 1860, 11in (28cm) long.
£105–120 / €160–180
$190–220 ⊞ WeA

An Elm oatmeal roller, Scottish, c1880, 14in (35.5cm) long.
£80–90 / €120–135
$150–170 ⊞ MFB

A sycamore rolling pin, c1880, 18in (45.5cm) long.
£15–20 / €22–30
$28–38 ⊞ Cot

A wooden miniature oatmeal roller, 1875–1900, 8½in (21.5cm) long.
£60–70 / €90–105
$110–125 ⊞ MSB

A glass rolling pin, painted with a love message, 1880–1900, 11¾in (30cm) long.
£70–80 / € 105–120
$135–150 ⊞ MSB

A beech rolling pin, c1900, 18in (45.5cm) long.
£25–30 / € 40–45
$50–55 ⊞ Cot

A wooden oatmeal roller, c1900, 12½in (32cm) long.
£40–45 / € 60–70
$75–85 ⊞ MSB

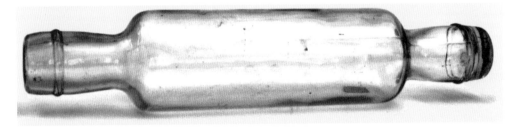

A glass rolling pin, cork or metal cap missing, early 20thC, 14in (35.5cm) long.
£10–15 / € 15–22
$20–25 ⊞ MSB

A wooden oatmeal roller, early 20thC, 19½in (49.5cm) long.
£40–45 / € 60–70
$75–85 ⊞ MSB

A **Thomas Farar Isobel ceramic rolling pin,** with wooden handles, c1910, 21in (53.5cm) long.
£135–150 / €200–230
$240–270 ⊞ B&R

A **T. G. Green ceramic Cornish Ware rolling pin,** c1920, 18½in (47cm) long.
£120–135 / €180–200
$220–250 ⊞ AL

A **ceramic rolling pin,** with beech handles, 1920s, 20in (51cm) long.
£200–230 / €300–350
$370–420 ⊞ BS

A **ceramic rolling pin,** with wooden handles, c1930, 18in (45.5cm) long.
£30–35 / €45–50
$55–65 ⊞ AL

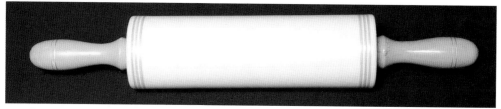

A **Sadler ceramic Kleen Ware rolling pin,** 1940s, 17in (43cm) long.
£50–60 / €75–90
$95–110 ⊞ SCH

A **T. G. Green ceramic Cornish Ware rolling pin,** stamped, 1950s, 17in (43cm) long.
£85–95 / €130–145
$160–180 ⊞ HSt

BAKING

Tins

A copper cake/roasting tin, c1880, 12½in (32cm) wide.
£65–75 / €100–115
$120–140 ⊞ **F&F**

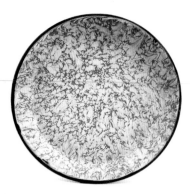

A graniteware pie pan, American,
1880–1910, 8¾in (22cm) diam.
£7–11 / €10–16
$16–20 ⊞ **MSB**

A graniteware pan, American, 1880–1910,
9¾in (25cm) diam.
£85–95 / €130–145
$155–175 ⊞ **MSB**

A metal bread pan, American, 1890–1910, 15¾in (40cm) long.
£80–90 / €120–135
$150–165 ⊞ **MSB**

A tin cake pan, American, c1900, 15¼in (38.5cm) long.
£40–45 / €60–70
$75–85 ⊞ **MSB**

A tin muffin baking pan, American, c1900,
13¼in (33.5) wide.
£35–40 / €50–60
$65–75 ⊞ **MSB**

A metal muffin baking pan, with an applied rack, c1900,
12½in (32cm) wide.
£60–70 / €90–105
$110–125 ⊞ **MSB**

◀ **A metal bread roll baking pan,** American, early 20thC,
12¾in (32.5cm) wide.
£15–20 / €22–30
$28–38 ⊞ **MSB**

A cast-iron bread roll baking pan, American, early 20thC, 12½ x 6¾in (15 x 26cm).
£35–40 / €50–60
$65–75 ⊞ MSB

A metal bread roll baking pan, American, c1900, 10¼in (26cm) wide.
£20–25 / €30–35
$35–45 ⊞ MSB

A galvanized-steel Hovis bread tin, c1920, 7in (18cm) wide.
£25–30 / €40–45
$50–55 ⊞ DaM

A tin baking pan, American, Chicago, early 20thC, 10¼in (26cm) wide.
£15–20 / €22–30
$28–38 ⊞ MSB

A metal Turog bread tin, c1920, 6in (15cm) wide.
£15–20 / €22–30
$28–38 ⊞ JWK
Bread tins with names are more desirable to collectors.

A tin cake baking pan, American, c1920s, 11in (28cm) wide.
£15–20 / €22–30
$28–38 ⊞ MSB

Two Hovis bread tins, c1920, 6in (15cm) diam.
£20–25 / €30–35
$35–45 each ⊞ JWK

Two bread tins, c1920, larger
8in (20.5cm) wide.
£4–8 / €6–12
$8–15 each ⊞ AL

Three bread tins, c1920, largest 13in (33cm) wide.
£4–8 / €6–12
$8–15 each ⊞ AL

An Allinson bread tin, c1920, 6in (15cm) wide.
£15–20 / €22–30
$28–38 ⊞ JWK

◄ **A Green's
flan tin,** 1930,
8in (20.5cm) diam.
£8–12 / €12–18
$15–22 ⊞ JWK

► **A Green's
sponge tin,**
1930, 7in
(18cm) diam.
£6–10 / €9–15
$12–19 ⊞ JWK

A bun tin, 1940s, 12in (30.5cm) wide.
£6–10 / €9–15
$12–18 ⊞ JWK

A tin pie pan, American, c1950s, 6¼in (16cm) diam.
£10–15 / €15–20
$20–25 ⊞ MSB

Weights & Measures

A set of dairy scales, 19thC, 18in (45.5cm) wide.
£90–100 / €135–150
$170–190 ⊞ B&R

▶ A set of A. K. & Sons iron imperial weights, c1880, largest 5¼in (13.5cm) diam.
£85–95
€130–145
$160–180 ⊞ SMI

A set of kitchen scales, Swedish, 19thC, 21in (53.5cm) wide.
£250–280 / €380–420
$460–510 ⊞ SWN

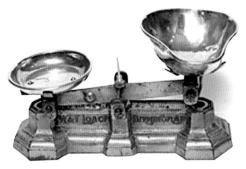

A set of W. T. Loach scales, with brass pans, late 19thC, 11in (28cm) wide.
£65–75 / €100–115
$120–140 ⊞ B&R

▶ A set of cast-iron and brass household scales, c1880, 18in (45.5cm) high.
£75–85
€115–130
$140–160
⊞ SMI

A set of cast-iron and brass butcher's scales, c1880, 26in (66cm) wide.
£180–200 / €270–300
$330–370 ⊞ SMI

BAKING

A set of cast-iron and brass sweet scales, c1880, 12in (30.5cm) wide.
£75–85 / €115–130
$140–160 ⊞ SMI

A set of cast-iron scales, with weights, c1880, 15in (38cm) wide.
£150–165 / €220–250
$270–300 ⊞ DaM

A set of cast-iron, brass and ceramic butter scales, c1880, 21in (53.5cm) wide.
£80–90 / €120–135
$150–170 ⊞ SMI

▶ **A set of brass bread scales,** late 19thC, 10¾in (27.5cm) wide.
£155–175
€230–260
$280–320
⊞ WeA

◀ **A brass measuring scoop,** possibly from a set of scales, American, 1890–1910, 12in (30.5cm) wide.
£35–40 / €50–60
$65–75 ⊞ MSB

A metal measuring jug, late 19thC, 5¼in (13.5cm) high.
£55–65 / €85–100
$100–120 ⊞ WeA

▶ **A set of cast-iron and brass scales,** 1890–1910, 18¾in (47.5cm) wide.
£50–60 / €75–90
$100–110 ⊞ MSB

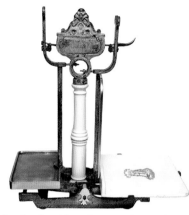

A set of five brass weights, early 20thC, in a wooden case, 8in (20.5cm) wide.
£25–30 / €45–50
$55–65 ⊞ MSB

A pair of cast-iron, brass and ceramic butcher's scales, 1900, 27in (68.5cm) high.
£470–530 / €710–800
$860–970 ⊞ SMI

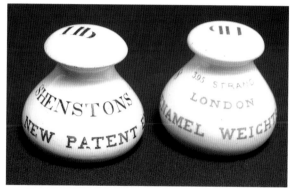

Two Shenstons ceramic 1lb weights, early 20thC, 3in (7.5cm) high.
£135–150 / €200–230
$250–280 each ⊞ SMI

◀ A pint measure, with a brass handle, c1910, 7in (18cm) high.
£45–50 / €70–80
$85–95 ⊞ YT

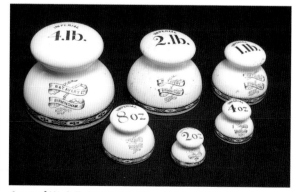

A set of W. & T. Avery ceramic weights, c1910, largest 4in (10cm) wide.
£1,350–1,500 / €2,000–2,250
$2,450–2,750 ⊞ SMI

◀ A set of three ceramic weights, largest 2½in (6.5cm) diam.
£220–250 / €330–380
$400–460 ⊞ B&R

◀ **A pair of Salter scales,** with a brass pan, c1920, 13in (33cm) high.
£65–75 / €100–115
$120–140 ⊞ AL

A Tremall's glass measure, 1920s, 6in (15cm) high.
£20–25 / €30–35
$35–45 ⊞ JWK

Two enamel measuring jugs, c1920, larger 6in (15cm) high.
£45–50 / €70–80
$85–95 ⊞ JWK

A Salter's butter balance, 1920s, 10½in (26.5cm) high.
£70–80 / €105–120
$130–150 ⊞ AL

A glass measuring cup, American, 1920s–30s, 3½in (9cm) high.
£10–14 / €15–21
$20–25 ⊞ MSB

A set of household scales, c1930, 13in (33cm) high.
£50–60 / €75–90
$95–110 ⊞ SMI

A pair of metal scales, with weights, c1930, 10in (25.5cm) wide.
£45–50 / €70–80
$85–95 ⊞ AL

An enamel measuring jug, 1930s, 6in (15cm) high.
£10–15 / €15–22
$19–28 ⊞ JWK

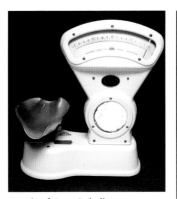

A set of Salter household scales,
No. 16, c1930, 11¾in (30cm) high.
£35–40 / €50–60
$65–75 ⊞ JWK

**A pair of Asco Bakelite
scales,** with a tin pan, 1930s,
19in (48.5cm) high.
£100–110 / €150–165
$180–200 ⊞ JWK

**A pair of Vancome & Hart metal
scales,** 1930s, 19in (48.5cm) high.
£100–110 / €150–165
$180–200 ⊞ JWK

BAKING

An enamel measuring jug, 1950s,
6¼in (16cm) high.
£6–10 / €9–15
$12–19 ⊞ WeA

A set of Salter metal scales, 1954, 9in (23cm) diam.
£30–35 / €45–50
$55–65 ⊞ JWK

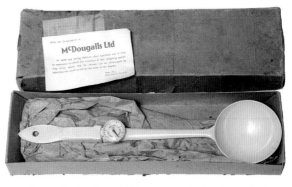

A set of Salter scales, c1960, 8¾in (22cm) high.
£20–25 / €30–35
$35–45 ⊞ JWK

A McDougalls plastic weighing spoon, 1950s, with original
box, 12in (30.5cm) long.
£45–50 / €70–80
$85–95 ⊞ DaM

Moulds

A salt-glazed mould, c1800, 9¾in (25cm) wide.
£40–45 / €60–70
$70–80 ⊞ B&R

A copper ring mould, stamped '522', 19thC,
6in (15cm) diam.
£140–165 / €210–250
$260–300 ⚒ TMA

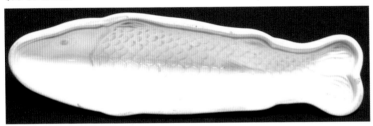

◀ **A ceramic creamware
mould,** in the form of
a fish, c1850,
8in (20.5cm) long.
£135–150 / €200–230
$250–270 ⊞ SMI

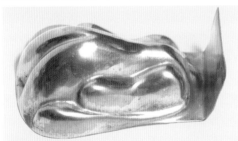

A Victorian miniature copper mould, in the form of a
chicken, 2¾in (7cm) long.
£15–20 / €25–30
$30–35 ⊞ WiB

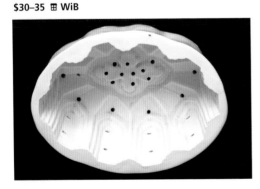

A tin cheese strainer, 1860–80, 5½in (14cm) wide.
£170–190 / €260–290
$310–350 ⊞ MSB

◀ **A Copeland ceramic cream cheese mould,**
cracked, c1870, 5in (12.5cm) high.
£50–60 / €80–90
$95–110 ⊞ AL

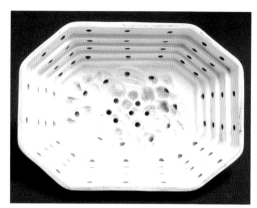

A ceramic curd mould, with raised fruit, c1880, 7in (18cm) high.
£115–130 / €175–195
$210–240 ⊞ SMI

A cast-iron mould, c1880, 15in (38cm) wide.
£40–45 / €60–70
$70–80 ⊞ DaM

A copper mould, c1880, 6in (15cm) high.
£120–135 / €180–200
$220–250 ⊞ WAC

A late Victorian copper mould, with lid, 6in (15cm) high.
£45–50 / €70–80
$80–95 ⊞ YT

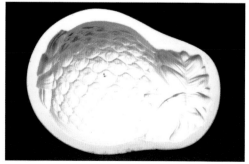

A Copeland ceramic mould, in the form of a pineapple, slight damage, c1890, 7in (18cm) long.
£50–60 / €75–90
$90–105 ⊞ B&R

A metal springerle mould, American, 1890–1910, 6¾ x 6½in (17 x 16.5cm).
£160–180 / €240–270
$290–330 ⊞ MSB
Springerle are moulded cookies.

MOULDS

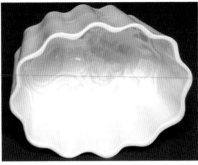

A ceramic mould, with a raised lion, c1900, 6in (15cm) high.
£50–55 / €75–85
$90–100 ⊞ AL

▶ **A metal springerle mould,** cast with animals and a butterfly, c1900, 4¾in (12cm) high.
£75–85
€115–130
$135–150
⊞ MSB

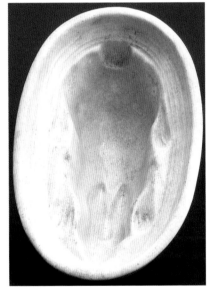

An Ironstone mould, in the form of a rabbit, c1900, 6½in (16.5cm) long.
£90–100 / €135–150
$165–185 ⊞ MSB

◀ **A Brown & Polson's ceramic blancmange mould,** decorated with a recipe, c1900, 4½in (11.5cm) high.
£90–100
€135–150
$165–185
⊞ AL

A ceramic cheese mould, French, c1900, 8in (20.5cm) wide.
£20–25 / €30–35
$35–45 ⊞ B&R

A tin candle mould, c1900, 10½in (26.5cm) high.
£110–125 / €165–190
$200–230 ⊞ B&R

A miniature tin mould, with a raised wheat sheaf, 1890–1900, 1¼in (3cm) wide.
£25–30 / €40–45
$45–50 ⊞ MSB

A miniature tin mould, with a raised ham, 1890–1900, 1¼in (3cm) wide.
£25–30 / €40–45
$45–50 ⊞ MSB

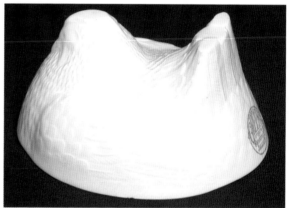

A miniature tin mould, with a raised walnut, 1890–1900, 2in (5cm) wide.
£25–30 / €40–45
$45–50 ⊞ MSB

A Green's ceramic mould, in the form of a chicken, c1910, 6½in (16.5cm) wide.
£50–60 / €80–90
$95–110 ⊞ AL

A Shelly ceramic mould, c1910, 5¾in (14.5cm) diam.
£80–90 / €120–135
$145–165 ⊞ AL

▶ **A Shelly ceramic mould,** c1910, 5¾in (14.5) diam.
£50–55 / €75–85
$90–100 ⊞ AL

MOULDS

A tin cheese mould, in the form of a heart, French, c1920, 6in (15cm) wide.
£25–30 / €40–45
$50–55 ⊞ B&R

A Brown & Polson's ceramic blancmange mould, decorated with a recipe, 1920s, 7in (18cm) wide.
£120–135 / €180–200
$220–250 ⊞ BS

A set of four aluminium moulds, each in the form of a rabbit, c1930, 5in (12.5cm) long.
£1–5 / €2–7
$3–9 each ⊞ AL

A glass mould, in the form of a tortoise, c1930, 7½in (19cm) long.
£15–20 / €25–30
$30–35 ⊞ AL

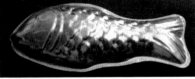

A set of five aluminium moulds, each in the form of a fish, c1950, largest 5in (12.5cm) long.
£1–5 / €2–7
$3–9 each ⊞ AL

A set of five aluminium moulds, each in the form of a dog, c1950, largest 5in (12.5cm) long.
£1–5 / €2–7
$3–9 each ⊞ AL

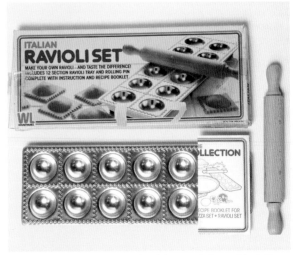

A set of W. L. Housewares aluminium ravioli moulds, Italian, c1970, 13in (33cm) wide, with box.
£25–30 / €40–45
$50–55 ⊞ DaM

Baking Moulds

A copper meat pie mould, with raised decoration, late 19thC, 9in (23cm) wide.
£300–330 / €450–500
$550–600 ⊞ B&R

A ceramic redware pudding mould, marked 'No 9', American, c1800, 9½in (24cm) diam.
£50–55 / €75–85
$90–100 ⊞ COBB

A copper game pie mould, moulded with deer, c1880, 8in (20.5cm) wide.
£180–200 / €270–300
$330–370 ⊞ SMI

A ceramic cake mould, French, Savoie, 1890, 9½in (24cm) diam.
£40–45 / €60–70
$70–80 ⊞ MLL

A sycamore shortbread mould, late 19thC, 9in (23cm) diam.
£35–40 / €50–60
$65–75 ⊞ WeA

A tin miniature pudding steamer, 1890–1910, 4in (10cm) high.
£30–35 / €45–50
$60–65 ⊞ MSB

A tin cake mould, in the form of a star, early 20thC, 8¾in (22cm) wide.
£20–25 / €30–40
$40–45 ⊞ MSB

MOULDS

A Brown & Polson's ceramic shortbread baking dish, early 20thC, 9in (23cm) wide.
£115–130 / € 175–195
$210–240 ⊞ WeA

A Grimwade Paragon ceramic blancmange and jelly mould, c1910, 7in (18cm) diam.
£135–150 / € 200–230
$250–270 ⊞ SMI

▶ **A wooden shortbread mould,** c1930,
5½in (14cm) diam.
£8–12 / € 12–18
$14–20 ⊞ AL

A tin cake mould, in the form of a horseshoe, American, 1900s–20s, 13in (33m) wide.
£100–120 / € 150–165
$180–200 ⊞ MSB

A set of Tala tin cake moulds, in the form of hearts, 1950s, 9in (23cm) wide, in original box.
£1–5 / € 2–7
$3–9 ⊞ DaM

A set of Tala metal castle pudding moulds, 1950s, 3¼in (8.5cm) high, with box.
£1–5 / € 2–7
$3–9 ⊞ JWK

Chocolate & Fondant Moulds

A sycamore double-sided fondant mould, c1860, 7in (18cm) wide.
£155–175 / €230–260
$280–320 ⊞ MFB

A copper double-sided chocolate mould,
in the form of a stag, c1850, 13in (33cm) high.
£400–450 / €600–680
$730–820 ⊞ SMI

A tin chocolate mould, in the form of a duck, c1890,
3½in (9cm) wide.
£105–120 / €160–180
$190–220 ⊞ WeA

A wooden maple sugar mould, hand-carved
with a heart, c1900, 6¼ x 5in (16 x 12.5cm).
£195–220 / €290–330
$360–400 ⊞ MSB

▶ **A steel chocolate mould,** in the form of a
skier, c1900, 5½in (14cm) high.
£80–90 / €120–135
$145–165 ⊞ B&R

MOULDS

A tin chocolate mould, in the form of a swan, c1900, 4in (10cm) wide.
£35–40 / €50–60
$65–75 ⊞ Cot

A chocolate mould, in the form of a fish, 1900–20, 18in (33cm) wide.
£65–75 / €100–115
$120–140 ⊞ CHAC

A metal lollypop mould, cast with rabbits, 1900–25, 7½in (19cm) long.
£60–70 / €90–105
$110–125 ⊞ MSB

A metal chocolate mould, in the form of a rabbit, 1900–20, 7½in (19cm) wide.
£35–40 / €50–60
$65–75 ⊞ CHAC

A wooden maple sugar mould, hand-carved with stars, American, 1900–25, 22in (56cm) long.
£320–360 / €480–540
$580–650 ⊞ MSB

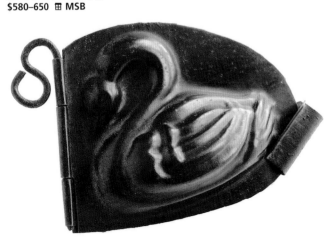

A chocolate mould, in the form of a turkey, c1910, 4in (10cm) high.
£80–90 / €120–135
$145–165 ⊞ WeA

◄ **A chocolate mould,** in the form of a swan, c1910, 2½in (6.5cm) wide.
£30–35 / €45–50
$55–65 ⊞ WeA

A **tin chocolate mould,** in the form of two birds, c1920,
11in (28cm) wide.
£85–95 / €130–145
$160–180 ⊞ SMI

A **chocolate mould,** in the form of a rabbit,
c1910, 5in (12.5cm) high.
£75–85 / €115–130
$140–160 ⊞ WeA

A **tin chocolate mould,** in the form of a pig,
Continental, c1920, 6in (15cm) wide.
£30–35 / €45–50
$55–65 ⊞ B&R

A **tin chocolate mould,** in the form of a tiger, Continental,
c1920, 6in (15cm) wide.
£35–40 / €50–60
$65–75 ⊞ B&R

A **tin chocolate mould,** in the form of a
cockerel, Continental, c1920, 5in (12.5cm) wide.
£35–40 / €50–60
$65–75 ⊞ B&R

◄ A **copper and tin double-sided
chocolate mould,** in the form of a horse and
a rider, 1930s, 13½in (34.5cm) wide.
£490–550 / €740–830
$900–1,000 ⊞ MSB

MOULDS

Ice Cream Moulds

A pewter three-piece ice cream mould, 19thC, 6in (15cm) high.
£150–165 / €230–250
$270–300 ⊞ BS

A pewter three-piece ice cream mould, by Benham & Froud, with raised fruit, 19thC, 7in (18cm) high.
£150–165 / €230–250
$270–300 ⊞ BS

A steel and copper ice cream mould, with raised fruit, 19thC, 7in (18cm) high.
£200–230 / €300–350
$370–430 ⊞ BS

A pewter three-piece banquet ice cream mould, with raised fruit, 1868, 7in (18cm) diam.
£350–390 / €530–590
$640–710 ⊞ BS

A copper ice cream mould, with a raised lion, 1875–1900, 5¾in (14.5cm) high.
£460–520 / €690–790
$850–950 ⊞ MSB

▶ **A copper ice cream mould,** with a raised quail, 1875–1900, 4½in (11.5cm) high.
£460–520
€690–790
$850–950
⊞ MSB

A pewter ice cream mould, with raised fruit, 19thC, 7in (18cm) high.
£160–180 / €240–270
$290–330 ⊞ MFB

A copper and tin ice cream ring mould, American, 1890–1910, 2¾in (7cm) high.
£75–85 / €115–130
$135–150 ⊞ MSB

A pewter three-piece jelly/ice cream mould, c1880, 6in (15cm) high.
£65–75 / €100–115
$120–135 ⊞ DaM

▶ **A pewter three-piece ice cream mould,** c1900, 10½in (26.5cm) high.
£80–90 / €120–135
$145–165 ⊞ BS

A tin ice cream mould, with raised fruit, 1890–1910, 6in (15cm) diam.
£110–125 / €165–190
$200–230 ⊞ MSB

A tin ice cream ring mould, American, early 20thC, 7¾in (19.5cm) diam.
£60–70 / €90–105
$115–130 ⊞ MSB

A tin ice cream ring mould, American, early 20thC, 7¾in (19.5cm) diam.
£60–70 / €90–105
$115–130 ⊞ MSB

A tin ice cream ring mould, with an indented top, American, early 20thC, 7¼in (18.5cm) diam.
£60–70 / €90–105
$115–130 ⊞ MSB

MOULDS

A tin ice cream mould, in the form of a castle, American, early 20thC, 5in (12.5cm) high.
£85–95 / €130–145
$155–175 ⊞ MSB

A tin ice cream mould, with artichoke-shaped peaks, American, early 20thC, 8in (20.5cm) diam.
£85–95 / €130–145
$155–175 ⊞ MSB

A tin ice cream mould, American, early 20thC, 4in (10cm) diam.
£40–45 / €60–70
$75–85 ⊞ MSB

A tin ice cream mould, with nine swirl-shaped peaks, American, early 20thC, 7¾in (19.5cm) diam.
£60–70 / €90–105
$115–130 ⊞ MSB

A pewter banquet ice cream mould, in the form of a basket, 1900–25, 11½in (29cm) wide.
£970–1,100 / €1,450–1,650
$1,800–2,000 ⊞ MSB

A pewter ice cream mould, in the form of a rose, 1925–50, 2½in (6.5cm) wide.
£40–45 / €60–70
$70–80 ⊞ MSB

Jelly Moulds

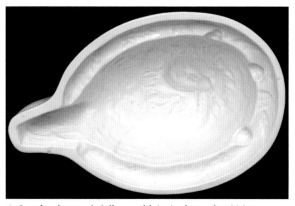

A Copeland ceramic jelly mould, in the form of a chicken, 19thC, 9in (23cm) wide.
£110–125 / €165–190
$200–230 ⊞ **BS**

A copper jelly/sponge mould, 19thC, 2¼in (5.5cm) high.
£60–70 / €90–105
$110–130 ⊞ **BS**

A Benham & Froud copper crown jelly mould, 19thC, 7in (18cm) wide.
£210–240 / €320–360
$380–440 ⊞ **BS**

A Benham & Froud copper jelly mould, 19thC, 4½in (11.5cm) high.
£130–145 / €195–200
$240–270 ⊞ **BS**

A Benham & Froud copper jelly mould, 19thC, 7in (18cm) high.
£500–550 / €760–830
$920–1,000 ⊞ **BS**

A steel and copper jelly mould, 19thC, 6in (15cm) wide.
£210–230 / €320–350
$380–420 ⊞ **BS**

A copper aspic mould, in the form of a crown, 19thC, 3in (7.5cm) high.
£70–80 / €105–120
$130–145 ⊞ **BS**

A copper aspic mould, in the form of a butterfly, 19thC, 2½in (6.5cm) wide.
£50–55 / €80–85
$95–100 ⊞ **BS**

Three copper jelly moulds, 19thC, largest 6in (15cm) diam.
£260–310 / €390–470
$580–570   ✐ G(L)

A copper aspic mould, in the form
of two golf clubs and balls, 19thC,
2¼in (5.5cm) wide.
£65–75 / €100–115
$120–135   ⊞ BS

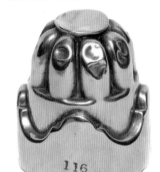

A Purssell Cornhill copper jelly mould, 19thC, 7in (18cm) diam.
£360–400 / €540–600
$660–730   ⊞ SEA

A copper jelly mould, c1820,
2½in (6.5cm) high.
£60–70 / €90–105
$110–130   ⊞ F&F

A Victorian copper jelly mould,
4in (10cm) high.
£155–175 / €230–260
$280–320   ⊞ WiB

A Victorian ceramic jelly mould, with a raised lion, 8in (20.5cm) wide.
£20–25 / €30–40
$35–45   ⊞ TOP

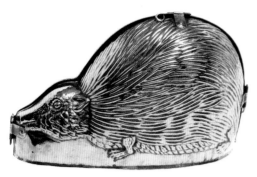

A copper jelly mould, in the form of a hedgehog, c1850, 9in (23cm) wide.
£360–400 / €540–600
$660–730 ⊞ SMI

A ceramic creamware footed jelly mould, c1850, 7in (18cm) wide.
£135–150 / €200–230
$250–270 ⊞ SMI

A ceramic jelly mould, in the form of a lobster, 1860s–90s, 3¼in (8.5cm) high.
£100–110 / €150–165
$180–200 ⊞ MSB

A copper aspic mould, in the form of a cutlet, 1875–1900, 3¼in (8.5cm) high.
£30–35 / €45–50
$55–65 ⊞ MSB

A copper aspic mould, in the form of a ham, 1875–1900, 2½in (6.5cm) high.
£30–35 / €45–50
$55–65 ⊞ MSB

A Wedgwood ceramic jelly mould, with a relief of a ewe and lamb, c1880, 4in (10cm) wide.
£135–150 / €200–230
$250–270 ⊞ SMI

A Wedgwood ceramic jelly mould, with a raised partridge, c1880, 5in (12.5cm) high.
£110–125 / €165–190
$200–230 ⊞ SMI

MOULDS

A copper and tin mould, late 19thC, 6in (15cm) wide.
**£70–80 / €105–120
$130–150 ⊞ B&R**

A copper and tin jelly mould, with a raised wheat sheaf, c1880, 6in (15cm) wide.
**£160–180 / €240–270
$290–330 ⊞ WeA**

A ceramic creamware jelly mould, c1880, 8in (20.5cm) wide.
**£115–130 / €175–195
$210–240 ⊞ SMI**

A copper aspic mould, in the form of a hare, c1890, 3in (7.5cm) wide.
**£40–45 / €60–70
$75–85 ⊞ WeA**

A ceramic jelly mould, with a relief of a lady and a milk churn, c1880, 7in (18cm) wide.
**£105–120 / €160–180
$190–220 ⊞ SMI**

A copper aspic mould, in the form of a horseshoe, c1890, 1½in (4cm) wide.
**£30–35 / €45–50
$55–65 ⊞ WeA**

A copper aspic mould, in the form of a fish, c1890. 4½in (11.5cm) long.
**£30–35 / €45–50
$55–65 ⊞ WeA**

A Copeland ceramic jelly mould, with a relief of a woman milking a cow, c1900, 8in (20.5cm) wide.
£105–120 / € 160–180
$190–220 ⊞ SMI

A copper and tin jelly mould, with a raised woodcock, American, early 20thC, 4in (10cm) high.
£100–110 / € 150–165
$180–200 ⊞ MSB

A copper and tin jelly mould, with a raised tulip, American, early 20thC, 3¼in (8.5cm) high.
£90–100 / € 135–150
$165–185 ⊞ MSB

A copper and tin jelly mould, with raised acorns, early 20thC, 3½in (9cm) high.
£110–125 / € 165–190
$200–230 ⊞ MSB

A stoneware salt-glazed jelly mould, early 20thC, 3¼in (8.5cm) high.
£40–45 / € 60–70
$75–85 ⊞ MSB

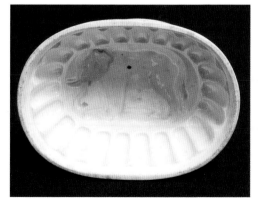

A ceramic jelly mould, with a relief of an elephant, c1910, 6in (15cm) wide.
£115–130 / € 175–195
$210–240 ⊞ SMI

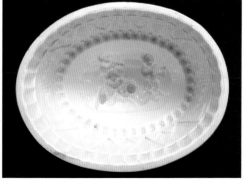

A Wedgwood ceramic jelly mould, with a relief of children playing musical instruments, c1910, 8in (20.5cm) wide.
£115–130 / € 175–195
$210–240 ⊞ SMI

MOULDS

A Grimwade ceramic mould, in the form of a lion, c1910, 11in (28cm) wide.
£90–100 / € 135–150
$165–180 ⊞ SMI

A Shelley ceramic jelly mould, in the form of an armadillo, 1912–25, 7in (18cm) wide.
£200–230 / € 300–350
$370–420 ⊞ BS

A stoneware jelly mould, with a relief of an elephant, c1920, 9in (23cm) wide.
£70–80 / € 105–200
$130–150 ⊞ SMI

A Shelley ceramic jelly mould, in the form of a hen, c1920, 8in (20.5cm) wide.
£220–250 / € 330–380
$400–460 ⊞ SMI

A Shelley ceramic jelly mould, in the form of a rabbit, c1920, 10in (25.5cm) wide.
£220–250 / € 330–380
$400–460 ⊞ SMI

A stoneware jelly mould, with a relief of a cow, c1920, 6in (15cm) wide.
£70–80 / € 105–200
$130–150 ⊞ SMI

A set of three Shelley ceramic jelly moulds, in the form of swans, c1920, largest 9in (23cm) wide.
£180–200 / € 270–300
$330–370 ⊞ SMI

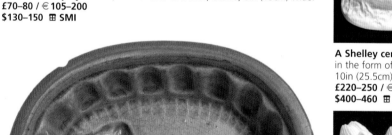

◄ **A stoneware jelly mould,** with a relief of a greyhound, c1920, 7in (18cm) wide.
£70–80 / € 105–200
$130–150 ⊞ SMI

A Shelley ceramic Cecil jelly mould, c1920–30, 8in (20.5cm) wide.
£35–40 / €50–60
$65–75 ⊞ HO

A stoneware jelly mould, with a raised horse's head, c1920, 8in (20.5cm) wide.
£70–80 / €105–120
$130–150 ⊞ SMI

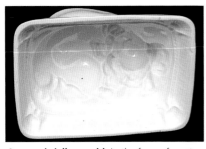

A ceramic jelly mould, in the form of a cat on a cushion, 1929, 6in (15cm) wide.
£80–90 / €120–135
$150–170 ⊞ BS

A Shelley ceramic jelly mould, 1920s, 4½in (11.5cm) wide.
£35–40 / €50–60
$65–75 ⊞ WiB

A metal jelly mould, with raised Disney characters, 1934, 7in (18cm) wide.
£35–40 / €50–60
$65–75 ⊞ HYP

MOULDS

A plastic jelly mould, in the form of a cat, 1980s, 8in (20.5cm) long.
£4–8 / €6–12
$8–15 ⊞ TWI

A plastic jelly mould, in the form of a space shuttle, 1980s, 10in (25.5cm) long.
£4–8 / €6–12
$8–15 ⊞ TWI

A plastic jelly mould, in the form of a spaceman, 1980s, 9½in (24cm) long.
£4–8 / €6–12
$8–15 ⊞ TWI

Cookware

A brass griddle, Scottish, 19thC, 4in (10cm) wide.
£135–150 / €200–230
$240–270 ⊞ SEA

A wrought-iron game crown, early 19thC, 12in (30.5cm) high.
£400–450 / €600–680
$730–820 ⊞ WeA

A wrought-iron harnen, mid-19thC, 16in (40.5cm) high.
£220–250 / €330–380
$400–460 ⊞ WeA
A harnen is an Irish toasting device that would have stood in an inglenook fireplace.

A wrought-iron harnen, Irish, c1850, 23in (58.5cm) high.
£690–790 / €1,050–1,200
$1,250–1,450 ⊞ STA

A tin pudding steamer, in the form of a heart, American, 1860–80, 7in (18cm) wide.
£170–190 / €260–290
$310–350 ⊞ MSB

An iron chestnut roaster, French, c1880, 26in (66cm) high.
£400–440 / €600–660
$730–810 ⊞ DaM

A tin and copper steamer, 1880–1910, 15½in (39.5cm) high.
£60–70 / €90–105
$110–125 ⊞ MSB

A copper hotplate, c1890, 27in (68.5cm) wide.
£200–230 / €300–350
$370–420 ⊞ DaM

A cast-iron griddle, Scottish, c1890, 12in (30.5cm) wide.
£50–60 / €75–90
$95–110 ⊞ DaM

A cast-iron griddle, 1890–1910, 20in (51.5cm) wide.
£50–55 / €75–85
$90–100 ⊞ MSB

A wrought-iron harnen, Irish, c1850, 23in (58.5cm) high.
£80–90 / €125–140
$145–165 ⊞ STA

A pigeon roaster, French, c1900, 10in (25.5cm) wide.
£60–70 / €90–105
$110–130 ⊞ B&R

A porcelain pudding steamer, with a metal cover, c1900, 6in (15cm) high.
£25–30 / €35–45
$45–50 ⊞ MSB

A metal steamer, early 1900s, 8in (20.5cm) wide.
£30–35 / €45–50
$55–65 ⊞ MSB

COOKWARE

A Hemmings ceramic baking dish, early 20thC,
7in (18cm) wide.
£25–30 / €35–45
$45–50 ⊞ WeA

A J. Lawrence & Co ceramic baking dish, early
20thC, 9in (23cm) wide.
£30–35 / €45–50
$55–65 ⊞ WeA

A tin apple roaster, French, c1920, 14in (35.5cm) wide.
£40–45 / €60–70
$75–85 ⊞ B&R

A Rippingille's paraffin stove, c1920,
16in (40.5cm) wide.
£90–100 / €135–150
$165–185 ⊞ AL

A Henley tin oven, c1930, 12in (30.5cm) high.
£35–40 / €50–60
$65–75 ⊞ AL

A Sotox aluminium pudding steamer, 1930s–50s,
6in (15cm) wide.
£25–30 / €40–45
$50–55 ⊞ DaM

Pots & Pans

Three cast-bronze posset pots, one marked 'Wasborough No. 2', 18thC, largest 8in (20.5cm) diam.
£170–190 / €260–290
$310–350 ⊞ COBB
Posset is a drink of hot milk, curdled with ale and flavoured with spices, that was formerly used as a remedy for colds.

A silver brandy saucepan, with a wooden handle, maker's mark partially worn, London 1728, 3½in (9cm) diam.
£220–260 / €330–390
$400–470 ⚒ WW

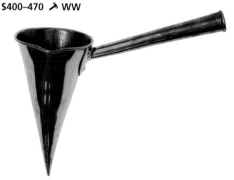

A copper ale muller, 19thC, 7½in (19cm) high.
£120–135 / €180–200
$220–250 ⊞ BS

A silver brandy saucepan, by William Fleming, London 1720, 3in (7.5cm) high.
£1,500–1,650 / €2,250–2,500
$2,700–3,000 ⊞ NS

A Britannia Standard silver brandy saucepan, with a wooden handle, probably by Edward Feline, London 1721, 3¾in (9.5cm) diam, 5oz.
£280–330 / €420–500
$510–600 ⚒ WW

A copper side-handled brandy saucepan, with a fruitwood handle, damaged, c1870, 4½in (11.5cm) high.
£50–55 / €75–85
$95–105 ⊞ F&F

COOKWARE

A Benham & Froud copper saucepan, 19thC, 4in (10cm) diam.
£55–65 / €85–100
$100–120 ⊞ BS

A Benham & Froud copper saucepan, with a cover, 19thC, 4¼in (10cm) diam.
£110–125 / €165–190
$200–230 ⊞ BS

A copper fish kettle, stamped '16', engraved 'H. A. B.', 19thC, 16¼in (41.5cm) long.
£220–260 / €330–390
$400–470 ⚒ SWO

A copper stock pot, with a cover, 19thC, 10in (25.5cm) high.
£270–300 / €400–450
$490–550 ⊞ BS

Two copper saucepans, with covers and iron handles, 19thC, larger 10¾in (27.5cm) diam.
£190–220 / €280–330
$350–400 ⚒ SWO

▶ **A copper saucepan,** with a cover and iron handle, c1800, 6¼in (16cm) diam.
£90–100 / €135–150
$165–185 ⊞ F&F

▶ **A silver brandy saucepan,** with an ivory handle, London 1825, 2in (5cm) diam.
£190–220 / €280–330
$350–400 ⚲ **GAK**

A brass and iron jam pan, c1820, 6in (15cm) diam.
£120–135 / €180–200
$220–250 ⊞ **SEA**

A copper saucepan, American, 1830–50, 8¾in (22cm) diam.
£95–110 / €145–165
$175–200 ⊞ **MSB**

A cast-iron cauldron, c1860, 20in (51cm) wide.
£450–500 / €680–750
$820–910 ⊞ **DaM**

A cast-iron cauldron, c1860, 13in (33cm) wide.
£200–220 / €300–330
$360–400 ⊞ **DaM**

▶ **A copper cooking pot,** c1880, 8in (20.5cm) diam.
£150–165 / €220–250
$270–300 ⊞ **YT**

COOKWARE

A copper fish kettle, c1880, 21in (53.5cm) long.
£270–300 / €400–450
$490–550 ⊞ NEW

A copper cooking pot, c1880, 8in (20.5cm) diam.
£130–145 / €195–220
$240–270 ⊞ YT

A copper fish kettle, c1880, 20in (51cm) long.
£540–600 / €820–910
$990–1,100 ⊞ DaM

◄ **A cast-iron griddle,** c1880, 11in (28cm) diam.
£60–70
€90–105
$110–130
⊞ DaM

A cast-iron cooking pot, c1880, 12in (30.5cm) diam.
£155–175 / €230–260
$280–320 ⊞ DaM

► **A Kenrick & Sons cast-iron cooking pot,** c1880, 18in (45.5cm) diam.
£100–110
€150–165
$180–200
⊞ DaM

A cast-iron cooking pot, No. 3, with three legs and a cover, c1880, 10in (25.5cm) wide.
£150–165 / €220–250
$270–300 ⊞ DaM

A spun-brass pail, with a cast-iron handle, 1880–1900, 6¾in (17cm) diam.
£50–55 / €75–85
$90–100 ⊞ MSB

An iron pan, c1890, 11in (28cm) wide.
£50–55 / €75–85
$95–105 ⊞ DaM

A brass jelly pan, 1880–1900, 15in (38cm) diam.
£110–125 / €165–190
$200–230 ⊞ MSB

► A cast-iron frying pan, c1890, 20in (51cm) wide.
£55–65
€85–100
$100–120
⊞ DaM

A copper, iron and ceramic double saucepan, with a wooden handle, c1890, 6in (15cm) high.
£175–195 / €260–290
$320–360 ⊞ WeA

▶ **A copper double saucepan,** with a wooden handle, 19thC, 6in (15cm) high.
£165–185 / €250–280
$300–340 ⊞ BS

A cast-iron cauldron, with a cover, on three legs, c1890, 15in (38cm) diam.
£110–125 / €165–190
$200–230 ⊞ DaM

A Kenrick & Sons cast-iron cooking pot, 1890–1900, 14in (35.5cm) diam.
£80–90 / €120–135
$150–170 ⊞ DaM

A cauldron, late 19thC, 15in (38cm) diam.
£65–75 / €100–115
$120–140 ⊞ DEB

A cast-iron pot, with a swing handle, c1890, 9in (23cm) diam.
£80–90 / €120–135
$150–170 ⊞ DaM

Further reading
Miller's Buying Affordable Antiques Price Guide, Miller's Publications, 2005

◀ **A Swain cast-iron frying pan,** marked, 1880–1900, 10in (25cm) diam.
£35–40 / €50–60
$65–75 ⊞ DaM

A tinplate fish kettle, c1920, 18in (45.5cm) diam.
£45–50 / €70–80
$85–95 ⊞ DaM

A Judge Ware enamel cooking pot, with a cast-iron
cover, c1890, 16in (40.5cm) diam.
£85–95 / €130–145
$160–180 ⊞ DaM

A graniteware pot, with a cover, c1920s,
6¼in (16cm) diam.
£40–45 / €60–70
$75–85 ⊞ MSB

An enamel jam pan, 1930s, 12½in (32cm) diam.
£25–30 / €40–45
$50–55 ⊞ JWK

An enamel double saucepan, 1940s, 6in (15cm) diam.
£15–20 / €22–30
$28–38 ⊞ JWK

◄ **A Judge Ware enamel saucepan,** late 1940s,
10in (25.5cm) diam.
£10–15 / €15–22
$18–28 ⊞ JWK

COOKWARE

Trivets & Stands

A brass iron trivet, c1830, 3½in (9cm) long.
£30–35 / €45–50
$55–65 ⊞ F&F

A Victorian beaded saucepan stand,
9in (23cm) square.
£105–120 / €160–180
$190–220 ⊞ CAL

A Victorian rosewood and petit point teapot stand, 9½in (24cm) square.
£40–45 / €60–70
$75–85 ⊞ BrL

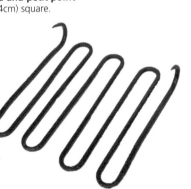

▶ **A wrought-iron range stand,** c1860, 8in (20.5cm) wide.
£20–25
€30–35
$35–45 ⊞ Cot

A cast-iron trivet, c1850, 24in (61cm) wide.
£110–125 / €165–190
$200–230 ⊞ DaM

A brass iron trivet, c1880, 9¾in (25cm) long.
£75–85 / €115–130
$140–160 ⊞ WeA

A cast-iron stand, c1890, 15in (38cm) diam.
£80–90 / €120–135
$150–170 ⊞ DaM

A cast-iron trivet, c1900, 6½in (16.5cm) long.
£10–15 / €15–22
$18–28 ⊞ AL

A cast-iron trivet, c1890, 13in (33cm) wide.
£100–110 / €150–165
$180–200 ⊞ DaM

A cast-iron trivet, c1900, 5½in (14cm) diam.
£10–15 / €15–22
$18–28 ⊞ AL

A metal trivet, c1920, 12in (30.5cm) extended.
£15–20 / €22–30
$28–38 ⊞ AL

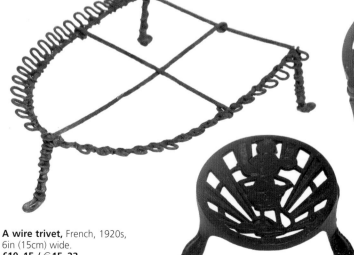

A metal trivet, depicting
Bonzo, 1930s,
6in (15cm) diam.
£20–25 / €30–35
$35–45 ⊞ HYP

◄ A metal trivet,
depicting Mickey Mouse,
1930s, 6in (15cm) diam.
£45–50 / €70–80
$85–95 ⊞ HYP

A wire trivet, French, 1920s,
6in (15cm) wide.
£10–15 / €15–22
$18–28 ⊞ AL

COOKWARE

Waffle Irons & Toasters

◀ A cast-iron waffle iron, with range cover No. 2, c1890, 10in (25.5cm) long.
£60–70
€75–95
$95–110
⊞ DaM

▶ A cast-iron waffle iron, c1890, 24in (61cm) long.
£60–70
€75–95
$95–110
⊞ DaM

A cast-iron waffle iron, c1890, 22in (56cm) long.
£60–70 / €75–95
$95–110 ⊞ DaM

A cast-iron waffle iron, c1890, 26in (66cm) long.
£60–70 / €75–95
$95–110 ⊞ DaM

A Kenrick & Sons waffle iron, No. 4, late 19thC, 4in (10cm) wide.
£75–85 / €115–130
$140–160 ⊞ WeA

A cast-iron waffle iron, with wooden handles, American, c1900, 12in (30.5cm) long.
£70–80 / €105–120
$135–150 ⊞ MSB

A Wagner Ware cast-iron waffle iron, with wooden handles, American, Ohio, c1900, 14in (35.5cm) long.
£70–80 / €105–120
$135–150 ⊞ MSB

A cast-iron Cloverleaf doughnut maker, American, Missouri, early 20thC, 13½in (34.5cm) wide.
£60–70 / €90–105
$110–125 ⊞ MSB

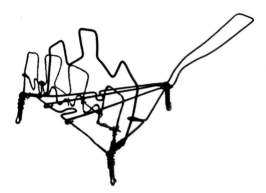

A wire toaster, French, c1920, 12in (30.5cm) long.
£35–40 / €50–60
$65–75 ⊞ AL

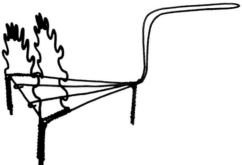

A wire toaster, French, c1920, 13in (33cm) long.
£40–45 / €60–70
$75–85 ⊞ AL

◀ A wire toaster, French, 1920s, 8in (20.5cm) wide.
£35–40 / €50–60
$65–75 ⊞ AL

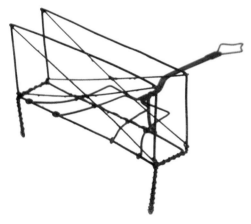

A Landers, Ferry & Clark chrome Universal electric toaster, American, Connecticut, 1920s, 9in (23cm) wide.
£40–45 / €60–70
$75–85 ⊞ TRA

A Landers, Ferry & Clark chrome Universal electric toaster, American, Connecticut, 1920s, 8in (20.5cm) wide.
£50–60 / €75–90
$95–110 ⊞ TRA

A Toastmaster chrome automatic electric toaster, American, 1930s, 10in (25.5cm) wide.
£35–40 / €50–60
$65–75 ⊞ TRA

COOKWARE

A Bersted chrome electric toaster, American, 1940s, 8in (20.5cm) high.
£20–25 / €30–35
$35–45 ⊞ TRA

A Kenwood chrome electric toaster, rewired, 1950.
£65–75 / €100–115
$120–140 ⊞ JAZZ

A Calor France aluminium electric toaster, 1930s, 8in (20.5cm) wide.
£30–35 / €45–50
$55–65 ⊞ TRA

A cast-aluminium Tid Bit Toast Tite sandwich grill, American, 1950s, 15½in (39.5cm) long.
£15–20 / €22–30
$28–38 ⊞ MSB

A cast-iron wafer iron, with wooden handles, 1950s, 16½in (42cm) long.
£15–20 / €22–30
$28–38 ⊞ MSB

A chrome electric toaster, 1960s, 8in (20.5cm) wide.
£15–20 / €22–30
$28–38 ⊞ TRA

A Son Chef chrome electric toaster, American, 1960s, 8in (20.5cm) high.
£15–20 / €22–30
$28–38 ⊞ TRA

Utensils

A bone apple corer, Welsh, 18thC, 4½in (11.5cm) long.
£135–150 / €200–230
$240–270 ⊞ SEA

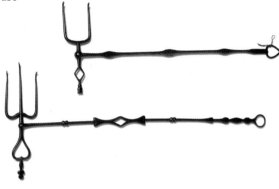

▶ **Two wrought-iron toasting forks,** Welsh, c1770, larger 23in (58.5cm) long.
£1,050–1,200
€1,600–1,800
$1,900–2,200
⊞ SEA

A pair of wrought-iron and brass nutcrackers, c1770, 5in (12.5cm) long.
£340–380 / €510–570
$620–700 ⊞ SEA

A fruitwood apple corer, c1770, 6in (15cm) long.
£450–500 / €680–760
$820–920 ⊞ SEA

An iron potato/bread hook, c1780, 14in (35.5cm) long.
£55–65 / €85–100
$100–120 ⊞ Cot

An iron cheese scoop, Welsh, c1770, 7in (18cm) long.
£430–480 / €650–720
$790–880 ⊞ SEA

A wrought-iron toasting fork, Welsh, c1780, 19in (48.5cm) long.
£400–450 / €600–680
$730–820 ⊞ SEA

▶ **A metal toasting fork,** with a laburnum handle, c1780, 21in (53.5cm) long.
£340–380 / €510–570
$620–700 ⊞ SEA

◄ **A steel toasting fork,** Welsh, c1790, 22in (56cm) long.
£430–480 / €650–720
$790–880 ⊞ SEA

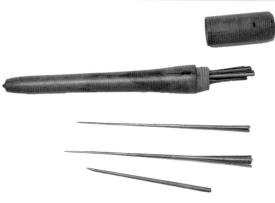

A set of steel larding needles, 19thC, in original wooden case, 10in (25.5cm) long.
£100–115 / €150–175
$180–210 ⊞ BS

A H. W. Garrard knife keener and buffer, 19thC, 16in (40.5cm) wide.
£340–380 / €510–570
$620–700 ⊞ SEA

◄ **A steel sugar cleaver,** probably Continental, early 19thC, 10½in (26.5cm) long.
£510–570 / €770–860
$930–1,050 ⊞ BS

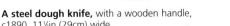

A pair of cast-iron sugar nips, early 19thC, 8in (20.5cm) long.
£55–65 / €85–100
$100–120 ⊞ WeA

A steel dough knife, with a wooden handle, c1890, 11½in (29cm) wide.
£105–120 / €160–180
$190–220 ⊞ WeA

A metal adjustable kitchen hook, mid-19thC, 25½in (65cm) long.
£180–200 / €270–300
$330–370 ⊞ WeA

◄ **A metal toasting iron,** with a wooden handle, c1880, 18in (45.5cm) long.
£135–150 / €200–230
$240–270 ⊞ WeA

A cast-iron skillet, c1890, 20in (51cm) long.
£25–30 / €40–45
$50–55 ⊞ DaM

A cast-iron chestnut shovel, c1890, 20in (51cm) long.
£35–40 / €50–60
$65–75 ⊞ DaM

An Enterprise cast-iron ice shredder, American, 1893, 8¼in (21cm) long.
£40–45 / €60–70
$75–85 ⊞ MSB

A pair of steel crab claw crackers, late 19thC, 9in (23cm) long.
£75–85 / €115–130
$140–160 ⊞ BS

A pickle fork, with a wooden handle, c1900, 7½in (19cm) long.
£20–25 / €30–35
$35–45 ⊞ JWK

A wooden egg timer, late 19thC, 3in (7.5cm) high.
£65–75 / €100–115
$120–140 ⊞ WeA

A bread knife, the wooden handle carved with a cornucopia, c1900, 12¾in (32.5cm) long.
£35–40 / €50–60
$65–75 ⊞ CHAC

A bread knife, with a wooden handle, 1900, 12¾in (32.5cm) long.
£30–35 / €45–50
$55–65 ⊞ JWK

▶ **A pair of metal nutcrackers,** c1900, 6in (15cm) long.
£25–30 / €40–45
$50–55 ⊞ AL

UTENSILS

A metal spatula, 1900, 14¼in (36cm) long.
£25–30 / €40–45
$50–55 ⊞ WeA

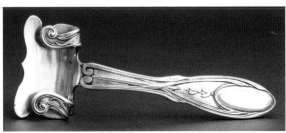

A silver-plated plate server, early 20thC, 7in (15cm) long.
£65–75 / €100–115
$115–135 ⊞ MSB

A metal meat tenderizer, American, c1900,
6½in (16.5cm) long.
£30–35 / €45–50
$55–65 ⊞ MSB

A wooden vegetable/herb masher, early 20thC,
4½in (11.5cm) diam.
£20–25 / €30–35
$35–45 ⊞ MSB

A pair of steel nutcrackers, 1901–10, 10in (25.5cm) long.
£140–160 / €210–240
$260–290 ⊞ PICA

A porcelain egg timer, c1910, 4in (10cm) high.
£15–20 / €22–30
$27–36 ⊞ HO

▶ **A ceramic meat tenderizer,** with a
wooden handle, c1910, 15in (38cm) long.
£60–70 / €75–90
$95–110 ⊞ SMI

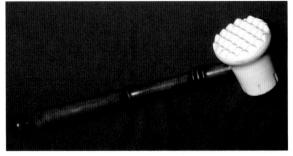

A pine bread shovel, Eastern European, c1920, 150in (381cm) long.
£15–20 / €22–30
$27–36 ⊞ HRQ

A pine bread shovel, Eastern European, c1920, 60in (152.5cm) long.
£15–20 / €22–30
$27–36 ⊞ HRQ

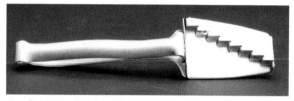

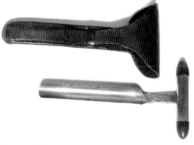

An aluminium ice shredder, 1925–50, 6¼in (16cm) long.
£1–5 / €2–6
$5–10 ⊞ MSB

A metal cheese taster, c1920,
7½in (19cm) long, with a leather case.
£50–60 / €75–90
$95–110 ⊞ AL

◀ **A tin corer,** 1920s–30s,
4¾in (12cm) high.
£1–5 / €2–6
$5–10 ⊞ MSB

An iron can opener, in the form of
a bull, c1930, 6in (15cm) long.
£20–25 / €30–35
$35–45 ⊞ TOP

▶ **A cast-aluminium pie divider,**
American,
c1930s, 7½in
(19cm) wide.
£9–13
€14–19
$20–25 ⊞ MSB

UTENSILS

An Ekco pie slice, with a wooden handle, 1940s, 11in (28cm) long.
£1–5 / €2–7
$3–9 ⊞ JWK

A Skyline pastry blender, 1940s,
5in (12.5cm) wide.
£1–5 / €2–7
$3–9 ⊞ JWK

A Nutbrown kitchen saw, 1950s, 10in (25.5cm) long,
with packaging.
£1–5 / €2–7
$3–9 ⊞ RTT

A Smith's Ringer Timer, c1950,
10in (25.5cm) wide, with box.
£15–20 / €22–30
$27–36 ⊞ JWK

A cast-iron Handi Hostess kit, comprising waffle iron and
moulds, 1950s, in original cardboard box, 11½in (29cm) wide.
£16–20 / €24–30
$30–35 ⊞ MSB

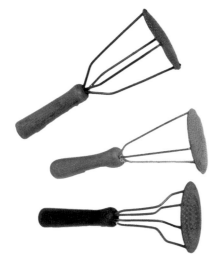

◄ **Three potato
mashers,** with wooden
handles, c1950,
largest 10in (25.5cm).
£4–8 / €6–12
$8–15 each ⊞ AL

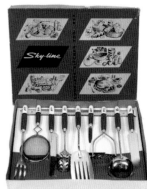

► **A set of Prestige Sky-
line kitchen utensils,**
1960s, boxed,
20in (51cm) wide.
£35–40 / €45–50
$55–65 ⊞ HSt

Bread Boards

A sycamore bread board, 19thC, 8¾in (22cm) wide.
£155–175 / €230–260
$280–320 ⊞ SEA

A sycamore bread board, with carved decoration, c1870, 12in (30.5cm) diam.
£105–120 / €160–180
$190–220 ⊞ SMI

A sycamore bread board, carved with flowers, c1890, 14in (35.5cm) diam.
£135–150 / €200–230
$240–270 ⊞ B&R

A wooden bread board, carved with wheat, 1890–1920, 11½in (29cm) diam.
£15–20 / €22–30
$27–36 ⊞ CHAC

A wooden bread board, inscribed 'Long Life and Happiness', c1900, 12in (30.5cm) diam.
£105–120 / €160–180
$190–220 ⊞ JWK

A sycamore bread board, with carved decoration, c1900, 15in (38cm) diam.
£135–150 / €200–230
$240–270 ⊞ B&R

A sycamore bread board, with carved decoration, c1900, 12in (30.5cm) diam.
£70–80 / €105–120
$130–150 ⊞ B&R

UTENSILS

A sycamore bread board, inscribed 'We Eat To Live Not To Eat', c1900, 12in (30.5cm) diam.
£70–80 / €105–120
$130–150 ⊞ B&R

A wooden bread board, c1900, 10in (25.5cm) diam.
£15–20 / €22–30
$27–36 ⊞ AL

A sycamore bread board, carved with fruit and flowers, c1900, 12in (30.5cm) diam.
£60–70 / €90–105
$110–130 ⊞ B&R

A sycamore bread board, with carved decoration, c1920, 6in (15cm) diam.
£60–70 / €90–105
$110–130 ⊞ SMI

A sycamore bread board, with carved decoration, c1920, 6in (15cm) diam.
£60–70 / €90–105
$110–130 ⊞ SMI

A pine chopping board, in the form of a fish, c1930, 31in (78.5cm) long.
£35–40 / €50–60
$65–75 ⊞ MLL

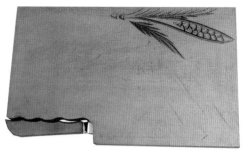

A sycamore bread board, with carved decoration, c1930, 12in (30.5cm) diam.
£25–30 / €40–45
$50–55 ⊞ AL

A sycamore wedding bread board, with carved decoration, 1936, 12in (30.5cm) diam.
£50–60 / €75–90
$95–110 ⊞ B&R

A wooden bread board, with a knife, c1950, 13in (33cm) wide.
£25–30 / €40–45
$50–55 ⊞ AL

Carvers & Sharpeners

A wrought-iron flesh fork, mid-18thC, 1740, 28in (71cm) long.
£430–480 / €650–720
$790–880 ⊞ SEA

An iron flesh fork, c1770, 22in (56cm) long.
£340–380 / €510–570
$620–700 ⊞ SEA

A wrought-iron flesh fork, c1780, 21in (53.5cm) long.
£250–280 / €380–420
$460–510 ⊞ SEA

A brass flesh fork, Welsh, 18thC, c1790, 16in (40.5cm) long.
£340–380 / €510–570
$620–700 ⊞ SEA

UTENSILS

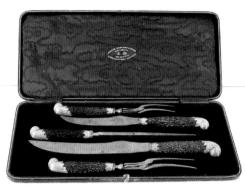

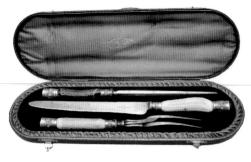

A Victorian steel carving set, comprising five pieces, with silver-mounted horn handles, hallmarked, with a fitted case, 13in (33cm) wide.
£115–135 / €170–200
$210–250 ✗ GAK

A Victorian steel carving set, comprising three pieces, with stag horn handles, in a fitted case.
£130–155 / €195–230
$240–280 ✗ G(L)

A butcher's steel, with a horn handle, c1880, 15in (38cm) long.
£85–95 / €130–145
$160–180 ⊞ SEA

A butcher's steel, c1900, 18in (45.5cm) long.
£25–30 / €40–45
$50–55 ⊞ Cot

A butcher's steel, c1900, 18in (45.5cm) long.
£30–35 / €45–50
$55–65 ⊞ Cot

▶ **A Sheffield steel carving set,** comprising three pieces, with ivory handles, c1910, in a fitted case, 15in (38cm) wide.
£15–20 / €22–30
$27–36 ⊞ CCO

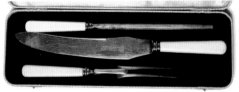

A steel meat fork, c1860, 17in (43cm) long.
£45–50 / €70–80
$85–95 ⊞ Cot

A Sky-line knife sharpener, 1940s, 7¼in (18.5cm) long.
£2–6 / €3–9
$4–11 ⊞ JWK

Choppers & Slicers

A meat cleaver, the wooden handle with a brass finial, 19thC, 21¾in (55.5cm) long.
£180–200 / € 270–300
$330–370 ⊞ WeA

▶ **A Gilpin steel vegetable chopper,**
19thC, 6½in (16.5cm) wide.
£60–70 / € 90–105
$110–130 ⊞ BS

A metal chopper, with a wooden handle,
French, c1800, 6in (15cm) wide.
£85–95 / € 130–145
$155–175 ⊞ MSB

A steel herb chopper,
with a wooden handle,
1778, 22in (56cm) long.
£130–145 / € 195–220
$240–270 ⊞ NEW

▶ **A wooden mandolin,**
c1860, 10½in
(26.5cm) long.
£100–110
€ 150–165
$180–200
⊞ WeA

A brass and steel chopper, mid-19thC,
6in (15cm) wide.
£120–140 / € 180–210
$220–260 ⊞ WeA

◀ **A steel herb chopper,**
European,
c1870, 11in
(28cm) long.
£165–185
€ 250–280
$300–340
⊞ NEW

UTENSILS

A boxwood slicer, 1880, 9¾in (25cm) long.
£60–70 / €90–105
$110–130 ⊞ WeA

A steel herb chopper, the brass handle with acorn finials, c1880, 7in (18cm) wide.
£85–95 / €130–145
$160–180 ⊞ SMI

A steel and brass herb chopper, with a wooden handle, c1880, 7in (18cm) wide.
£70–80 / €105–120
$130–150 ⊞ SMI

A steel herb chopper, with a wooden handle, c1880, 9in (23cm) wide.
£90–100 / €135–150
$165–185 ⊞ SMI

A steel herb chopper, with a wooden handle, marked S. C. J. Clark , c1880, 8in (20.5cm) wide.
£120–140 / €180–210
$220–260 ⊞ SMI

A metal chopper, with a wooden handle, late 19thC, 7in (18cm) high.
£60–70 / €90–105
$110–130 ⊞ WeA

A steel chopper, with a wooden handle, late 19thC, 9¼in (23.5cm) high.
£75–85 / €115–130
$140–160 ⊞ WeA

A steel herb chopper, late 19thC,
5½in (14cm) high.
£40–45 / €60–70
$75–85 ⊞ B&R

A steel chopper, with a wooden handle, late 19thC, 11in (28cm) high.
£25–30 / €40–45
$50–55 ⊞ B&R

A metal herb chopper, c1900,
6¾in (17cm) wide.
£15–20 / €22–30
$27–36 ⊞ AL

A metal herb chopper, c1900, 6in (15cm) wide.
£15–20 / €22–30
$27–36 ⊞ AL

A metal chopper, with a wooden
handle, c1900, 7in (18cm) wide.
£20–25 / €30–35
$40–45 ⊞ MSB

► **A metal
chopper,** with a
wooden handle,
c1900, 9¾in
(25cm) high.
£45–50
€65–75
$80–90 ⊞ MSB

UTENSILS

A metal chopper, with a wooden handle, c1900, 6½in (16.5cm) wide.
£20–25 / €30–35
$35–45 ⊞ MSB

A metal chopper, early 20thc, 5in (12.5cm) wide.
£20–25 / €30–35
$35–45 ⊞ MSB

A metal chopper, with a wooden handle, early 20thC, 5½in (14cm) wide.
£20–25 / €30–35
$35–45 ⊞ MSB

A metal food chopper, American, early 20thC, 7in (18cm) wide.
£30–35 / €45–50
$55–65 ⊞ MSB

A wooden slaw cutter, with a metal blade, early 20thC, 20in (51cm) long.
£70–80 / €105–120
$130–145 ⊞ MSB

A metal food chopper, with a wooden handle, American, early 20thC, 5¾in (14.5cm) wide.
£30–35 / €45–50
$55–65 ⊞ MSB

◄ **An aluminium apple cutter,** 1950s, 7in (18cm) wide, with box.
£25–30 / €40–45
$50–55 ⊞ DaM

Drainers & Strainers

A brass strainer, maker's cross and pellet mark, c1680, 21in (53.5cm) long.
£440–490 / €660–740
$810–900 ⊞ SEA

A wrought-iron and brass straining ladle, c1780, 31in (78.5cm) long.
£340–380 / €510–570
$620–700 ⊞ SEA

An iron and brass straining ladle, c1780, 24in (61cm) long.
£200–230 / €300–350
$370–420 ⊞ MFB

A copper straining spoon, with a mahogany handle, 19thC, 23in (58.5cm) long.
£240–270 / €360–410
$440–490 ⊞ BS

A brass and iron straining ladle, c1780, 23in (58.5cm) long.
£380–430 / €570–650
$700–790 ⊞ SEA

A brass and steel colander, Dutch, early 19thC, 24in (61cm) long.
£340–380 / €510–570
$620–700 ⊞ NEW

▶ **A Spode ceramic drainer,** decorated with Star pattern, c1820, 14in (35.5cm) wide.
£340–390 / €510–590
$620–710 ⊞ CoS

A stoneware colander, c1880, 9in (23cm) wide.
£45–50 / €70–80
$85–95 ⊞ Cot

A tin colander, c1900, 6¼in (16cm) diam.
£13–17 / €20–25
$25–30 ⊞ MSB

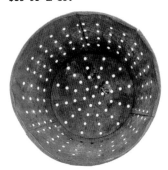

A tin colander, c1900,
8¾in (22cm) diam.
£4–8 / €6–12
$8–15 ⊞ MSB

A tin strainer, American, c1900, 9in (23cm) long.
£25–30 / €40–45
$50–55 ⊞ MSB

A tin colander, c1900,
10½in (26.5cm) diam.
£11–15 / €17–22
$20–25 ⊞ MSB

A copper strainer, c1900, 20in (51cm) long.
£75–85 / €115–130
$140–160 ⊞ BS

◀ A ceramic colander,
c1900, 9in (23cm) diam.
£35–40 / €50–60
$65–75 ⊞ AL

▶ A tin strainer,
American, c1900,
7in (18cm) long.
£13–17 / €20–25
$25–30 ⊞ MSB

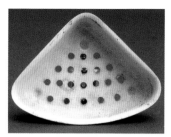

A metal sink drainer, early 20thC, 3in (7.5cm) wide.
£20–25 / €30–35
$35–45 ⊞ MSB

A porcelain drainer, transfer-printed with Willow pattern, early 20thC, 5¾in (14.5cm) wide.
£40–45 / €60–70
$75–85 ⊞ MSB

A wire salad spinner, early 20thC, 9½in (24cm) diam.
£55–65 / €85–100
$100–120 ⊞ WeA

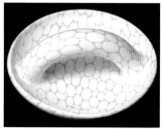

A Maling ceramic cabbage press, decorated with Cobblestone pattern, c1920, 5in (12.5cm) diam.
£50–60 / €75–90
$95–110 ⊞ B&R

An enamel colander, 1930s, 9½in (24cm) diam.
£10–15 / €15–22
$19–28 ⊞ JWK

An enamel colander, 1930s, 7½in (19cm) diam.
£4–8 / €6–12
$7–14 ⊞ JWK

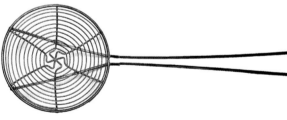

A wire strainer, 1950s, 16in (40.5cm) long.
£6–10 / €9–15
$11–18 ⊞ AL

A wire strainer, 1950s, 16in (40.5cm) long.
£6–10 / €9–15
$11–18 ⊞ AL

◀ **An enamel colander,** c1960, 11in (28cm) diam.
£20–25 / €30–35
$35–45 ⊞ AL

UTENSILS

Gadgets

A Geo. Fowler Lee & Co cucumber slicer, 19thC, 9in (23cm) high.
£150–165 / €220–250
$270–300 ⊞ BS

A cast-iron Ezy raisin seeder, American,
19thC, 6in (15cm) long.
£310–350 / €470–530
$570–640 ⊞ BS

▶ **A Reading
Hardware Co
metal apple
peeler,** with a
wooden handle,
American,
Philadelphia,
1875–1900,
9in (23cm) wide.
**£40–45
€60–70
$75–85 ⊞ MSB**

A Lockey & Holland apple peeler,
American, 1856, 8in (20.5cm) high.
£200–230 / €300–350
$370–420 ⊞ BS

LOCATE THE SOURCE
The source of each illustration in Miller's
can be found by checking the code
letters below each caption with the Key
to Illustrations, pages 313–315.

An oak potato press,
Romanian, c1880, 55in
(139.5cm) wide.
£35–40 / €50–60
$65–75 ⊞ Byl

A cast-iron apple peeler, c1880,
9in (23cm) high.
£240–270 / €360–400
$440–490 ⊞ BS

A steel coconut grater, 1880–1920, 9in (23cm) wide.
£120–135 / €180–200
$220–250 ⊞ DaM

A Hudson & Co cast-iron Little Star apple peeler, 1885, 10in (25.5cm) wide.
£150–165 / €220–250
$270–300 ⊞ BS

A metal apple peeler, with a wooden handle, American, 1880, 9½in (24cm) wide.
£40–45 / €60–70
$75–85 ⊞ MSB

A metal apple peeler, American, Baltimore, late 19thC, 6in (15cm) wide.
£155–175 / €230–260
$280–320 ⊞ WeA

► **A Shaw's brass bottlejack,** with a clockwork spit, late 19thC, 13¾in (35cm) long.
£180–200 / €270–300
$330–370 ⊞ WeA

A cast-iron raisin seeder, American, 1896, 6in (15cm) wide.
£120–135 / €180–200
$220–250 ⊞ BS

A cast-iron slicer/mincer, c1890, 18in (45.5cm) wide.
£75–85 / €115–130
$140–160 ⊞ DaM

► **A Canwheat iron pie and tart machine,** 1890–1900, 18in (45.5cm) high.
£115–130 / €175–195
$210–240 ⊞ DaM

A Salter brass clockwork spit, with key, c1900, 13in (33cm) wide.
£210–240 / €320–360
$380–440 ⊞ BS

A cast-iron double cherry stoner, American, c1900, 7in (18cm) wide.
£165–185 / €250–280
$300–340 ⊞ BS

A cast-iron potato slicer, American, c1900, 8in (20.5cm) long.
£200–230 / €300–350
$370–420 ⊞ BS

A cast-iron cherry stoner, American, c1900, 11in (28cm) high.
£165–185 / €250–280
$300–340 ⊞ BS

◀ **A Harras metal bean slicer,** with a wooden handle, German, early 20thC, 10½in (26.5cm) long.
£30–35 / €45–50
$55–65 ⊞ MSB

A Harras metal bean slicer, with a wooden handle, German, early 20thC, 12¼in (31cm) long.
£30–35 / €45–50
$55–65 ⊞ MSB

◀ **A metal Little Star apple peeler,** American, early 20thC, 10½in (26.5cm) long.
£30–35 / €45–50
$55–65 ⊞ MSB

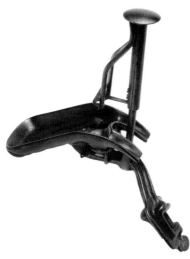

A cast-iron table-mounted cheese/bread grater, with a beechwood pushing block, 1900–20, 9in (23cm) high.
£35–40 / €50–60
$65–75 ⊞ BS

A cast-iron double cherry stoner, American, 1917, 11in (28cm) high.
£165–185 / €250–280
$300–340 ⊞ BS

A Parnall & Sons meat slicer, on a wooden base, maker's mark, 1920–30, 17in (43cm) wide.
£35–40 / €45–50
$55–65 ⊞ DaM

◄ **A meat press,** c1920, 10in (25.5cm) high.
£10–15 / €15–22
$18–27 ⊞ AL

An apple peeler and tin opener, 1920s, 9½in (24cm) wide.
£50–55 / €75–85
$95–105 ⊞ WeA

A metal food mill, 1950s, 9½in (24cm) diam.
£30–35 / €45–50
$55–65 ⊞ WeA

UTENSILS

Graters & Grinders

An iron coffee grinder, 19thC, 12in (30.5cm) long.
£155–175 / €230–260
$280–320 ⊞ SEA

A brass pestle and mortar, c1750,
4in (10cm) high.
£55–65 / €85–100
$100–120 ⊞ F&F

A Kenrick & Sons cast-iron coffee grinder, 19thC,
5in (12.5cm) high.
£300–340 / €450–510
$550–630 ⊞ SEA

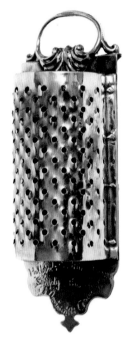

**A lignum vitae
pestle,** 19thC,
11in (28cm) long.
£80–90
€120–135
$150–170 ⊞ BS

**A Holland's brass
cheese grater,** c1870,
12in (30.5cm) long.
£180–200 / €270–300
$330–370 ⊞ SMI

◀ **A nutmeg grater,** America, 1869,
5in (12.5cm) long.
£360–400 / €540–600
$660–730 ⊞ BS

◀ A metal grater, on a wooden base, French, c1880, 12in (30.5cm) long.
£50–60 / €75–90
$95–110 ⊞ Cot

A W. Bullock cast-iron coffee grinder, c1880, 6in (15cm) high.
£135–150 / €200–230
$240–270 ⊞ SMI

A cast-iron coffee grinder, with a brass funnel, c1880, 28in (71cm) high.
£500–550 / €760–830
$920–1,000 ⊞ SMI

A metal coffee grinder, with a wooden handle, c1880, 6in (15cm) high.
£200–220 / €300–330
$370–400 ⊞ WeA

A Peugeot Frères metal coffee grinder, French, 1880–90, 14in (35.5cm) high.
£170–190 / €260–290
$310–350 ⊞ PaA

A nutmeg grater, American, c1880, 3in (7.5cm) wide.
£290–320 / €430–480
$530–590 ⊞ BS

◀ An ACME tin nut grater, 1888, 7in (18cm) long.
£40–45 / €60–70
$75–85 ⊞ BS

UTENSILS

A **cast-iron spice grinder,** with a wooden handle, American, 1880–1910, 7in (18cm) high.
£60–70 / €90–105
$110–125 田 MSB

A **Kenrick & Sons cast-iron grinder,** in the form of the font at York Minster, 1895, 7in (18cm) high.
£430–480 / €650–720
$790–880 田 MFB

A **metal nutmeg grater,** with a wooden handle, 1890–1910, 4¼in (11cm) high.
£60–70 / €90–105
$110–125 田 MSB

A **cast-iron pestle and mortar,** late 19thC, 2¾in (7cm) diam.
£65–75 / €100–115
$120–140 田 WeA

A **nutmeg grater,** American, late 19thC, 7in (18cm) long.
£310–350 / €470–530
$570–640 田 BS

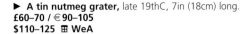

▶ A **tin nutmeg grater,** late 19thC, 7in (18cm) long.
£60–70 / €90–105
$110–125 田 WeA

A Kenrick & Sons cast-iron and brass coffee grinder, c1900, 5in (12.5cm) high.
£155–185 / €230–280
$280–340 ⊞ BS

A tin bread/nutmeg grinder, c1900, in an embossed box, 4¾in (12cm) wide.
£75–85 / €115–130
$135–150 ⊞ MSB

A tin nutmeg grater, with a wooden handle, 1900, 5¼in (13.5cm) wide.
£55–65 / €85–100
$100–120 ⊞ WeA

A Kenrick & Sons cast-iron and brass coffee grinder, c1900, 5in (12.5cm) high.
£90–100 / €135–150
$165–185 ⊞ SMI

◄ A cast-iron spice grinder, with a wooden handle, c1900, 9½in (24cm) wide.
£50–55 / €75–85
$90–100 ⊞ MSB

UTENSILS

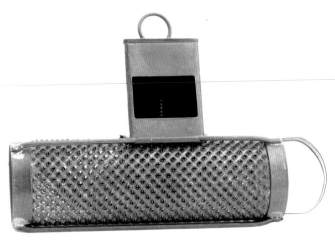

A tin chocolate grater, early 20thC, 8¾in (22cm) wide.
£170–190 / €250–280
$310–350 ⊞ MSB

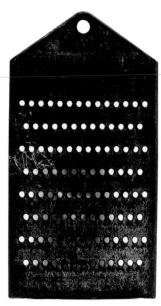

A 3-in-1 Lightning Shredder, early
1900s, 6¾in (17cm) long.
£20–25 / €30–35
$35–40 ⊞ MSB

◄ **A Beatrice cast-iron
Popular Coffee Mill,**
1908, 5in (12.5cm) wide.
£40–45 / €60–70
$75–85 ⊞ BS

**A Peugeot Frères cast-iron coffee
grinder,** with a wooden handle,
1900–25, 17in (43cm) high.
£170–190 / €250–280
$310–350 ⊞ MSB

A Christofle nutmeg grater,
1920s–30s, 4¾in (12cm) long.
£70–80 / €105–120
$130–150 ⊞ MSB

A brass coffee grinder, French,
1920s, 11in (28cm) high.
£85–95 / €130–145
$160–180 ⊞ DaM

Juicers & Funnels

► **A brass juicer,** on a wooden base, 1880, 13¾in (35cm) wide.
£200–220
€300–330
$360–400
⊞ SMI

A wooden juicer, c1870, 5½in (14cm) long.
£90–100 / €135–150
$165–185 ⊞ WeA

A Holborn cast-iron and ceramic lemon squeezer, c1880, 10in (25.5cm) high.
£180–200 / €270–300
$330–370 ⊞ SMI

A cast-iron juicer, with an enamel pourer, c1880, 13in (33cm) high.
£100–110 / €150–165
$180–200 ⊞ DaM

A wood and ceramic juicer, c1890, 10in (25.5cm) long.
£50–55 / €75–85
$95–105 ⊞ AL

► **A wood and ceramic juicer,** c1890, 10in (25.5cm) long.
£45–50 / €70–80
$85–95 ⊞ AL

A T. G. Green squeezer, 20thC, 5in (12.5cm) diam.
£85–95 / €130–145
$160–180 ⊞ TAC

UTENSILS

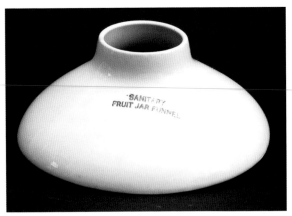

A ceramic Sanitary Fruit Jar Funnel, 1900–25, 6in (15cm) wide.
£20–25 / €30–35
$35–45 ⊞ MSB

◀ A copper and brass beer funnel, c1920, 9in (23cm) diam.
£30–35 / €45–50
$55–65 ⊞ AL

A copper funnel, 1900–25, 4in (10cm) diam.
£15–19 / €22–28
$30–35 ⊞ MSB

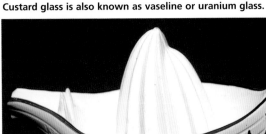

A Sunkist custard glass squeezer, American, 1900–25, 3¾in (9.5cm) high.
£60–70 / €90–105
$110–130 ⊞ MSB
Custard glass is also known as vaseline or uranium glass.

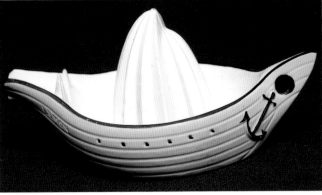

A squeezer, c1930, 2in (5cm) high.
£55–65 / €85–100
$100–120 ⊞ BET

A Torquay pottery squeezer, 1930, 6½in (16.5cm) wide.
£30–35 / €45–50
$55–65 ⊞ BET

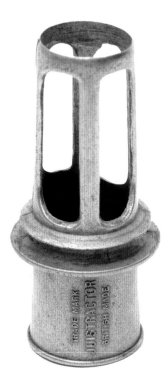

A glass squeezer, American, 1930s, 4in (10cm) high.
£15–20 / €22–30
$27–36 ⊞ MSB

◀ **An aluminium Juistractor,** 1935, 2in (5cm) high.
£20–25 / €30–35
$35–45 ⊞ BS

▶ **A glass squeezer,** American, 1930s, 5¼in (13.5cm) high.
£30–35 / €45–50
$55–65 ⊞ MSB

A majolica two-piece squeezer, in the form of duck, Japanese, 1930s, 4¾in (12cm) high.
£27–32 / €40–50
$50–60 ⊞ MSB

A cast-iron juicer, American, 1930s, 9in (23cm) long.
£4–8 / €6–12
$8–15 ⊞ MSB

▶ **A ceramic squeezer,** in the form of a clown, Japanese, 1940s, 7in (18cm) high.
£140–160
€210–240
$260–290
⊞ SCH

A Bakelite squeezer, 1930–40s, 5½in (14cm) diam.
£50–60 / €75–90
$95–110 ⊞ BS

Ladles & Spoons

A brass ladle, maker's mark, c1710, 19in (48.5cm) long.
£340–380 / € 510–570
$620–700 ⊞ SEA

A sycamore spoon, marked 'A. R.', Welsh, 1796, 7in (18cm) long.
£350–390 / € 530–590
$640–710 ⊞ SEA

A wooden spoon, c1870, 12in (30.5cm) long.
£8–12 / € 12–18
$14–22 ⊞ AL

A cast-iron spoon, c1890, 12in (30.5cm) long.
£30–35 / € 45–50
$55–65 ⊞ DaM

An iron and brass ladle,
c1790, 21in (53.5cm) long.
£340–380 / € 510–570
$620–700 ⊞ SEA

A Rumford Saltsman tin slotted spoon, early 20thC, 12¼in (31cm) long.
£13–17 / € 20–25
$25–30 ⊞ MSB

A brass bran scoop, with
a turned wood handle,
c1800, 16in (40.5cm) long.
£300–330 / € 450–500
$540–600 ⊞ MFB

A wooden spoon, 1930s, 14in (35.5cm) long.
£1–5 / € 2–7
$3–9 ⊞ JWK

Slices & Peels

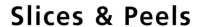

A brass fish slice, maker's cross and pellets mark, 1670–80, 17in (43cm) long.
£360–400 / €540–600
$660–730 ⊞ SEA

A wooden galette turner, French, late 19thC, 21in (53.5cm) long.
£20–25 / €30–35
$35–45 ⊞ B&R

A bannock turner, c1820, 14in (35.5cm) long.
£110–125 / €165–190
$200–230 ⊞ Cot

A brass fish slice, 1702–14,
18in (45.5cm) long.
£340–380 / €510–570
$620–700 ⊞ SEA

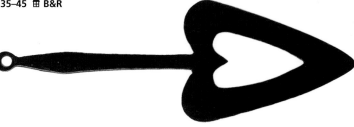

An iron fish slice, c1870, 21in (53.5cm) long.
£40–45 / €60–70
$75–85 ⊞ Cot

A sycamore pie peel, mid-19thC,
17¼in (44cm) long.
£220–250 / €330–380
$400–460 ⊞ WeA

A metal slice, with a wooden handle, late 19thC,
18in (45.5cm) long.
£60–70 / €90–105
$110–130 ⊞ WeA

◀ **A brass slice,**
late 19thC, 18¾in
(47.5cm) long.
£60–70
€90–105
$110–130
⊞ WeA

▶ **An
aluminium fish
slice,** 1940s.
£1–5 / €2–7
$3–9 ⊞ JWK

UTENSILS

Thermometers

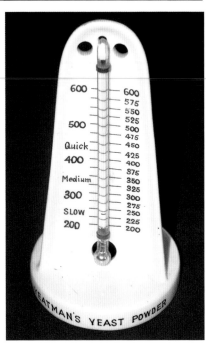

A Dunham's Cocoanut Shred brass and glass thermometer,
1900–50, 11¾in (30cm) diam.
£100–110 / €150–165
$180–200 ⊞ MSB

A Yeatman's Yeast Powder thermometer,
early 20thC, 6½in (16.5cm) high.
£105–120 / €160–180
$190–220 ⊞ WeA

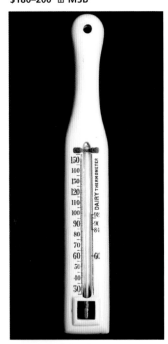

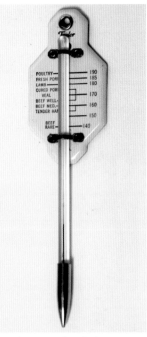

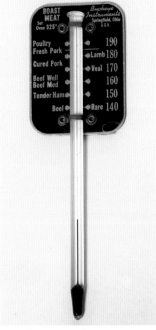

A ceramic dairy thermometer,
c1910, 14in (35.cm) long.
£220–250 / €330–380
$400–460 ⊞ SMI

A Taylor enamel and glass meat thermometer, c1930, 6in (15cm) long.
£65–75 / €100–115
$120–140 ⊞ Cot

A Buckeye meat thermometer,
American, c1940, 6in (15cm) high.
£35–40 / €50–60
$65–75 ⊞ Cot

Whisks & Beaters

A metal rotary egg whisk, American, 1871, 10in (25.5cm) long.
£35–40 / €50–60
$65–75 ⊞ WeA

A ceramic Patent egg beater, c1820,
4in (10cm) high.
£220–250 / €330–380
$400–460 ⊞ SMI

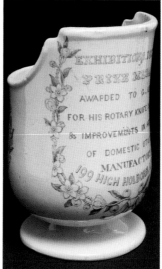

**A Kent's ceramic and
metal whisk and beater,**
c1880, 7in (18cm) high.
£310–350 / €470–530
$570–640 ⊞ SMI

**A Kent's ceramic egg whisk and
beater stand,** c1880,
7in (18cm) high.
£135–150 / €200–230
$240–270 ⊞ SMI

◀ **A Holborn ceramic egg whisk
stand,** c1880, 5in (12.5cm) high.
£135–150 / €200–230
$240–270 ⊞ SMI

A metal whisk, with a wooden handle, American, 1886, 13in (33cm) long.
£85–95 / €130–145
$150–170 ⊞ MSB

**A Diadem ceramic and
metal egg beater,**
c1880, 11in (28cm) high.
£135–150 / €200–230
$240–270 ⊞ SMI

A Dover tin rotary egg beater, 1880s, 11½in (29cm) long.
£15–20 / €22–30
$27–36 ⊞ MSB

A Dairy Outfit Co ceramic and metal Speedy egg beater, c1900, 8¾in (22cm) high.
£140–160 / €210–240
$260–290 ⊞ WeA

A Gourmet ceramic and metal egg beater, 20thC, 6in (15cm) high.
£65–75 / €100–115
$120–140 ⊞ JWK

A Keystone cast-iron and glass egg and cream beater, early 1900s, 11¼in (28.5cm) high.
£60–70 / €90–105
$110–125 ⊞ MSB

A tin egg beater, early 1900s, 10½in (26.5cm) high.
£40–45 / €60–70
$75–85 ⊞ MSB

A cast-iron and glass mixer, early 1900s, 13in (33cm) high.
£170–190 / €250–280
$310–350 ⊞ MSB

◄ A metal egg beater, with a wooden handle, American, 1908, 10¾in (27.5cm) long.
£27–32 / €40–50
$50–60 ⊞ MSB

A set of graduated Gourmet ceramic and metal egg beaters, c1910, largest 9in (23cm) high.
£105–120 / €160–180
$190–220 each ⊞ SMI

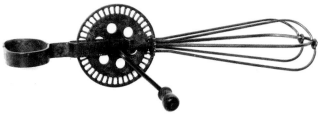

A metal rotary whisk, c1920, 12in (30.5cm) long.
£25–30 / €40–45
$50–55 ⊞ Cot

A wire whisk, with a wood handle, French, c1920, 9in (23cm) long
£10–15 / €15–22
$18–27 ⊞ Cot

A metal spring-loaded whisk, with a wood handle, c1920, 11in (28cm) long.
£20–25 / €30–35
$35–45 ⊞ Cot

◄ **A metal beater,** with a wood handle and a glass measuring jug, 1920s–30s, 11¼in (28.5cm) high.
£30–35 / €45–50
$55–65 ⊞ MSB

LOCATE THE SOURCE
The source of each illustration in Miller's can be found by checking the code letters below each caption with the Key to Illustrations, pages 313–315.

► **A Wesson Oil tin and glass mayonnaise beater,** 1920s–30s, 13in (33cm) high.
£15–20 / €22–30
$27–36 ⊞ MSB

UTENSILS

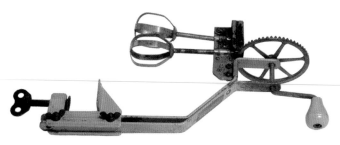

A Nutbrown whisk, c1930, 16in (40.5cm) high.
£25–30 / €40–45
$50–55 ⊞ AL

A metal rotary whisk, c1940, 12in (30.5cm) long.
£4–8 / €6–12
$8–15 ⊞ JWK

A Hamilton Beach Co metal and enamel electric drink mixer,
1930s–50s, 19in (48.5cm) high.
£60–70 / €90–105
$110–125 ⊞ MSB

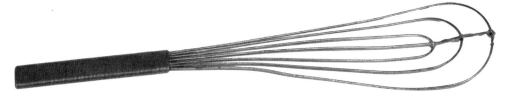

A metal whisk, 1940s, 12¼in (31cm) long.
£1–5 / €2–7
$3–9 ⊞ JWK

A Sky-line metal egg whisk, 1940s, 10in (25.5cm) high.
£2–6 / €3–9
$4–11 ⊞ JWK

A Sky-line metal egg whisk, 1940s, 10in (25.5cm) high.
£3–7 / €4–10
$5–12 ⊞ JWK

A Pifco chrome-plated battery-operated drink mixer, 1950s, 6in (15cm) long, with box.
£25–30 / €40–45
$50–55 ⊞ DaM

Tableware

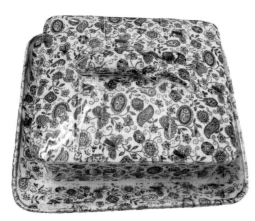

A Victorian ceramic sardine dish, 7¼in (18.5cm) wide.
£100–110 / €150–165
$180–200 ⊞ TASV

A ceramic spongeware dish, c1900, 7in (18cm) diam.
£75–85 / €115–130
$135–155 ⊞ MSB

A ceramic yellow ware dish, c1900, 8½in (21.5cm) diam.
£40–45 / €60–70
$75–85 ⊞ MSB

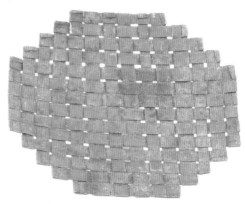

A tin table protector, early 20thC, 7¾in (19.5cm) wide.
£14–18 / €25–30
$25–35 ⊞ MSB

A tin mesh dish cover, early 20thC, 14½in (37cm) wide.
£30–35 / €45–55
$55–65 ⊞ MSB

▶ A glass cake stand, early 20thC, 10in (25.5cm) diam.
£60–70 / €90–105
$110–130 ⊞ MSB

A Maucheline ware napkin ring, 1900, 2in (5cm) diam.
£25–30 / €40–45
$50–55 ⊞ MSB

A silver menu holder, embossed with cherubs, early 20thC, 3in (7.5cm) high.
£60–70 / €90–105
$110–130 ⊞ MSB

A Copeland Spode ceramic Tranfield's Salmon Paste dish, c1930, 6in (15cm) wide.
£25–30 / €40–45
$45–55 ⊞ B&R

A silver-plated three-tier cake stand, c1930, 18in (45.5cm) high.
£70–80 / €105–120
$130–145 ⊞ BEV

▶ **An etched glass syphon,** c1930, 11in (28cm) high.
£25–30 / €40–45
$45–55 ⊞ AL

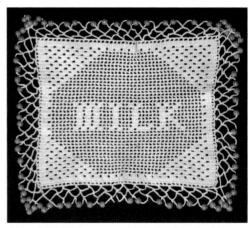

A beaded milk jug cover, 1930s, 7in (18cm) wide.
£6–10 / €9–15
$13–20 ⊞ JWK

◀ **A Fryer Tunstall ceramic cake plate,** 1930s, 8½in (21.5cm) diam.
£25–30 / €40–45
$45–55 ⊞ TAC

A beaded milk jug cover, 1930s, 7in (18cm) wide.
£6–10 / €9–15
$13–20 ⊞ JWK

▶ **A glass and aluminium pinch bottle and four glasses,** American, 1930s, bottle 11½in (29cm) high.
£40–45 / €60–70
$75–85 ⊞ MSB

A glass cake stand, 1930s–1940s, 11in (28cm) diam.
£60–70 / €90–105
$110–130 ⊞ MSB

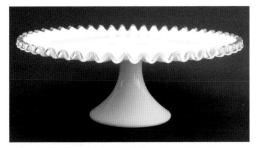

A Fostoria glass cake stand, American, c1940, 13in (33cm) diam.
£30–35 / €45–50
$55–65 ⊞ MSB

▶ **A Victoria Biscuits tin tray,** American, c1940, 10in (25.5cm) diam.
£30–35 / €45–50
$55–65 ⊞ MSB

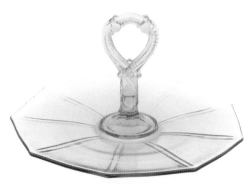

A glass cake plate, American, 1930s, 10¾in (27.5cm) diam.
£30–35 / €45–55
$55–65 ⊞ MSB

A ceramic sugar bowl and cover, 1950,
3in (7.5cm) high.
£15–20 / €22–30
$27–36 ⊞ BrL

A pressed glass and chrome cake stand, 1950s,
11in (28cm) diam.
£8–12 / €12–18
$15–22 ⊞ BAC

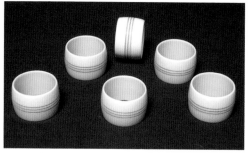

A Midwinter ceramic Red Domino cake stand,
1950s, 8¼in (21cm) diam.
£30–35 / €45–50
$55–65 ⊞ FLD

A set of six T. G. Green plastic napkin rings,
1950s, 2in (5cm) diam.
£40–45 / €60–70
$75–80 ⊞ SCH

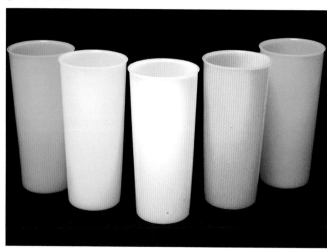

A set of six Tupperware plastic beakers, 1970, 6in (15cm) high.
£30–35 / €45–50
$55–65 ⊞ Mo

**A set of six Tupperware plastic
sundae glasses,** 1960s–1970s,
6in (15cm) high.
£20–25 / €30–35
$35–45 ⊞ Mo

Butter & Cheese Dishes

A ceramic butter dish, with a pierced cover, decorated with Willow pattern, 19thC, 6¼in (16cm) high.
£170–200 / €260–300
$310–370 ➹ **TMA**

▶ **A Leeds Pottery butter dish,** decorated with The Wanderer pattern, c1810, 6½in (16.5cm) wide.
£250–280 / €380–420
$460–510 ⊞ **SCO**

A cheese coaster, c1810, 16¼in (41.5cm) wide.
£540–600 / €820–910
$990–1,100 ⊞ **F&F**

A Staffordshire ceramic Stilton stand, decorated with Willow pattern, 1860–80, 11in (28cm) diam.
£60–70 / €90–105
$110–130 ⊞ **MCC**

A ceramic butter dish, with a pierced cover, c1910, 6in (15cm) diam.
£65–75 / €100–115
$120–140 ⊞ **B&R**

A ceramic butter dish, c1910, 8in (20.5cm) diam.
£135–150 / €200–230
$240–270 ⊞ **SMI**

◀ **A wooden cheese board,** with carved decoration, on three feet, c1910, 10in (25.5cm) diam.
£135–150
€200–230
$240–270
⊞ SMI

An Adams ceramic cheese dish, c1914, 7in (18cm) wide.
£105–120 / €160–180
$195–220 ⊞ CoCo

A ceramic butter dish, with wooden surround, the dish decorated with Willow pattern, 1920, 6¾in (17cm) diam.
£25–30 / €40–45
$45–55 ⊞ CHAC

A wooden butter dish surround, ceramic dish replaced, c1920, 6½in (16.5cm) diam.
£25–30 / €40–45
$45–55 ⊞ AL

A ceramic butter dish, with wooden surround, the dish decorated with Willow pattern, c1920, 6in (15cm) diam.
£20–25 / €30–35
$35–45 ⊞ AL

A ceramic butter dish, c1920, 8in (20.5cm) diam.
£90–100 / €135–150
$165–185 ⊞ SMI

A **Bretby ceramic butter dish,** damaged, early 20thC, 7½in (19cm) diam.
£35–40 / €50–60
$65–75 ⊞ B&R

A **stoneware butter dish,** 1920s.
£60–70 / €90–105
$110–130 ⊞ MSB

A **glass butter dish,** with wooden surround, c1930, 9in (23cm) diam.
£25–30 / €40–45
$45–55 ⊞ AL

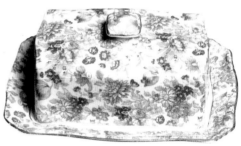

A **Royal Winton ceramic butter dish,** decorated with Kinver Chintz pattern, c1930, 6in (15cm) wide.
£105–120 / €160–180
$195–220 ⊞ BD

◀ A **ceramic cheese plate,** c1930, 10in (25.5cm) diam.
£45–50 / €70–80
$80–95 ⊞ SMI

A **Bagley glass butter dish,** 1930s, 7in (18cm) wide.
£8–12 / €12–18
$15–22 ⊞ BAC

◀ A **T. G. Green ceramic Polka Dot butter dish,** 1930s, 6in (15cm) diam.
£30–35 / €45–50
$55–65 ⊞ CAL

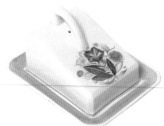

◄ **A Susie Cooper ceramic cheese dish,** decorated with Blue Gentian pattern, 1930s, 8in (20.5cm) wide.
£30–35
€**45–55**
$**55–65** ⊞ HO

A Crown Ducal ceramic cheese dish, decorated with Orange Tree pattern, 1930s, 8in (20.5cm) wide.
£125–140 / €**190–210**
$**230–260** ⊞ JOA

A Carlton Ware ceramic butter dish, 1930s, 6in (15cm) diam.
£240–270 / €**360–410**
$**440–490** ⊞ CCs

A T. G. Green ceramic Blue Domino cheese dish, c1940, 7in (18cm) wide.
£100–110 / €**150–165**
$**180–200** ⊞ CAL

A Falcon Pottery ceramic butter dish, c1936, 5in (12.5cm) square.
£15–20 / €**22–30**
$**27–36** ⊞ HO

A T. G. Green ceramic Cornish Ware butter dish, 1950s, 6in (15cm) diam.
£90–100 / €**135–150**
$**165–185** ⊞ CAL

◄ **A Portmeirion ceramic butter dish,** decorated with Totem pattern, c1963, 8in (20.5cm) wide.
£60–70 / €**90–105**
$**110–130** ⊞ CHI

Cruets

A Staffordshire pottery condiment pot, c1800, 6in (15cm) high.
£100–110 / €150–165
$180–200 ⊞ DHA

A Staffordshire pottery pepper pot, modelled as Roger Giles, c1825, 5in (12.5cm) high.
£540–600 / €820–910
$990–1,100 ⊞ DAN

A pewter caster, c1850, 5½in (14cm) high.
£60–70 / €90–105
$110–130 ⊞ MFB

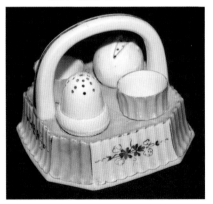

A lustreware egg cup and cruet set, c1880, 5in (12.5cm) square.
£20–25 / €30–35
$35–45 ⊞ POS

An Allertons ceramic Toby pepper pot, c1860, 6in (15cm) high.
£110–125 / €160–190
$200–230 ⊞ DHA

A Bovril ceramic pepper pot, 1915, 2¾in (7cm) high.
£80–90 / €120–135
$145–165 ⊞ BS

◀ **A Noritake ceramic cruet set,** maker's mark, c1920.
£80–90 / €120–135
$145–165 ⊞ DgC

A Noritake ceramic cruet set, maker's mark, c1920.
£50–55 / €75–85
$90–100 ⊞ DgC

A ceramic Happy Hounds cruet set, Japanese, c1930,
2in (5cm) high.
£25–30 / €40–45
$50–55 ⊞ CoCo

A ceramic cruet set, modelled as beehives, Japanese,
c1930, 3½in (9cm) high.
£35–40 / €50–60
$65–75 ⊞ CoCo

A ceramic cruet set, modelled as birds, Japanese,
c1930, 2in (5cm) high.
£15–20 / €22–30
$27–36 ⊞ CoCo

A ceramic cruet set, modelled as clowns, Japanese,
c1930, 3in (7.5cm) high.
£25–30 / €40–45
$50–55 ⊞ CoCo

▶ **A ceramic cruet set,** modelled as a chicken on a
nest, c1930, 3in (7.5cm) high.
£25–30 / €40–45
$50–55 ⊞ CoCo

A Clarice Cliff Bizarre ceramic cruet set, decorated with Solomon's Seal pattern, c1930.
£200–240 / €300–360
$370–440 🪚 **G(L)**

A Clarice Cliff ceramic cruet set, decorated with Crocus pattern, c1930, 3¼in (8.5cm) high.
£420–470 / €630–710
$770–860 ⊞ **JFME**

A ceramic cruet set, modelled as two children standing by an oven, German, 1930s, 3½in (9cm) high.
£40–45 / €60–70
$75–85 ⊞ **BET**

▶ **A Midwinter ceramic and chrome cruet set,** decorated with Springtime pattern, 1930s, 4½in (11.5cm) wide.
£70–80
€105–120
$130–145 ⊞ **JOA**

A T. G. Green ceramic Cornish Ware cruet set, with tray, 1930–80, 2½in (6.5cm) high.
£50–60 / €75–90
$95–110 ⊞ **CAL**

A plastic and glass cruet set, French, 1930s, 5in (12.5cm) wide.
£45–50 / €70–80
$85–95 ⊞ **GRo**

▶ **A Carlton ceramic cruet set,** modelled as fruit, c1950, 7in (18cm) wide.
£40–45 / €60–70
$75–85 ⊞ **BET**

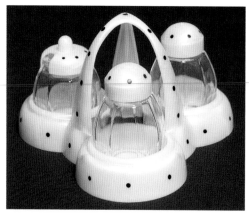

A plastic cruet set, 1950s, 3½in (9cm) high.
£35–40 / €50–60
$65–75 ⊞ BET

A Carlton ceramic cruet set, decorated with Australian pattern, 1950s, 3½in (9cm) high.
£20–25 / €30–35
$35–45 ⊞ GRo

A Midwinter ceramic Red Domino cruet set, 1950s, 4½in (11.5cm) diam.
£20–25 / €30–35
$35–45 ⊞ FLD

A composition cruet set, modelled as Noddy and Big Ears, on a wooden base, 1950s, 5in (12.5cm) wide.
£110–125 / €165–190
$200–230 ⊞ HYP

A Carlton Ware ceramic cruet set, modelled as vegetables, 1950s, 9in (23cm) wide.
£45–50 / €70–80
$85–95 ⊞ RTT

▶ A Wedgwood ceramic Summer Sky cruet set, 1950s, tray 6in (15cm) diam.
£50–55 / €75–85
$90–100 ⊞ CHI

A **Sandland ceramic cruet set,** depicting Jack Hobbs and Maurice Tate, some wear, 1950s, 4in (10cm) high.
£70–80 / €105–130
$130–155 ⚒ VS

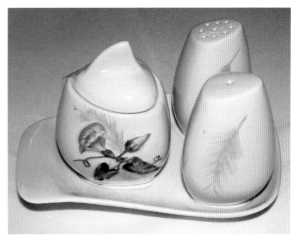

A **Carlton Ware ceramic cruet set,** 1950s–60s, 5½in (14cm) wide.
£25–30 / €40–45
$50–55 ⊞ HEI

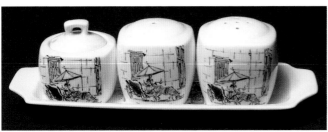

A **Midwinter ceramic Stylecraft cruet set,** designed by Sir Hugh Casson, decorated with Riviera pattern, c1954, 9in (23cm) wide.
£90–100 / €135–150
$165–185 ⊞ CHI

A **Carlton Ware ceramic Guinness pepper pot,** c1958, 4in (10cm) high.
£35–40 / €50–60
$65–75 ⊞ PrB

◄ A **T. G. Green ceramic Channel Isles cruet set,** designed by Judith Onions, 1968, 10in (25.5cm) wide.
£35–40 / €50–60
$65–75 ⊞ CAL

◄ A **Hornsea ceramic Image pepper pot,** 1980, 3in (7.5cm) high.
£12–16
€18–24
$22–30 ⊞ CHI

A **porcelain cruet set,** modelled as pigs, c2000, 3in (7.5cm) high.
£4–8 / €6–12
$7–14 ⊞ BAC

Cutlery

A Worcester ceramic honey spoon,
decorated with Mansfield pattern, c1758,
5in (12.5cm) long.
£1,500–1,700 / €2,250–2,550
$2,750–3,100 ⊞ JUP

▶ **A set of six silver forks,** London 1818,
7in (18cm) long.
£175–195 / €260–290
$320–360 ⊞ LaF

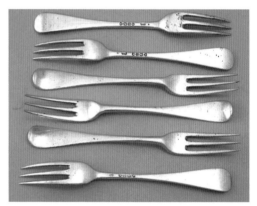

A set of six silver-plated fruit knives and forks, with
engraved decoration, c1870, knife 8½in (21.5cm) long,
in a fitted case.
£130–145 / €195–220
$240–270 ⊞ FOX

A set of six silver dessert forks, by George Adams,
London 1872, 8oz.
£150–180 / €230–270
$280–330 ⚒ G(L)

A set of six kitchen knives, forks and spoons, with wooden handles, late 19thC, knife 9½in (24cm) long.
£115–130 / €175–195
$210–240 ⊞ WeA

A set of six kitchen knives, forks and spoons, by Wardrobe & Pierce, Sheffield, with bone handles, late 19thC, knife 10in (25.5cm) long.
£115–130 / €175–195
$210–240 ⊞ WeA

◀ **An engraved silver preserve spoon,** by Tiffany & Co, American, c1900, 6in (15cm) long, 1oz.
£40–45
€60–70
$75–85 ⚒ WW

▶ **A silver-plated bread fork,** with a mother-of-pearl handle, c1910, 6in (15cm) long.
£15–20
€22–30
$27–36 ⊞ HO

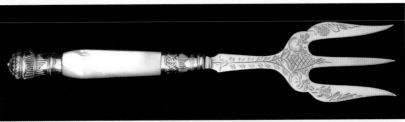

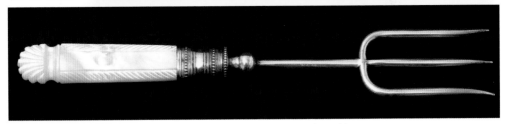

A silver-plated bread fork, with a mother-of-pearl handle, c1910, 6in (15cm) long.
£15–20 / €22–30
$27–36 ⊞ HO

A metal Virol spoon, 1920s, 8in (20.5cm) long.
£7–10 / €10–15
$10–20 ⊞ WeA

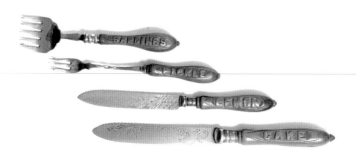

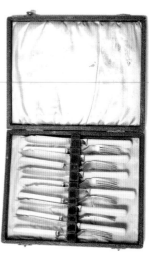

A set of four silver-plated knives and forks, with carved wooden handles, c1920.
£45–50 / €70–80
$80–90 ⊞ SMI

A set of six silver-plated fish knives and forks, with bone handles, 1920s, 8 x 9½in (20.5 x 24cm), in a fitted case,
£25–30 / €40–45
$50–55 ⊞ CCO

A metal Bovril spoon, 1920s, 5¾in (14.5cm) long.
£7–10 / €10–15
$10–20 ⊞ WeA

Items in the Cutlery section have been arranged in date order.

A metal Dairy Tea spoon, 1920s, 5in (12.5cm) long.
£7–12 / €10–15
$10–20 ⊞ WeA

A set of silver knives, forks and spoons, by Edward Viner, comprising 42 pieces, Sheffield, 1960–63, 52oz.
£400–480 / €600–720
$730–880 ⚒ G(L)

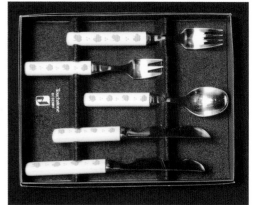

A set of Denby Touchstone knives, forks and spoons, decorated with Falling Leaves pattern, 1984.
£35–40 / €50–60
$65–75 ⊞ CHI

Honey Pots

◀ **A Spode ceramic honey pot,** decorated with Broseley pattern, 1820, 5in (12.5cm) diam.
£540–600
€**820–910**
$990–1,100
⊞ **GN**

A Wemyss ceramic honey box, designed by Thomas Goode, impressed mark, c1900, 7½in (19cm) square.
£720–800 / €**1,050–1,200**
$1,300–1,450 ⊞ **RdeR**

A Wemyss ceramic honey box, c1900, 7½in (19cm) square.
£740–820 / €**1,100–1,250**
$1,350–1,500 ⊞ **GLB**

◀ **A Wemyss ceramic honey pot,** some damage, painted mark, c1910, 4¾in (12cm) high.
£260–310
€**390–470**
$480–570
⚒ **SWO**

A Wemyss ceramic honey pot, c1900, 5in (12.5cm) high.
£270–300 / €**400–450**
$490–550 ⊞ **RdeR**

▶ **A Belleek ceramic honey pot,** Third Period, 1926–46, 6½in (16.5cm) high.
£630–700
€**950–1,050**
$1,150–1,300
⊞ **SCH**

◄ **A Royal Winton ceramic honey pot,** 1930s, 5in (12.5cm) high.
£145–160
€ **210–240**
$270–300
⊞ **SCH**

► **A Crown Devon ceramic honey pot,** c1930, 5in (12.5cm) high.
£80–90
€ **120–135**
$145–165
⊞ **CoCo**

A Carlton Ware ceramic honey box, 1930s, 7in (18cm) square.
£360–400 / € 540–600
$660–730 ⊞ CCs

A Carter, Stabler & Adams ceramic honey box, 1930, 5in (12.5cm) square.
£340–380 / € 510–570
$620–700 ⊞ CCs

A ceramic honey pot, 1930s, 5in (12.5cm) high.
£60–70 / € 95–105
$110–130 ⊞ CCs

► **A Shorter & Sons ceramic honey box,** c1930, 5in (12.5cm) square.
£105–120 / € 160–180
$195–220 ⊞ CCs

◄ **A Clarice Cliff ceramic honey pot,** decorated with Liberty Stripes pattern, c1930, 4in (10cm) high.
£430–480
€650–720
$790–880 ⊞ **TDG**

► **A Clarice Cliff ceramic honey pot,** decorated with Delicia Pansies pattern, c1930, 4in (10cm) high.
£320–380
€480–570
$590–700 ⚒ **G(L)**

A Clarice Cliff ceramic honey pot, decorated with Geometric pattern, signature mark, c1930, 3in (7.5cm) high.
£230–260 / €350–390
$420–480 ⚒ **SWO**

A Marutomo ware ceramic honey box, Japanese, 1930s, 4in (10cm) square.
£50–60 / €75–90
$95–110 ⊞ **BAC**

◄ **A Wadeheath ceramic honey pot,** c1930, 4½in (11.5cm) high.
£40–45 / €60–70
$70–80 ⊞ **CoCo**

► **A ceramic honey pot,** Czechoslovakian, 1930s, 5in (12.5cm) high.
£8–12 / €12–18
$15–20 ⊞ **BAC**

A commemorative ceramic honey pot,
1937, 5in (12.5cm) high.
£70–80 / €105–120
$130–145 ⊞ BAC

A Crown Devon ceramic honey box, 1940, 5in (12.5cm) square.
£150–165 / €220–250
$270–300 ⊞ CCs

A Goebel ceramic honey pot, modelled as a
bee, 1940s, 4¾in (12cm) high.
£65–75 / €100–115
$120–135 ⊞ BET

A Marutomo ware ceramic honey pot, 1940s, 4in (10cm) diam.
£40–45 / €60–70
$70–80 ⊞ BAC

A ceramic honey pot, 1950s,
5in (12.5cm) high.
£25–30 / €40–45
$50–55 ⊞ BAC

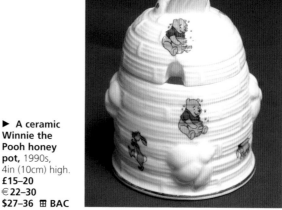

► A ceramic
Winnie the
Pooh honey
pot, 1990s,
4in (10cm) high.
£15–20
€22–30
$27–36 ⊞ BAC

Jugs & Boats

A copper jug, c1850, 5in (12.5cm) high.
£110–125 / €165–190
$200–230 ⊞ YT

▶ **A ceramic Mochaware jug,** c1880, 8in (20.5cm) high.
£360–400 / €540–600
$660–730 ⊞ SMI

A ceramic Mochaware jug, decorated with banding, c1880, 8in (20.5cm) high.
£220–250 / €340–380
$400–460 ⊞ SMI

▶ **A Dairy Outfit ceramic cream jug,** late 19thC, 8in (20.5cm) high.
£540–600 / €820–910
$990–1,100 ⊞ SMI

A copper jug, c1860, 15in (38cm) high.
£360–400 / €540–600
$660–730 ⊞ NEW

Two ceramic Mochaware jugs, c1880, larger 8in (20.5cm) high.
£220–250 / € 340–380
$400–460 each ⊞ SMI

A Doulton Lambeth stoneware jug,
decorated with portraits of W. G. Grace,
George Giffin and Ranji, marked, 1890s,
7¼in (18.5cm) high.
£920–1,100 / € 1,400–1,650
$1,700–2,000 ⚒ VS

◀ **A glazed stoneware jug,** 1890–1900,
5½in (14cm) high.
£25–30 / € 40–45
$50–55 ⊞ MSB

Two Copeland ceramic milk jugs, c1910,
larger 11in (28cm) high.
£135–150 / € 200–230
$240–270 each ⊞ SMI

An Adams ceramic milk jug, 1891–1917, 5in (12.5cm) high.
£70–80 / € 105–120
$130–145 ⊞ CoCo

▶ **A Wedgwood ceramic milk jug,** c1910, 13in (33cm) high.
£310–350 / € 470–530
$570–640 ⊞ SMI

A silver-plated Guernsey milk jug, c1910,
6in (15cm) high.
£50–60 / €75–90
$95–110 ⊞ AL

A T. G. Green ceramic Mochaware jug, 1910–20,
8in (20.5cm) high.
£160–180 / €240–270
$290–330 ⊞ CAL

A Burleigh ceramic milk jug, 1920, 7in (18cm) high.
£50–60 / €75–90
$95–110 ⊞ YT

A ceramic jug, with transfer-printed decoration, c1920,
10in (25.5cm) high.
£220–250 / €340–380
$400–460 ⊞ SMI

◄ **An enamel
jug,** French,
c1920, 14½in
(37cm) high.
£90–100
€135–150
$165–185 ⊞ AL

► **Three pottery
water jugs,**
1920s, largest
7in (18cm) high.
£14–18
€15–30
$25–35 ⊞ AL

▶ **An enamel jug,** with a hinged cover, French, 1920, 6½in (16.5cm) high.
£30–35
€**45–50**
$55–65 ⊞ **AL**

◀ **An enamel jug,** French, c1920, 15in (38cm) high.
£60–70
€**90–105**
$110–130 ⊞ **AL**

A T. G. Green ceramic jug, 1920s, 7½in (19cm) high.
£80–90 / €**120–135**
$145–165 ⊞ **CAL**

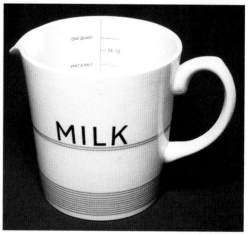

A Sadler ceramic Kleen Ware milk jug, 1920s, 5½in (14cm) high.
£25–30 / €**40–45**
$45–50 ⊞ **SCH**

A T. G. Green ceramic jug, c1925, 5in (12.5cm) high.
£25–30 / €**40–45**
$45–50 ⊞ **CAL**

▶ **A United Dairies ceramic cream jug,** c1925, 2¾in (7cm) high.
£15–20
€**22–30**
$25–35 ⊞ **HUX**

An enamel jug, 1930s, 4in (10cm) high.
£20–25 / €30–35
$35–45 JWK

An enamel jug, 1930s, 4in (10cm) high.
£20–25 / €30–35
$35–45 JWK

An Ovaltine ceramic jug, 1930s,
8in (20.5cm) high.
£35–40 / €50–60
$65–75 SMI

A T. G. Green ceramic jug, 1930s, 5½in (14cm) high.
£70–80 / €105–120
$130–145 SCH

◄ **An enamel
jug,** French,
c1930, 9½in
(24cm) high.
£20–25
€30–35
$35–40 AL

An enamel milk jug and cover, Continental, c1930,
6in (15cm) high.
£35–40 / €50–60
$65–75 AL

An enamel jug, French, c1930,
11in (28cm) high.
£50–55 / €75–85
$90–100 ⊞ AL

A T. G. Green ceramic Polka Dot milk jug, 1930s,
4in (10cm) high.
£15–20 / €22–30
$25–35 ⊞ CAL

**A T. G. Green ceramic Cornish Ware milk
jug,** 1930, 4½in (11.5cm) high.
£45–50 / €70–80
$80–90 ⊞ CoCo

An enamel jug, French,
c1930, 14¾in (37.5cm) high.
£25–30 / €40–45
$50–55 ⊞ CHAC

A pressed glass water jug, 1930s,
8in (20.5cm) high.
£8–12 / €12–18
$15–20 ⊞ BAC

A T. G. Green ceramic jug, 1930s,
7in (18cm) high.
£140–160 / €210–240
$260–290 ⊞ CAL

A T. G. Green ceramic cream jug, decorated with Alpha pattern,
1930s, 2in (5cm) high.
£70–80 / €105–120
$130–145 ⊞ CAL

A glass jug and six tumblers, American, 1930s, jug 8½in (21.5cm) high.
£60–70 / €90–105
$110–130 ⊞ MSB

◀ **A glass jug,** American, 1930s, 8½in (21.5cm) high.
£45–50
€70–80
$80–90 ⊞ MSB

A glass jug, with a metal handle and cover, American, 1930s, 8½in (21.5cm) high.
£60–70 / €90–105
$110–130 ⊞ MSB

▶ **A glass jug,** with a hinged tin cover, American, 1930s, 6½in (16.5cm) high.
£35–40 / €50–60
$65–75 ⊞ MSB

A T. G. Green ceramic Cornish Ware jug, c1940, 5in (12.5cm) high.
£90–100 / €135–150
$165–185 ⊞ CHI

A T. G. Green ceramic Blue Domino milk jug, c1940, 4in (10cm) high.
£75–85 / €115–130
$140–160 ⊞ CHI

A T. G. Green ceramic Cornish Ware jug, 1940s,
3¼in (8.5cm) high.
£25–30 / €40–45
$50–55 ⊞ **JWK**

A Royal Cauldon ceramic milk jug, c1940,
4in (10cm) high.
£6–10 / €9–15
$11–18 ⊞ **HO**

A T. G. Green ceramic sauce boat, 1950s,
7½in (19cm) wide.
£10–15 / €15–22
$18–27 ⊞ **CAL**

▶ **A T. G. Green ceramic Cornish Ware jug,** designed
by Judith Onions, 1966, 5in (12.5cm) high.
£40–45 / €60–70
$75–85 ⊞ **CAL**

A T. G. Green ceramic jug, 1960s, 5in (12.5cm) high.
£25–30 / €40–45
$50–55 ⊞ **CAL**

A T. G. Green ceramic jug, 1970, 6in (15cm) high.
£45–50 / €70–80
$85–95 ⊞ **CAL**

Preserve Pots

A Goss ceramic preserve pot, decorated with strawberries, c1890, 4in (10cm) high.
£85–95 / €130–145
$160–180 ⊞ HO

A glass preserve dish, with a silver-plated stand, c1895, 5½in (14cm) diam.
£120–135 / €180–200
$220–250 ⊞ GRI

A Wemyss ceramic preserve pot, painted with strawberries, impressed mark, c1900, 4½in (11.5cm) high.
£270–300 / €400–450
$490–550 ⊞ RdeR

▶ **A Wemyss ceramic preserve pot,** painted with oranges, impressed marks, c1900, 5½in (14cm) high.
£270–300 / €400–450
$490–550 ⊞ RdeR

◀ **A Wemyss ceramic preserve pot,** painted with sprays of roses, c1900, 5in (12.5cm) high.
£400–450 / €600–680
$730–820 ⊞ GLB

Further reading

Miller's Antiques Buyers Guide, Miller's Publications, 2004

A Wemyss ceramic preserve pot, painted with plums, c1900, 5in (12.5cm) high.
£180–200 / €270–300
$330–370 ⊞ RdeR

A cranberry glass preserve dish, with a silver cover, hallmarked, c1905, 4in (10cm) high.
£175–195 / €260–290
$320–360 ⊞ GRI

A Wemyss ceramic preserve pot, painted with plums, c1910, 5in (12.5cm) high.
£380–430 / €570–650
$700–790 ⊞ GLB

A silver preserve pot, with a glass liner, Birmingham 1911, 2¾in (7cm) high.
£70–80 / €105–120
$130–150 ⚒ G(L)

A Moorcroft ceramic preserve pot, decorated with Pomegranate pattern, impressed mark, c1920, 3½in (9cm) high.
£260–310 / €400–470
$470–560 ⚒ G(L)

A Clarice Cliff ceramic preserve pot, decorated with Blue Chintz pattern, c1930, 4in (10cm) high.
£500–550 / €750–830
$900–1,000 ⊞ TDG

A Minton ceramic preserve pot, c1930, 5in (12.5cm) high.
£80–90 / €120–135
$145–165 ⊞ BET

◀ **A Clarice Cliff ceramic preserve pot,** decorated with Crocus pattern, c1930, 4in (10cm) diam.
£320–360
€480–540
$590–660
⊞ TDG

A Marutomo ware ceramic preserve pot, with hand-painted decoration, 1930s, 3½in (9cm) high.
£35–40 / €50–60
$65–75 ⊞ BET

A Royal Winton ceramic preserve pot, modelled as a
Pekingese, 1930s, 5in (12.5cm) wide.
**£160–180 / €240–270
$290–330 ⊞ SCH**

A Clarice Cliff ceramic preserve pot,
decorated with Berries pattern, c1930,
3½in (9cm) high.
**£670–750 / €1,000–1,150
$1,200–1,350 ⊞ BD**

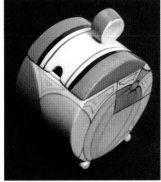

**► A Clarice Cliff ceramic preserve
pot,** decorated with Gayday pattern,
printed and painted marks, slight
damage, c1930, 3in (7.5cm) high.
**£130–155 / €195–230
$240–280 ✗ WW**

**A Clarice Cliff ceramic Bonjour
preserve pot,** decorated with Melons
pattern, c1930, 4½in (11.5cm) high.
**£720–800 / €1,050–1,200
$1,300–1,450 ⊞ BD**

**A Clarice Cliff ceramic Bonjour
preserve pot,** decorated with
Honolulu pattern, c1930,
4in (10cm) high.
**£590–650 / €890–980
$1,050–1,200 ⊞ BD**

**◄ A Clarice Cliff ceramic Biarritz
preserve pot,** decorated with
Rhodanthe pattern, printed marks,
c1930, 5in (12.5cm) diam.
**£120–140 / €180–210
$220–260 ✗ SWO**

**► A Clarice Cliff ceramic Biarritz
preserve pot,** decorated with
Delicia Citrus pattern, printed mark,
c1930, 5in (12.5cm) diam.
**£320–380 / €480–570
$590–700 ✗ SWO**

A Shelley ceramic preserve pot, with hand-painted decoration, 1930s, 4½in (11.5cm) high.
£40–45 / €60–70 $75–85 ⊞ TAC

A Clarice Cliff ceramic Celtic Harvest preserve pot, 1930, 5in (12.5cm) high.
£125–140 / €190–210 $230–260 ⊞ CoCo

A Shelley ceramic Harmony Banded Ware preserve pot, c1930, 4in (10cm) high.
£45–50 / €70–80 $80–95 ⊞ HEW

◄ **A Clarice Cliff ceramic preserve pot,** decorated with Rhodanthe pattern, c1930, 2in (5cm) high.
£310–350 / €480–540 $580–640 ⊞ RH

► **A Clarice Cliff ceramic preserve pot,** decorated with Secrets pattern, c1930, 4in (10cm) high.
£590–650 / €890–980 $1,050–1,200 ⊞ RH

A Clarice Cliff ceramic preserve pot, decorated with Poplar pattern, c1930, 4in (10cm) high.
£670–750 / €1,000–1,150 $1,200–1,350 ⊞ RH

A Poole Pottery ceramic preserve pot, designed by Truda Carter, painted by Phyllis Allen, 1934–35, 5in (12.5cm) high.
£85–95 / €130–145 $155–175 ⊞ PGO

A Portmeirion ceramic preserve pot, decorated with Totem pattern, c1963, 4in (10cm) high.
£50–55 / €75–85 $90–100 ⊞ CHI

Sugar Sifters

A Staffordshire salt-glazed stoneware sugar sifter, with moulded decoration, c1760, 5¼in (13.5cm) high.
**£620–740 / €950–1,100
$1,150–1,350** ⚒ WW

A silver sugar sifter, by Hester Bateman, London 1784, 5½in (14cm) high.
**£810–900
€1,200–1,350
$1,500–1,650** ⊞ NOR

A parcel-gilt sugar sifter, decorated with engraved scrolling and winged angel masks, Continental, 19thC, 6¼in (16cm) high.
**£240–280 / €360–420
$440–520** ⚒ G(L)

A George II-style silver sugar caster, by Charles Fox, engraved with a crest, some wear, London 1823, 9½in (24cm) high, 15oz.
**£340–400 / €510–600
$620–730** ⚒ WW

A silver sugar caster, with pierced sides and glass liner, late 19thC, 3¾in (9.5cm) high.
**£60–70 / €90–105
$110–130** ⚒ G(L)

A Victorian silver-plated sugar caster, in the form of a thistle, 6in (15cm) high.
**£400–450 / €600–680
$730–820** ⊞ SHa

▶ **A cranberry glass sugar caster,** with a silver-plated cover, c1900, 6in (15cm) high.
**£90–100 / €135–150
$165–185** ⊞ GRI

A silver sugar caster, by Deakin & Francis, Birmingham 1901, 7in (18cm) high.
**£290–320 / €430–480
$530–590** ⊞ GRe

A silver sugar caster, by
Charles & George Asprey,
London 1904,
9in (23cm) high.
£210–240 / €330–370
$400–440 ⊞ PGO

A white metal sifter spoon, with a silver handle, Sheffield 1908, 7in (18cm) long.
£30–35 / €45–50
$55–65 ⊞ CoCo

A cranberry glass sugar
caster, with a silver-plated
cover, c1910,
6in (15cm) high.
£110–125 / €170–190
$200–230 ⊞ GRI

A silver sugar caster,
Birmingham 1911,
7in (18cm) high.
£200–230 / €300–350
$370–420 ⊞ EXC

A silver-mounted glass
sugar caster, by H & O,
Birmingham 1921,
5½in (14cm) high.
£60–70 / €90–105
$110–130 ⊞ WAC

A Minton ceramic sugar
caster, 1920s,
5in (12.5cm) high.
£70–80 / €105–120
$130–145 ⊞ TAC

▶ A Clarice Cliff
ceramic Bonjour sugar
caster, decorated with
Taormina pattern, c1930,
5in (12.5cm) high.
£500–550 / €750–830
$900–1,000 ⊞ TDG

A Crown Devon ceramic
sugar caster, with hand-
painted decoration, 1930s,
4½in (11.5cm) high.
£45–50 / €70–80
$80–90 ⊞ TAC

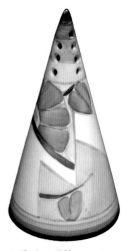

A Clarice Cliff ceramic
sugar caster, decorated
with Moonflower pattern,
c1930, 5in (12.5cm) high.
£720–800
€1,050–1,200
$1,300–1,450 ⊞ RH

◄ **A silver sugar caster,** modelled as a milk canister, American, c1930, 11in (28cm) high.
£1,050–1,200
€ **1,600–1,800**
$1,900–2,200 ⊞ GoW

A Clarice Cliff ceramic sugar caster, decorated with Nasturtium pattern, c1930, 6in (15cm) high.
£540–600 / € **820–910**
$990–1,100 ⊞ BD

A Clarice Cliff ceramic sugar caster, decorated with Crocus pattern, c1930, 5½in (14cm) high.
£560–620
€ **850–940**
$1,000–1,150 ⊞ TDG

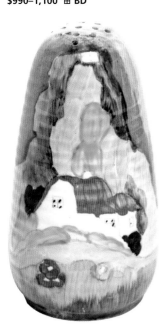

A Clarice Cliff ceramic Lynton sugar caster, decorated with Newlyn pattern, c1930, 5in (12.5cm) high.
£720–800 / € **1,050–1,200**
$1,300–1,450 ⊞ BD

A Clarice Cliff ceramic Bonjour sugar caster, decorated with Idyll pattern, c1930, 5in (12.5cm) high.
£500–600 / € **750–900**
$920–1,100 ⚒ G(L)

A Clarice Cliff ceramic Bonjour sugar caster, decorated with Crocus pattern, c1930, 5in (12.5cm) high.
£670–750
€ **1,000–1,150**
$1,200–1,350 ⊞ BD

A Barker Brothers ceramic sugar caster, c1930, 8in (20.5cm) high.
£90–100 / €135–150
$165–185 ⊞ BD

A Royal Winton ceramic sugar caster, decorated with Delphinium pattern, c1930, 7in (18cm) high.
£135–150 / €200–230
$240–270 ⊞ BD

A Clarice Cliff ceramic sugar caster, decorated with Secrets pattern, c1932, 5½in (14cm) high.
£830–930
€1,250–1,400
$1,500–1,700 ⊞ TDG

A Clarice Cliff ceramic sugar caster, decorated with Taormina pattern, c1936, 5½in (14cm) high.
£440–530 / €670–800
$810–970 ⚒ G(L)

A Portmeirion ceramic sugar caster, decorated with a Chemist print, 1970s, 6½in (16.5cm) high.
£20–25 / €30–35
$35–45 ⊞ CHI

A Burslem ceramic sugar caster, 1940, 6in (15cm) high.
£25–30 / €40–45
$45–55 ⊞ BrL

◀ **A silver sugar caster,** with engraved inscription, London 1957, 8in (20.5cm) high.
£100–110 / €150–165
$180–200 ⊞ CoHA

Tea & Coffee Pots

A Copeland Spode ceramic teapot, decorated with Italian pattern, handle cracked, 19thC.
£330–390 / €500–590
$600–710 ⚒ G(L)

A copper chocolate pot, c1850, 11in (28cm) high.
£400–440 / €600–660
$730–810 ⊞ MFB

A tin coffee pot, with original paint, c1870, 11in (28cm) high.
£65–75 / €100–115
$120–140 ⊞ Cot

A cast-iron hot water urn, with a brass tap, c1880, 21in (53.5cm) high.
£240–270 / €360–410
$440–490 ⊞ DaM

A copper and brass coffee pot, with an acorn finial and wooden handle, c1900, 10in (25.5cm) high.
£50–60 / €75–85
$90–100 ⊞ WAC

▶ **A copper and brass Bovril urn,** 1900, 19in (48.5cm) high.
£800–900
€1,200–1,350
$1,500–1,650 ⊞ AL

A copper electric water heater, c1915, 20in (51cm) high.
£110–125 / €165–190
$200–230 ⊞ YT

An enamel coffee pot, French, c1920, 13in (33cm) high.
£70–80 / €105–120
$130–145 ⊞ AL

A T. G. Green ceramic teapot, cream jug and sugar bowl, decorated with Dickens Days pattern, 1930, teapot 4in (10cm) high.
£180–200 / € 270–300
$330–370 ⊞ CAL

A T. G. Green ceramic hot water pot, 1930s, 5in (12.5cm) high.
£130–145 / € 195–220
$240–270 ⊞ SCH

A T. G. Green ceramic Polka Dot coffee service, comprising 23 pieces, 1930s, coffee pot 6in (15cm) high.
£135–150 / € 200–220
$250–280 ⊞ CAL

A T. G. Green ceramic Blue Domino teapot, 1940s, 5in (12.5cm) high.
£145–160 / € 220–250
$270–300 ⊞ CHI

◄ **A Royal Winton ceramic breakfast set,** decorated with Welbeck pattern, with associated toast rack, 1940s.
£130–155
€ 195–230
$240–280
⚒ CHTR

► **A T. G. Green ceramic Polo ware coffee service,** 1950s, jug 3in (7.5cm) high.
£50–60
€ 75–90
$90–100
⊞ CAL

An enamel urn, c1950, 15in (38cm) high.
£55–65 / € 85–100
$85–100 ⊞ AL

A T. G. Green ceramic Tally Ho teapot,
1950s, 4½in (11.5cm) high.
£110–125 / €170–190
$200–230 ⊞ CAL

A T. G. Green ceramic Cornish Ware
cafetière, marked, 1950, 6in (15cm) high.
£200–220 / €300–330
$360–400 ⊞ CAL

◄ **A Midwinter ceramic Red Domino tea**
service, designed by Jessie Tait, c1953, cup
3in (7.5cm) high.
£120–135 / €180–200
$220–250 ⊞ CHI

A Heatmaster ceramic and chrome coffee pot, c1960, 9in (23cm) high.
£25–30 / €40–45
$45–55 ⊞ LUNA

▶ **A T. G. Green ceramic Channel Isles coffee pot,** designed by Judith Onions and Martin Hunt, decorated with Jersey Blue pattern, 1968, 8in (20.5cm) high.
£60–70 / €90–105
$110–130 ⊞ CAL

◀ **A T. G. Green ceramic Cornish Ware coffee pot,** designed by Judith Onions, 1966, 7in (18cm) high.
£65–75 / €100–115
$120–135 ⊞ CAL

A T. G. Green ceramic Sark coffee service, designed by Judith Onions, 1968, coffee pot 8½in (21.5cm) high.
£70–80 / €105–120
$130–145 ⊞ CAL

Toast Racks

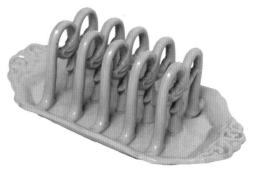

A Spode ceramic toast rack, decorated with Filigree pattern, c1820, 8in (20.5cm) wide.
£450–500 / €680–760
$820–920 ⊞ SCO

A Copeland pottery toast rack, c1870, 9in (23cm) wide.
£140–160 / €210–240
$260–290 ⊞ HUM

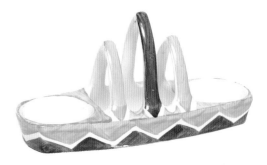

A Shelley ceramic toast rack, 1920s, 5in (12.5cm) wide.
£35–40 / €50–60
$65–75 ⊞ TAC

An Ivory ceramic toast rack, with hand-painted decoration, c1930, 7½in (19cm) wide.
£45–50 / €70–80
$80–90 ⊞ BET

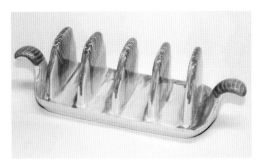

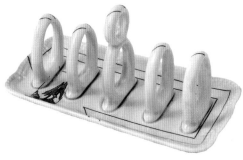

◄ **A Shelley ceramic toast rack,** 1930s, 7in (18cm) wide.
£50–60 / €75–85
$90–100 ⊞ TAC

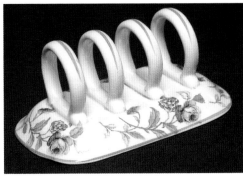

A Solian Ware ceramic toast rack, 1930s,
5in (12.5cm).
£40–45 / €60–70
$75–80 ⊞ BET

◄ **A Clarice Cliff ceramic Bizarre toast rack,**
painted with fir trees, c1930, 6½in (16.5cm) wide.
£130–155 / €195–230
$240–280 ⚒ G(L)

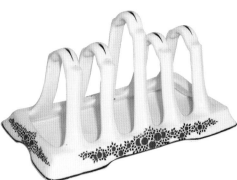

A Crown Ducal ceramic toast rack, decorated with
Orange Tree pattern, 1930s, 6in (15cm) wide.
£125–140 / €190–210
$230–260 ⊞ JOA

A Royal Winton ceramic toast rack, decorated with
Hazel pattern, c1940, 4½in (11.5cm) wide.
£125–140 / €185–210
$230–260 ⊞ RH

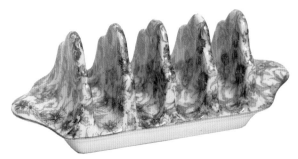

A Royal Winton ceramic toast rack, decorated with Kew
pattern, c1940, 7in (18cm) wide.
£150–170 / €230–260
$280–310 ⊞ RH

A ceramic Golly toast rack, 1980s–1990s,
5in (12.5cm) wide.
£45–50 / €70–80
$80–90 ⊞ HYP

Scullery
Brushes

A Vowless & Co clothes brush, c1920, 10in (25.5cm) long.
£15–20 / €22–30
$28–38 ⊞ SDA

A bottle brush, with a wooden handle, c1920, 18in (45.5cm) long.
£1–5 / €2–7
$3–9 ⊞ AL

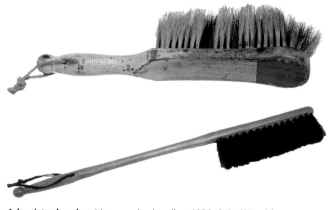

◄ **A cleaning brush,** with a wooden handle, c1930, 12in (30.5cm) long.
£2–6 / €3–9
$4–11 ⊞ AL

A banister brush, with a wooden handle, c1930, 24in (61cm) long.
£3–7 / €4–10
$6–13 ⊞ AL

A cleaning brush, with a wooden handle, c1950, 14in (35.5cm) long.
£3–7 / €4–10
$6–13 ⊞ AL

A straw brush, 1940s, 10in (25.5cm) long.
£5–9 / €8–13
$10–16 ⊞ JWK

Cleaning Equipment

A maid's pine box, c1890, 10in (25.5cm) wide.
£90–100 / €135–150
$165–185 ⊞ AL
It is unusual for this type of box to still
have its tray.

A maid's metal bucket,
1890–1920, 11in (28cm) wide.
£30–35 / €45–50
$55–65 ⊞ CHAC
This tin bucket would have been
available in a variety of colours.

A pan scourer, with a
wooden handle, c1900,
5in (12.5cm) long.
£20–25 / €30–35
$35–45 ⊞ Cot

A Domex Housemaid's Box,
c1910, 16in (40.5cm) wide.
£40–45 / €60–70
$75–85 ⊞ Cot
It is unusual for this type of box
to have retained its original label.

**A Kiwi painted tin shoe polishing
stand,** c1930, 17in (43cm) wide.
£115–130 / €175–195
$210–240 ⊞ B&R

◄ **A Ewbank wooden carpet
sweeper,** c1910, 20½in (52cm) high.
£65–75 / €100–115
$120–140 ⊞ AL

An enamel soap dish, 1940s,
7in (18cm) wide.
£10–15 / €15–22
$18–28 ⊞ JWK

A metal and cloth mop, 1940s, 10in (25.5cm) long.
£1–5 / €2–7
$3–9 ⊞ JWK

Kettles

A copper kettle, 18thC,
12in (30.5cm) high.
£310–350 / €**470–530**
$570–640 ⊞ **SEA**

A brass kettle, Dutch, mid-18thC,
12in (30.5cm) high.
£230–260 / €**350–390**
$420–480 ⊞ **SEA**

A copper kettle, c1820,
11in (28cm) high.
£310–350 / €**470–530**
$570–640 ⊞ **SEA**

Buying Kettles

Although mainly purchased as decorative items today,
kettles that are in good condition can still be used.
They are available in all shapes and sizes and can be
made from enamel, tin, cast-iron, copper and brass,
although buyers should be aware that there are many
reproductions on the market, many of which are made
of copper and cast-iron. Original cast-iron kettles are
very popular for use with Aga-style stoves and open
fires, but it is advisable to check for cracks before
making a purchase.

◄ **A copper and brass
kettle,** c1880,
10in (25.5cm) high.
£100–115 / €**150–175**
$180–210 ⊞ **AL**

A copper kettle, c1820, 12in (30.5cm) high.
£220–250 / €**330–380**
$400–460 ⊞ **YT**

► **A copper
kettle,** c1880,
15in (38cm) high.
£200–230
€**300–350**
$370–420 ⊞ **YT**

A Victorian painted hot water can,
8in (20.5cm) high.
£90–100 / €**135–150**
$165–185 ⊞ **Cot**
**Hot water cans were available in three
different sizes. It is unusual to find
examples with their original paint.**

A steel and brass kettle, c1880,
10in (25.5cm) high.
£80–90 / €120–135
$150–170 ⊞ SMI

A copper kettle, c1890, 11½in (29cm) high.
£120–135 / €180–200
$220–250 ⊞ AL

Two cast-iron kettles, one with a brass handle, c1890,
larger 5in (12.5cm) high.
£110–125 / €165–190
$200–230 ⊞ SMI
**It is very rare to find such
small kettles, hence the higher price.**

A copper picnic kettle, c1910,
6in (15cm) high.
£35–40 / €50–60
$65–75 ⊞ AL
**This kettle would have been part
of a picnic set.**

An enamel kettle, c1920s,
11in (28cm) high.
£35–40 / €50–60
$65–75 ⊞ AL
**This colour enamel is very
popular in America.**

A picnic kettle and stand, 1920,
9½in (24cm) high.
£35–40 / €50–60
$65–75 ⊞ AL

An enamel kettle, c1960,
8in (20.5cm) high.
£10–15 / €15–22
$18–28 ⊞ AL

Laundry

An iron stand, Irish, 19thC, 14in (35.5cm) long.
£75–85 / €115–130
$140–160 ⊞ STA

A painted birchwood mangle, Scandinavian, 1817, 23½in (59.5cm) long.
£540–600 / €820–910
$990–1,100 ⊞ NEW

A brass double goffering iron,
pokers missing, early 19thC,
11½in (29cm) high.
£270–300 / €400–450
$490–550 ⊞ WeA

A Dowsings cast-iron electric iron, c1870, 10in (25.5cm) long.
£60–70 / €90–105
$110–130 ⊞ FST

A Carron's Foundry goose iron,
c1850, 10in (25.5cm) long.
£25–30 / €40–45
$50–55 ⊞ FST

A C. E. Sheldon cast-iron mangle,
Irish, c1860, 60in (152.5cm) high.
£165–185 / €250–275
$300–330 ⊞ HON

◀ **A Kenrick flat iron,** c1880,
6in (15cm) long.
£45–50 / €70–80
$85–95 ⊞ SMI

A brass ox tongue iron, Austrian,
c1880, 8in (20.5cm) long.
£680–750 / €1,050–1,200
$1,250–1,400 ⊞ SEA

A Beetall cast-iron gas steam iron, with a wooden handle, c1880, 11in (28cm) long.
£135–150 / €200–230
$250–270 ⊞ SMI

A goffering iron, poker missing, late 19thC, 3in (7.5cm) high.
£80–90 / €120–135
$150–170 ⊞ WeA

A set of three Mrs Potts irons, detachable handle restored, c1885, 6½in (16.5cm) wide.
£65–75 / €100–115
$120–140 ⊞ AL
Mary Florence Potts patented her iron in the USA in 1871. It was a set of three irons that came with a detachable wooden handle which could be removed while the iron was heating so that it was always cold to the touch.

A W. Parnall & Co ceramic washing dolly, c1880, 16½in (42cm) high.
£360–400 / €540–600
$660–730 ⊞ WeA

A cast-iron iron heating stove, French, c1900, 19in (48.5cm) wide.
£220–250 / €330–380
$400–460 ⊞ B&R

A wood and steel mangle, c1910, 24in (61cm) wide.
£450–500 / €680–760
$820–920 ⊞ FST

▶ **A glass washboard,** c1920, 22½in (57cm) high.
£15–20 / €22–30
$28–38 ⊞ AL

A wood and tin washboard, American, early 1900s, 13¾in (35cm) wide.
£30–35 / €45–50
$55–65 ⊞ MSB

Packaging

A Charlot Extra Cream Shoe Polish tin,
c1920, 1¾in (4.5cm) diam.
£20–25 / €30–35
$35–45 ⊞ HUX

◄ **A Plynine Household Ammonia bottle,**
Scottish, c1900, 12in (30.5cm) high.
£25–30 / €40–45
$50–55 ⊞ YT

A Wellington Knife Polish tin,
c1900, 4½in (11.5cm) high.
£55–65 / €85–100
$100–120 ⊞ BS

A CWS Pelaw Polish tin, c1920s,
2in (5cm) diam.
£40–45 / €60–70
$75–85 ⊞ HUX
CWS (Cooperative Wholesale Society)
items are very collectable.

**A Kohler of Kohler
Superior Cleanser tin,**
American, 1920s–30s,
7in (18cm) high.
£14–18 / €21–27
$26–30 ⊞ MSB

A Kewpie Klenser tin, c1920s,
5in (12.5cm) high.
£35–40 / €50–60
$65–75 ⊞ HUX

► **A W. C. Nixey's Black Lead box,** c1920, 10in (25.5cm) wide.
£20–25 / €30–35
$35–45 ⊞ B&R

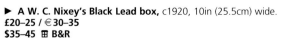

A Borax Soap Chips free sample,
American, 1920s–30s,
7in (18cm) high.
£8–12 / €12–18
$15–22 ⊞ MSB

A L'Ebène polish tin, 1930s,
1½in (4cm) diam.
£20–25 / €30–35
$35–45 ⊞ HUX

A Brown Beauty shoe polish tin,
1930s, 3in (7.5cm) diam.
£2–6 / €3–9
$4–11 ⊞ Do

▶ **Three tablets of Fairy
household soap,** with original box,
1940s, 7in (18cm) wide.
£6–10 / €9–15
$12–19 ⊞ NFR

A Brasso sample tin, 1950,
2in (5cm) high.
£15–20 / €22–30
$28–38 ⊞ HUX

▶ **A Lifebuoy soap box,** 1950s,
3in (7.5cm) wide.
£1–5 / €2–7
$3–9 ⊞ Do

A box of Sprinkleen, 1950–60,
8in (20.5cm) wide.
£2–6 / €3–9
$4–11 ⊞ RTT

A Sprinko cleaner
packet, c1950s,
9in (23cm) high.
£10–15 / €15–22
$19–28 ⊞ RTT

Trugs & Baskets

A basket, American, 1890–1910, 11½in (29cm) high.
£45–50 / €70–80
$85–95 ⊞ MSB

A wicker bottle basket, early 20thC, 20½in (52cm) wide.
£55–65 / €85–100
$100–120 ⊞ WeA

A woven basket, with wooden handles, American, early 20thC, 12¾in (32.5cm) wide.
£110–125 / €165–190
$200–230 ⊞ MSB

A miniature woven basket, signed, American, North Carolina, 1900–25, 3in (7.5cm) high.
£85–95 / €130–145
$155–175 ⊞ MSB

A wood and metal picnic basket, 1900–25, 19½in (49.5cm) wide.
£35–40 / €50–60
$65–75 ⊞ MSB

A pine trug, French, c1920, 18½in (47cm) wide.
£30–35 / €45–50
$55–65 ⊞ AL

A wooden Sussex trug, c1938, 24in (61cm) wide.
£35–40 / €50–60
$65–75 ⊞ HOP

A wooden Sussex trug, c1938, 21in (53.5cm) wide.
£45–50 / €70–80
$85–95 ⊞ HOP

A wooden Sussex trug,
with original paint, c1938,
22in (56cm) wide.
£45–50 / €70–80
$85–95 ⊞ HOP
Trugs with their original
paint are very popular
with the American
market.

▶ **A wicker basket,**
1940s, 15in (38cm) wide.
£15–20 / €22–30
$28–38 ⊞ JWK

A wicker basket, 1930s, 13½in (34.5cm) wide.
£15–20 / €22–30
$28–38 ⊞ JWK

◀ **A wicker
basket,** 1950s,
8in (20.5cm) wide.
£8–12
€12–18
$15–22 ⊞ JWK

A wicker basket, 1950s, 15in (38cm) wide.
£15–20 / €22–30
$28–38 ⊞ JWK

Books

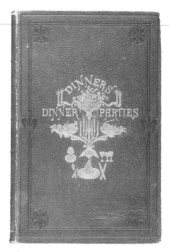

Mrs A. M. Collins, *The Great Western Cookbook*, American, New York, 1857, 7½ x 5¼in (19 x 13.5cm).
£60–70 / €90–105
$110–125 ⊞ MSB

Dinners & Dinner Parties, 1862, 7½ x 5¼in (19 x 13.5cm).
£60–70 / €90–105
$110–125 ⊞ MSB

Mrs M. Parloa, *Miss Parloa's Cook Book*, American, Boston, 1857, 7½ x 5¼in (19 x 13.5cm).
£40–45 / €60–70
$70–80 ⊞ MSB

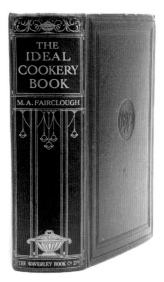

▶ **G. H. Ellwanger,** *The Pleasures of the Table*, American, New York, 1902, 9½ x 6in (24 x 15cm).
£35–40 / €50–60
$65–75 ⊞ MSB

M. A. Fairclough, *The Ideal Cookery Book*, published by Waverley Book Co, London, UK, early 20thC, 10¼ x 9¾in (26 x 25cm).
£50–55 / €75–85
$90–100 ⊞ MSB

M. L. Doods, *Practical Cookery*, with a silver cover, 1906, 2½ x 2in (6.5 x 5cm).
£90–100 / €135–150
$165–185 ⊞ SMI

LOCATE THE SOURCE
The source of each illustration in Miller's can be found by checking the code letters below each caption with the Key to Illustrations, pages 313–315.

▶ **Mildred Maddocks,** *Good Housekeeping Family Cookbook*, American, New York, 1906, 9½ x 4in (24 x 10cm).
£25–30 / €40–45
$45–50 ⊞ MSB

W. Whipple, *The Minute Man Cookbook,* published by the Minute Tapioca Co, American, Massachussetts, 1909, 7 x 5in (18 x 12.5cm).
£35–40 / €50–60
$65–75 ⊞ MSB

The Cookery Book, published by Richard Edward King, London, UK, c1910, 7in (18cm) high.
£15–20 / €/20–25
$25–35 ⊞ LBM

◄ **Marion Harris Neil,** *The Something-Different Dish,* American, 1915, 8 x 5½in (20.5 x 14cm).
£15–20 / €20–25
$35–40 ⊞ MSB

McLaren, *The Pan Pacific Cookbook,* American, San Francisco, 1915, 7¾ x 5¼in (19.5 x 13.5cm).
£35–40 / €50–60
$65–75 ⊞ MSB

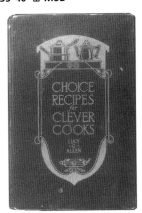

Lucy G. Allen, *Choice Recipes for Clever Cooks,* American, Boston, 1929, 8½ x 5½in (21.5 x 14cm).
£20–25 / €30–35
$40–45 ⊞ MSB

◄ **Miss Tuxford's Modern Cookery for the Middle Classes,** published by John Heywood, Manchester, UK, 1920s, 7 x 5in (18 x 12.5cm).
£6–10 / €9–15
$11–18 ⊞ COB

► **Frederick Phillip Stieff,** *Eat, Drink and Be Merry in Maryland,* illustrated by Edwin Tunis, American, 1932, 8¼ x 6½in (21.5 x 16.5cm).
£15–20 / €20–25
$35–40 ⊞ MSB

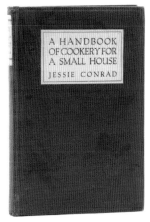

Jessie Conrad, *A Handbook of Cookery For A Small House,* American, 1923, 7½ x 5in (19 x 12.5cm).
£50–55 / €75–85
$90–100 ⊞ MSB

Della T. Lutes, *The Country Kitchen*, American, 1936, 7½ x 5in (19 x 12.5cm).
£9–13 / €15–20
$20–25 ⊞ MSB

The Radiation Recipe Book, published by Radiation Publications, UK, 1940s, 8½ x 5½in (21.5 x 14cm).
£1–5 / €2–7
$3–9 ⊞ JWK

R. B. Wilcox, *Friends Seminary Cookbook*, 1951, 7½ x 5¼in (19 x 13.5cm).
£15–20 / €20–25
$35–40 ⊞ MSB

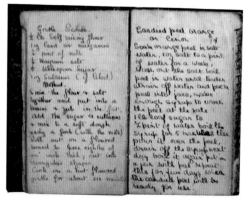

► **A book of recipes,** written by Elsie Jones, Welsh, c1950, 6¾in (17cm) high.
£4–8 / €6–12
$8–15 ⊞ LBM

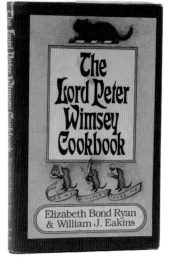

Metropolitan Cookbook, 1960s, 8in (20.5cm) high.
£1–5 / €2–7
$3–9 ⊞ DaM

Marguerite Patten, *Marguerite Patten's Everyday Cookbook*, published by Hamlyn, London, UK, 1970, 10¼in (26cm) high.
£8–12 / €12–18
$15–22 ⊞ LBM

◄ **Elizabeth Bond Ryan and William J. Eakins,** *Lord Peter Wimsey Cookbook*, American, 1981, 9½ x 6½in (24 x 16.5cm).
£25–30 / €40–45
$50–55 ⊞ MSB
Lord Peter Wimsey is a fictional character in a series of detective novels by Dorothy L. Sayers.

Home Management

Good Things, published by
Goodall, Backhouse & Co, Leeds,
UK, 1887, 5½ x 3¾in (14 x 9.5cm).
£20–25 / €30–35
$40–45 MSB

Virginia E. James, *Mother James'
Key To Good Cooking*, American,
1892, 10 x 7¾in (25.5 x 19.5cm).
£35–40 / €50–60
$65–75 MSB

▶ **Margaret Greenleaf and
Helen R. Churchill,** *My Home –
why not yours?*, published by Pratt
& Lambert, American, 1915,
9 x 6in (23 x 15cm).
£15–20 / €22–30
$28–38 MSB

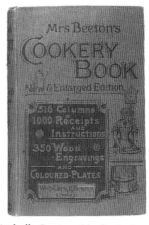

Isabella Beeton, *Mrs Beeton's
Cookery Book*, published by Ward,
Lock & Bowden, London, UK, early
20thC, 7¾ x 5¼in (19.5 x 13.5cm).
£45–50 / €65–75
$80–90 MSB

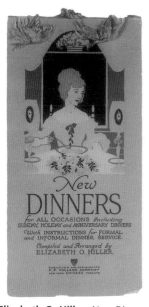

Elizabeth O. Hiller, *New Dinners
For All Occasions*, booklet, published
by P. F. Volland & Co, American,
c1910, 7¾ x 5¼in (19.5 x 13.5cm).
£35–40 / €50–60
$65–75 OPB

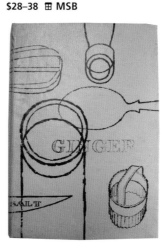

Isabella Beeton, *Mrs Beeton's All
About Cookery*, published by Ward,
Lock & Co, London, UK, first edition,
1961, 8in (20.5cm) high.
£15–20 / €20–25
$25–35 LBM

▶ **Georgina Horley,** *Good Food on a Budget*, published by Penguin Books,
London, UK, 1980, 7in (18cm) high.
£1–5 / €2–7
$3–9 LBM

Speciality Recipe Books

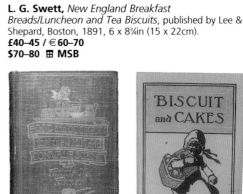

L. G. Swett, *New England Breakfast Breads/Luncheon and Tea Biscuits*, published by Lee & Shepard, Boston, 1891, 6 x 8¾in (15 x 22cm).
£40–45 / €60–70
$70–80 ⊞ MSB

A. L. Guyot, *La Patissière des Petits Ménages*, French, Paris, 1860, 6¾ x 5¼in (17 x 13.5cm).
£60–70 / €90–105
$110–125 ⊞ MSB

Hood's Book of Homemade Candies, published by C. I. Hood & Co, American, Boston, 1888, 7 x 4½in (18 x 11.5cm).
£25–30 / €40–45
$45–50 ⊞ MSB

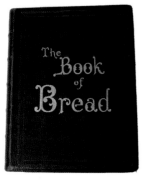

◀ **Owen Simmons,** *The Book of Bread*, published by Maclaren, London, UK, limited edition of 350, 1900, with original photographs, leather, 12in (30.5cm) high.
£105–120
€160–180
$190–220
⊞ B&R

Fannie M. Farmer, *Food and Cookery for the Convalescent*, American, Boston, 1904, 7¾ x 5½in (19.5 x 14cm).
£25–30 / €40–45
$50–60 ⊞ MSB

Biscuit and Cakes, published by Reliable Flour Co, American, 1915, 6 x 3¾in (15 x 9.5cm).
£12–16 / €18–24
$25–30 ⊞ MSB

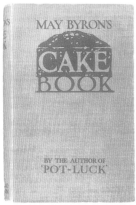

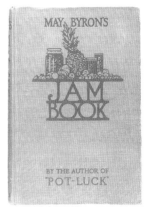

May Byron, *May Byron's Cake Book*, published by Hodder & Stoughton, London, UK, 1915, 8¼ x 5¾in (21 x 14.5cm).
£15–20 / €25–30
$30–35 ⊞ MSB

Dainty Desserts for Dainty People, by the makers of Knox gelatine, published by Charles B. Knox, American, 1916, 6¾ x 4¾in (17 x 12cm).
£20–25 / €30–35
$40–45 ⊞ MSB

May Byron, *May Byron's Jam Book*, published by Hodder & Stoughton, London, UK, 1917, 8¼ x 5¾in (21 x 14.5cm).
£15–20 / €25–30
$30–35 ⊞ MSB

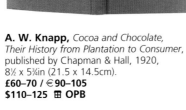

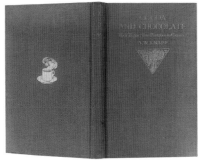

Ceresota Cook Book,
published by The
Northwestern Consolidated
Miling Co, American,
Minnesota, c1920,
7½ x 5in (19 x 12.5cm).
£25–30 / €40–45
$45–50 ⊞ MSB

A. W. Knapp, *Cocoa and Chocolate,*
Their History from Plantation to Consumer,
published by Chapman & Hall, 1920,
8½ x 5¾in (21.5 x 14.5cm).
£60–70 / €90–105
$110–125 ⊞ OPB

Alice Foote MacDougall,
Coffee and Waffles, published by
Doubleday Page & Co, 1926,
7½ x 5¼in (19 x 13.5cm).
£20–25 / €30–35
$40–45 ⊞ MSB

◄ *All About Icing,* published by
Tala, UK, 1920s, 6½ x 4½in
(16.5 x 11.5cm).
£3–7 / €5–11
$6–13 ⊞ JWK

► *Chocolate Candies*
You Can Make,
pamphlet, 1925–50,
6 x 6¼in (15 x 16cm).
£4–8 / €6–10
$10–15 ⊞ MSB

Mrs Rufus Taylor, *French Sauces*
and Entrees, published by Clark-
Sprague Printing Co, American,
Missouri, 1934, 7¼ x 5½in
(18.5 x 14cm).
£35–40 / €50–60
$65–75 ⊞ MSB

Sea Food Explanation
Card Suggestions,
published by M. F. Foley Co,
American, Boston, 1920s,
9 x 4½in (23 x 11.5cm).
£20–25 / €30–35
$40–45 ⊞ MSB

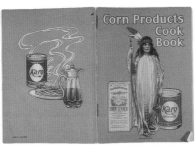

◄ **E. C. Hewitt,** *Corn Products*
Cookbook, 1930s, 7¼ x 5½in
(18.5 x 14cm).
£15–20 / €25–30
$30–35 ⊞ MSB

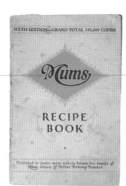

◀ *Mums Recipe Book,* Australian, c1950s, 7in (18cm) high.
£1–5 / €2–7
$3–9 ⊞ DaM

▶ *McDougall's Cookery Book,* UK, c1950s, 7in (18cm) high.
£1–5 / €2–7
$3–9 ⊞ DaM

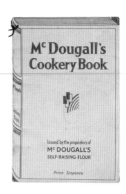

Elizabeth Craig, *Borwick's Baking Powder,* booklet, UK, 1940s, 8½ x 5½in (21.5 x 14cm).
£3–7 / €5–11
$6–13 ⊞ JWK

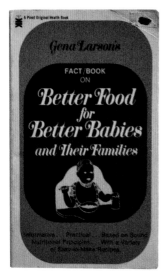

Margaret Powell, *Sweetmaking for Children,* published by Pan Books, London, 1972, 7½in (19cm) high.
£1–5 / €2–7
$3–9 ⊞ LBM

Robin Howe, *Rice Cooking,* published by André Deutsch, London, UK, 1959, 7½in (19cm) high.
£50–60 / €75–90
$95–110 ⊞ MSB

Gena Larson, *Better Food for Better Babies and their Families,* published by Pivet Original Health Editions, South Africa, 1972, 7in (18cm) high.
£1–5 / €/2–7
$3–9 ⊞ LBM

▶ **Michael Smith,** *Fine English Cookery,* published by Faber & Faber, London, UK, 1973, 10in (25.5cm) high.
£6–10 / €/9–15
$12–19 ⊞ LBM

David and Rose Mabey, *The Penguin Book of Jams, Pickles and Chutneys,* published by Penguin Books, 1978, 7¾in (19.5cm) high.
£2–6 / €/3–9
$4–11 ⊞ LBM

Directory of Specialists

If you require a valuation for an item it is advisable to check whether the dealer or specialist will carry out this service, and whether there is a charge. Please mention Miller's when making an enquiry. Having found a specialist who will carry out your valuation, it is best to send a description and photograph of the item to them, together with a stamped addressed envelope for the reply. A valuation by telephone is not possible. Most dealers are only too happy to help you with your enquiry, however, they are very busy people and consideration of the above points would be welcomed.

Berkshire

Below Stairs, 103 High Street, Hungerford, RG17 0NB Tel: 01488 682317 hofgartner@belowstairs.co.uk www.belowstairs.co.uk
Antiques and collectables including kitchenware, textiles and lighting.

Dreweatt Neate, Donnington Priory, Donnington, Newbury, RG14 2JE
Tel: 01635 553553
donnington@dnfa.com
www.dnfa.com/donnington
Auctioneers.

Buckinghamshire

Gillian Neale Antiques, PO Box 247, Aylesbury, HP20 1JZ Tel: 01296 423754/ 07860 638700 gillianneale@aol.com www.gillannealeantiques.co.uk
Blue & white transfer printed pottery 1780–1860.

Cambridgeshire

Mark Seabrook Antiques, PO Box 396, Huntingdon, PE28 0ZA Tel: 01480 861935 or 07770 721931
enquiries@markseabrook.com
www.markseabrook.com
Early English oak, country furniture, metalware, treen, ceramics.

Essex

20th Century Marks, Whitegates, Rectory Road, Little Burstead, Near Billericay, CM12 9TR Tel: 01268 411 000 or 07831 778992
info@20thcenturymarks.co.uk
www.20thcenturymarks.co.uk
Original 20th century design.

Debden Antiques, Elder Street, Debden, Saffron Walden, CB11 3JY Tel: 01799 543007 info@debden-antiques.co.uk debden-antiques.co.uk
Large selection of 16th–20thC oak, mahogany and pine furniture, watercolours and oil paintings, rugs, ceramics, silver and jewellery. Plus garden furniture and ornaments.

Sworders, 14 Cambridge Road, Stansted Mountfitchet, CM24 8BZ
Tel: 01279 817778
auctions@sworder.co.uk
www.sworder.co.uk
Auctioneers.

Gloucestershire

Cottage Collectibles, Long Street Antiques, 14 Long Street, Tetbury, G18 8AQ Tel: 01666 500850
sheila@cottagecollectibles.co.uk
English and Continental country antiques and kitchenalia. Showroom at Eccleshall, Staffordshire. Open by appointment only – 01785 850210.

Durham House Antiques, Sheep Street, Stow-on-the-Wold, GL54 1AA
Tel: 01451 870404
30+ dealers. Town and country furniture, metalware, books, ceramics, kitchenalia, sewing ephemera, silver, jewellery and samplers.

Newsum Antiques, 2 High Street, Winchcombe, GL54 5HT
Tel: 01242 603446/07968 196668
mark@newsumantiques.co.uk
www.newsumantiques.co.uk
Oak & country furniture, treen, metalware and kitchenalia.

Peter Scott 0117 986 8468 or 07850 639770
Blue & white transferware.

The Top Banana Antiques Mall, 1 New Church Street, Tetbury, GL8 8DS Tel: 0871 288 1102
info@topbananaantiques.com
www.topbananaantiques.com

Hampshire

Cedar Antiques Ltd, High Street, Hartley Wintney, RG27 8NY
Tel: 01252 843222 or 01189 326628
ca@cedar-antiques.com
www.cedar-antiques.com
Museum of T. G. Green pottery.

Millers Antiques Ltd, Netherbrook House, 86 Christchurch Road, Ringwood, BH24 1DR Tel: 01425 472062 mail@millers-antiques.co.uk www.millers-antiques.co.uk
Majolica and Quimper, decorative items, English and continental furniture.

Kent

Tenterden Antiques Centre, 66–66A High Street, Tenterden TN30 6AU Tel: 01580 765655/765885
Furniture, Art Deco, china, clocks,
silver, jewellery, militaria, postcards, porcelain, bric-a-brac.

Tenterden Antiques & Silver Vaults, 66 High Street, Tenterden, TN30 6AU
Tel: 01580 765885
Clocks, silver, china, furniture, glass, collectables, jewellery.

Wenderton Antiques Tel: 01227 720295 (by appointment only)

Lincolnshire

Skip & Janie Smithson Antiques
Tel: 01754 810265 or 07831 399180
smithsonantiques@hotmail.com
Specialist dealers in kitchen, laundry, dairy and related advertising items.

London

Banana Dance Ltd, 155A Northcote Road, Battersea, SW11 6QT
Tel: 01634 364539 or 07976 296987
jonathan@bananadance.com
www.bananadance.com
Decorative Arts of the 1920's and the 1930's.

Beth, GO 43–44, Alfies Antique Market, 13–25 Church Street, Marylebone, NW8 8DT Tel: 020 7723 5613/0777 613 6003

Beverley, 30 Church Street, Marylebone, NW8 8EP Tel: 020 7262 1576 or 07776136003
Art Deco furniture, glass, figures, metalware and pottery.

Jasmin Cameron, Antiquarius, 131–141 King's Road, SW3 4PW
Tel: 020 7351 4154 or 077 74 871257
jasmin.cameron@mail.com
Specializing in drinking glasses and decanters 1750–1910.

Liz Farrow T/As Dodo, Stand F071/73, Alfie's Antique Market, 13–25 Church Street, NW8 8DT Tel: 020 7706 1545
Sats only 9am–4pm. Posters and old advertising.

David Huxtable, Saturdays at: Portobello Road, Basement Stall 11/12, 288 Westbourne Grove, W11
Tel: 07710 132200 david@huxtins.com
www.huxtins.com
Old advertising collectables.

Geoffrey Robinson, GO77–78, GO91–92 (Ground floor), Alfies Antique Market, 13–25 Church Street, Marylebone, NW8 8DT Tel: 020 7723 0449 info@alfiesantiques.com www.alfiesantiques.com
Mirrors, Art Pottery, glass, small furniture, china, Art Deco and post-war lighting.

Rogers de Rin, 76 Royal Hospital Road, SW3 4HN Tel: 020 7352 9007
Wemyss pottery.

Twinkled, 1st Floor, Old Petrol Station, 11–17 Stockwell Street, Greenwich, SE10 9JN Tel: 020 8269 0864 info@twinkled.net www.twinkled.net
Purveyors of fine homeware from the 1950's, 60's and 70's.

Staffordshire
The 40's Room, Unit 40 Rugeley Antiques Centre, Main Road, Brereton, Rugeley, WS15 1DX Tel: 01889 577166 info@cc41homefrontdisplays.co.uk

East Sussex
The Brighton Lanes Antique Centre, 12 Meeting House Lane, Brighton, BN1 1HB Tel: 01273 823121 peter@brightonlanes-antiquecentre.co.uk www.brightonlanes-antiquecentre.co.uk
Fine selection of furniture, silver, jewellery, glass, porcelain, clocks, pens, watches, lighting and decorative items.

Church Hill Antiques Centre, 6 Station Street, Lewes, BN7 2DA Tel: 01273 474842 churchhilllewes@aol.com www.church-hill-antiques.com
Antiques centre with a good range of antiques and decorative items including, kitchenware and collectables.

Gorringes inc Julian Dawson, 15 North Street, Lewes, BN7 2PD Tel: 01273 478221 auctions@gorringes.co.uk www.gorringes.co.uk
Auctioneers.

Jupiter Antiques, PO Box 609, Rotting-dean, BN2 7FW Tel: 01273 302865
Specializing in English porcelain from 18thC factories and Royal Worcester and Royal Crown Derby.

Ann Lingard, Ropewalk Antiques, Rye, TN31 7NA Tel: 01797 223486 ann-lingard@ropewalkantiques.freeserve. co.uk
Kitchenware and collectables.

Rin Tin Tin, 34 North Road, Brighton, BN1 1YB Tel: 01273 672424 rick@rintintin.freeserve.co.uk
Original old advertising and promotional material, magazines, early glamour, games, toys, plastics and miscellaneous 20thC collectables.

Trudi's Treasures, Post Office House, Crowborough Hill, Crowborough, TN6 2EG Tel: 01892 667671 www.trudis-treasures.co.uk
Specialists in pine, painted furniture, china, kitchenalia, linen and more.

Jane Wicks Kitchenalia, Country Ways, Strand Quay, Rye Tel: 01424 713635 or 07754 308269 Janes_kitchen@hotmail.com
Specializing in kitchen, garden and textiles collectables.

West Sussex
Rupert Toovey & Co Ltd, Spring Gardens, Washington, RH20 3BS Tel: 01903 891955 auctions@rupert-toovey.com www.rupert-toovey.com
Monthly specialist auctions of antiques, fine art and collectors' items. Regular specialist auctions of collectors' toys and dolls and antiquarian and collectors' books.

Nicholas Shaw Antiques, Virginia Cottage, Lombard Street, Petworth, GU28 0AG Tel: 01798 345146/01798 345147 silver@nicholas-shaw.com www.nicholas-shaw.com
Silver.

Warwickshire
Bread & Roses Tel: 01926 817342
Kitchen antiques 1800–1950's.
Also at The Ark Angel, Long Street, Tetbury, Glos 01666 505820 and Zani Lady, Corfe Street, Ludlow, Shropshire Tel: 01584 877200
Kitchenware.

Chinasearch Ltd, 4 Princes Drive, Kenilworth, CV8 2FD Tel: 01926 512402 helen.rush@chinasearch.uk.com www.chinasearch.uk.com
Discontinued dinner, tea and collectable ware bought and sold.

West Midlands
Martin's Antiques & Collectibles, The Shed Antiques Collectibles Centre Tel: 01386 438387/07951 600573 Jackiem743710633@aol.com. www.martinsantiquescollectibles.co.uk
Kitchen collectables and other affordable antique collectables dating from the 19thC through to various sections of the early 20thC.

Wiltshire
Woolley & Wallis, Salisbury Salerooms, 51–61 Castle Street, Salisbury, SP1 3SU Tel: 01722 424500/411854 junebarrett@woolleyandwallis.co.uk ww.woolleyandwallis.co.uk
Auctioneers.

Worcestershire
Worcester Antiques Centre, Reindeer Court, Mealcheapen Street, Worcester, WR1 4DF Tel: 01905 610680 WorcsAntiques@aol.com
Porcelain & pottery, furniture, silver and dining room accessories, jewellery, period watches & clocks, scientific instrumentation, Arts & Crafts, Nouveau, Deco, antique boxes, Mauchline & Tartan wares, books, ephemera, militaria and kitchenalia, with full restoration and repair services on all of the above.

Yorkshire
Country Collector, 11–12 Birdgate, Pickering, YO18 7AL Tel: 01751 477481 www.country-collector.co.uk
Art Deco ceramics, blue & white, pottery & porcelain.

Glasstastique, (by appointment only) Tel: 0113 287 9308 office or 07967 337795/07967 345952 glasstastique@aol.com www.glasstastique.com
18th, 19th and 20thC glassware.

USA
Absolutely Staffordshire, Etc, 6924 Harper Valley Lane, Clemmons, NC 27012
English ceramics.

Marilynn & Sheila Brass, PO Box 380503, Cambridge, MA 02238-0503 Tel: 617 492 1491 shelmardesign1@aol.com

Cobbs Auctioneers LLC, Noone Falls Mill, 50 Jaffrey Rd, Peterborough, NH 03458 Tel: 603 924 6361 info@thecobbs.com www.thecobbs.com

Home Grown Antiques, Michele L. Anderson-Laidlaw, PO Box 232, Cut Bank, MT 59903 info@homegrownantiques.com www.homegrownantiques.com
Quality collectible American-made dinnerware, glassware and pottery from the 20thC.

Kings Way Books and Antiques, 774 Main St, (Rte. 6A), West Brewster, Brewster, MA, Tel: 508 896 3639
Out-of-print and rare books, including a large medieval section, plus small antiques, kitchenware, china, glass, silver, coins, and linens.

Middlebury Antique Center, on the corner of Rte. 7 & 116, Box 378, East Middlebury, VT 05740 Tel: 802 388 6229 midantct@together.net

Olde Port Bookshop, 18 State Street, Newburyport, Massachusetts 01950 Tel: 978 462 0100 Oldeport@ttlc.net

Directory of Collectors' Clubs

**Association of Coffee
Mill Enthusiasts**
John White, 5941 Wilkerson Road, Rex,
GA 30273, USA Tel: 770 474 0509

Blue & White Pottery Club
Howard Gardner, 224 12th Street
N.W., Cedar Rapids, Iowa 52405,
USA Tel: 319 362 8116

British Iron Collectors
Julia Morgan, 87 Wellsway Road,
Bath BA2 4RU

**British Novelty Salt & Pepper
Collectors Club**
Ray Dodd (Secretary), Coleshill, Clayton
Road, Mold, Flintshire CH7 1SX
www.bnspcc.com

**The Burleigh Ware International
Collectors Circle**
Tel: 01664 454570

Butter Pat Collectors' Notebook
5955 S.W. 179th Ave, Beaverton,
OR 97007, USA

**Butter Pats International
Collectors Club**
Alice Black, 38 Acton Street,
Maynard, MA 01754, USA

**Campbell Soup Collectors
International Association**
Betty Campbell Madden (President),
305 East Main Street, Ligonier,
PA 15658, USA

**Carlton Ware Collectors
International**
Carlton Factory Shop, Carlton Works,
Copeland Street, Stoke-on-Trent,
Staffordshire ST4 1PU
Tel: 01782 410504

Chintz Collectors Club (US)
PO Box 50888, Pasadena,
CA 91115, USA

Clarice Cliff Collectors' Club
Fantasque House, Tennis Drive,
The Park, Nottingham NG7 1AE
www.claricecliff.com

Cook Book Collectors Club
Barbara Gelink, 4756 Terrace Drive,
San Diego, CA 92116-2514, USA
Tel: 619 281 8962
cookwithbabs@home.com

**Cook Book Collectors Club of
America, Inc**
Col. Bob Allen, PO Box 56,
St James, MO 65559-0056, USA
Tel: 573 265 8296

Cookie Cutters Collectors Club
Ruth Capper, 1167 Teal Road S.W.,
Dellroy, OH 44620-9704, USA

Cornish Collectors Club
PO Box 58, Buxton, Derbyshire
SK17 0FH

Cream Separator Association
Dr. Paul Dettloff (Secretary),
Rte. 3 Box 189, Arcadia, WI 54612,
USA Tel: 608 323 7470

**Crunch Club (Breakfast Cereal
Collectables)**
John Cahill, 9 Weald Rise, Tilehurst,
Reading, Berkshire RG30 6XB

Devon Pottery Collectors Group
Mrs Joyce Stonelake, 19 St Margarets
Avenue, Torquay, Devon TQ1 4LW
Tel: 01803 327277
Virginia.Brisco@care4free.net

Egg Cup Collectors' Club of GB
Sue Wright (Subs Secretary), PO Box
39, Llandysul, Wales SA44 5ZD
suewright@suecol.freeserve.co.uk
www.eggcupworld.co.uk

Eggcup Collectors' Corner
Dr. Joan M. George, 67 Stevens Ave,
Old Bridge, NJ 08857, USA
drjgeorge@nac.net

Egg Cup International Club
Dr. J. Hahsemi, 22 Eastcote Lane,
Hampton in Arden, Solihull, West
Midlands B92 0AS Tel: 01675 442175

**The European Honeypot
Collectors' Society**
John Doyle, The Honeypot, 18 Victoria
Road, Chislehurst, Kent BR7 6DF
Tel: 020 8289 7725
johnhoneypot@hotmail.com
www.geocities.com/tehcsuk

Friends of Blue Ceramic Society
Terry Sheppard, 45a Church Road,
Bexley Heath, Kent DA7 4DD
www.fob.org.uk

**Griswold & Cast Iron Cookware
Association**
David G. Smith, PO Drawer B,
Perrysburg, NY 14129-0301, USA
Tel: 716 532 5154
DGSpanman@aol.com
www.C1web.com/panman

Honiton Pottery Collectors' Society
Robin Tinkler (Chairman), 2 Redyear
Cottages, Kennington Road, Ashford,
Kent TN24 0TF hpcs@moshpit.cix.co.uk
www.hpcs.info

**Hornsea Pottery Collectors' and
Research Society**
c/o Peter Tennant, 128 Devonshire
Street, Keighley, West Yorkshire BD21
2QJ hornsea@pdtennant.fsnet.co.uk
www.hornseacollector.co.uk

**Inner-Seal Collectors Club
(National Biscuit Co and
Nabisco Memorabilia)**
Charlie Brown, 6609 Billtown Road,
Louisville, KY 40299, USA

**International Society for Apple
Parer Enthusiasts**
G. W. Laverty, 735 Cedarwood
Terrace, Apt 735B, Rochester,
NY 14609, USA

**The International Society of
Antique Scale Collectors (ISASC)**
Steve Beare (Membership Chairman),
7E Brookland Ave, Wilmington,
DE 19805, USA

**James Sadler International
Collectors Club**
Customer Services, Churchill
China PLC, High Street, Tunstall,
Stoke-on-Trent, Staffordshire
ST6 5NZ Tel: 01782 577566
diningin@churchillchina.plc.uk
www.james-sadler.co.uk

**Kitchen Antiques &
Collectibles News**
Dana & Darlene Demore,
4645 Laurel Ridge Drive,
Harrisburg, PA 17119, USA

**Midwest Antique Fruit Jar
& Bottle Club**
Norman & June Barnett, PO Box 38,
Flat Rock, IN 47234, USA
Tel: 812 587 5560

Milk Bottle News
Paul & Lisa Luke, 60 Rose Valley
Crescent, Stanford-le-Hope,
Essex SS17 8EF
www.milkbottlenews.org.co.uk

**National Association of Milk
Bottle Collectors, Inc – The
Milkroute (NAMBC)**
Box 105, Blooming Grove,
NY 10914, USA
milkroute@yahoo.com

**National Autumn Leaf
Collectors Club**
Dianna Kowallis, PO Box 7929,
Moreno Valley, CA 92552-7929, USA
www.nalcc.org

National Reamer Collectors Association
Deborah Gillham, 47 Midline Court, Gaithersburg, MD 20878, USA
reamers@erols.com www.reamers.org

Novelty Salt & Pepper Shakers Club
Lula Fuller (Membership Coordinator), PO Box 3617, Lantana, FL 33465, USA
Tel: 561 588 5368

Nutcracker Collectors' Club
Susan Otto, 12204 Fox Run Drive, Chesterland, OH 44026, USA
Tel: 440 729 2686
nutsue@adelphia.net

The Old Hall Collectors' Club
Nigel Wiggin, Sandford House, Levedale, Stafford ST18 9AH Tel: 01785 780376
oht@gnwiggin.freeserve.co.uk
www.oldhallclub.co.uk

The Pewter Society
Llananant Farm, Penallt, Monmouth NP25 4AP secretary@pewtersociety.org
www.pewtersociety.org

Pillsbury Collectors InfoLine
Donna L. McDaniel, 4224 Independence Drive, Flint, MI 48506, USA Tel: 810 736 0933
Cookbknut@aol.com

Poole Pottery Collectors Club
Poole Pottery Limited, Sopers Lane, Poole, Dorset BH17 7PP
Tel: 01202 666200
www.poolepottery.com

Potteries of Rye Society
Barry Buckton (Membership Secretary), 2 Redyear Cottages, Kennington Road, Ashford, Kent TN24 0TF
Tel: 01233 647898
www.potteries-of-rye-society.co.uk

Rocky Mountain Cutups – Cookie Cutter Collector Club
Kristi Gardner, 9483 Desert Willow Way, Littleton, CO 80129, USA

Royal Winton International Collectors' Club
Dancers End, Northall, Bedfordshire LU6 2EU

The Shelley Group
4 Fawley Road, Regents Park, Southampton, Hampshire SO2 1LL

The Silver Spoon Club of Great Britain
Daniel Bexfield, 26 Burlington Arcade, Mayfair, London W1J 0PU Tel: 020 7491 1730 antiques@bexfield.co.uk

Society for Tin Box Collectors
K. Hughes, 121 Preston Drive, Brighton, East Sussex BN1 6LE

The Spode Society
Mrs R. Pulver, PO Box 1812, London NW4 4NW

Susie Cooper Collectors Club
Panorama House, 18 Oakley Mews, Aycliffe Village, Co Durham DL5 6JP
www.susiecooper.co.uk

The Teapot Collectors Club
Ian & Lesley Rogers, Unit 4b, Ephraim Court, Ephraim Street, Hanley, Stoke-on-Trent, Staffordshire ST1 3SH
Tel: 01782 769453
ian@noveltyteapots.freeserve.co.uk
www.noveltyteapots.co.uk

Tin Container Collectors Association
PO Box 440101, Aurora, CO 80044, USA

Toaster Collector Association
PO Box 485, Redding Ridge, CT 06876, USA

Torquay Pottery Collectors' Society
Membership Secretary, c/o Torre Abbey, The Kings Drive, Torquay, Devon TQ2 5JX
www.torquaypottery.com

Totally Teapots – The Novelty Teapot Collectors Club
Vince McDonald, Euxton, Chorley, Lancashire PR7 6EY
Tel: 01257 450366
vince@totallyteapots.com
www.totallyteapots.com

UK Spoon Collectors Club
David Cross (General Secretary), 72 Edinburgh Road, Newmarket, Suffolk CB8 0DQ Tel: 01638 665457
david@ukspoons.fsnet.co.uk

UK Sucrologists Club
Membership Secretary, 14 Marisfield Place, Selsey, West Sussex PO20 0PD

Museums & Websites

All Vintage Store
http://allvintagestore.com/
Online vintage store for vintage kitchenware, housewares, vintage table linen, etc.

AntiqueClimax
http://members.rogers.com/kensue/
Home page for two antique bottle, jar, stoneware and pottery collectors.

Antique-Irons.com and Antique Pressing Iron & Stove Museum
http://www.antique-irons.com/
The original community page for antique pressing iron collectors, including the Shaker Brook Farm Antique Pressing Iron & Stove Museum.

Antique Pressing Irons
http://www.shirbil.com/
Collection of pressing irons online.

Bakelite Man
www.bakeliteman.com
Jools Zauscinski's site dedicated to all things Bakelite including specialist sections of kitchenalia, toys and a history of plastics.

Bill's Milk Bottle Page
www.gotmilkbottles.com/
Bill Kaiser's milk bottle collectors site featuring items from his collection and bottles for sale.

Bob's Eggcup World
http://members.lycos.co.uk/Bob_eggcupmad/index.htm
Bob Paton's eggcup collection.

Clarice Cliff Collectors Club
www.claricecliff.com/
The official website for collectors of Clarice Cliff pottery.

Collectible-Hunter.com
http://www.collectible-hunter.com/

auction/Housewares-and-Kitchenware_c13905/
Buy housewares and kitchenware collectibles online.

Collectics Antiques & Collectibles
www.collectics.com/kitchenware.html
Online shopping for vintage kitchenware.

Collecting Eggcups
http://www.angelfire.com/fl/eggcups/index.html
Site dedicated to the world of eggcup collecting.

Collectormania
www.collectormania.com.au
Australia's monthly collector's trading paper with specialist sections including breweriana and collectibles. Includes online listings and editorial articles each month.

The Cornishware Collectors Site
www.feeandme
Cornishware and T. G. Green collectors
site from Fee & Me Antiques about
blue and white, yellow and white,
Domino and other T. G. Green items.

Country Joe's Collectible Stuff
www.countryjoescollectiblestuff.com
Kitchen collectibles online.

Days Gone By
www.daysgoneby.net
Vintage cookbooks.

Dec a Diner.com
www.veryartique.com
Vintage kitchenware and Barware,
also cookbooks.

**Early American Workshop: The Milk
Bottle Collectors Website**
www.earlyamericanworkshop.com/
A milk bottle collector's and dealer's
site including history and information
on bottles, caps and reproductions
and links to other related sites.

Egg-Coddlers.com
www.egg-coddlers.com
Website dedicated to the study of egg
coddlers, providing an information
resource and a forum for collectors
of egg coddlers to meet and share
their experience.

The Fruit Jar Collector Web Site
http://members.intertek.net/~pmurfe/
fruitjars/main.html
Phil Murphy's online collection of
fruit jars.

Gramas Attic
www.gramasattic.net/
A collectors' resource for vintage
tablecloths and other antique linens.

Guardian Service Cookware Corner
http://hcprobate.homestead.com/
guardian.html
Website dedicated to the Guardian
Service cookware collector, user
and fan.

Hall China Collecting
http://www.inter-services.com/
HallChina/
Website for the use and enjoyment
of Hall China collectors and anyone
who is interested in learning more
about Hall China.

Honeypot Collector Site
www.hjb-honeypot.org.uk
The online home of honeypot collector
Helen Butcher.

**The International Central Services
Toaster Museum**
www.toastermuseum.com/
Online toaster collection of
Jens Veerbeck.

Kim's Salt and Pepper Shaker Page
http://kimmykay.tripod.com/snppage/
Website giving advice on collecting salt
and pepper shakers, including history
of shakers, places to buy, etc.

L & J Antiques & Collectibles
www.landjantiques.net
Collectible reamers.

**Medium Green Fiestaware
Collectors**
www.mediumgreen.com/
Collectors site for Homer Laughlin
China Company's Fiestaware which
includes a Fiestaware database,
information on colours, a discussion
board and a search facility.

**The Museum of Beverage
Containers and Advertising**
www.nostalgiaville.com/museum/
Website for the Tennessee museum
devoted to beverage cans and
advertising collectibles, which includes
contact information, admission times
and prices, a history of beverage cans
and collectors information.

**My Granny's Attic Antique
& Collectibles**
www.mygrannysatticantiques.com
Vintage and antique kitchen utensils.

Nick's Antique Fruit Jar Collection
http://glassjunkie.coolfreepages.com/
A site devoted to collecting Ball
fruit jars.

The Old Hall Club
www.oldhallclub.co.uk
The home of the club for Old
Hall stainless steel tableware
on the internet.

**The Pillsbury Doughboy and Green
Giant Sprout Collector page**
http://users.stargate.net/~glshir/
Collectors page dedicated to Pillsbury
character advertising items.

Potted Meat Museum
www.pottedmeatmuseum.com
Online museum featuring a diverse
collection of tinned meat cans from
around the world, which can be
browsed according to brand or
meat type.

The Pyrex Files
http://dragonfire1.50megs.com/Pyrex/
Pyrex.htm
Reference page for Pyrex patterns
and items.

**The Restaurant Ware Collectors
Network**
www.restaurantwarecollectors.com
The RWCN is a community of
Restaurant Ware collectors, sellers
and buyers dedicated to research,

identification and valuation of all kinds
of commercial china. Areas of interest
include transportation china (railroad,
steamship, airline) and hotel ware
(china produced for use in dining
concerns such as restaurants, hotels,
resorts, diners, burger joints, donut
shops, inns, cafes, amusement parks,
sporting concerns, country clubs,
government concerns, etc).

Ruby Lane
www.rubylane.com
Shop for vintage kitchen items
cookware, graniteware and baskets.

Second Impression Palace
http://www.antiquepalace.com/
kitchen.htm
Kitchen collectibles.

The Stove Collector
http://stovecollector.tripod.com/
Site specializing in stoves that includes
a discussion board, database of stoves
and articles examining fuel types,
saftey issues and restoration FAQ.

Texas 4 Treasures
http://www.tias.com/stores/txt/
Glass and collectibles including Tiara,
early American Prescut, L. E. Smith,
Anchor Hocking, Pyrex, Indiana and
Westmoreland.

T. G. Green Pottery Collectors
www.zyworld.com/tggreen/
Collectors site for T. G. Green Pottery
items including information on the
pottery's history, designs and recent
news regarding the company and
its products.

**Tin & Graniteware General Store
Measures**
www.ontera.net/~johnell/
Collectors site providing information
about collecting tin, graniteware and
copper measures, manufacturers and
verification stamps.

The Toaster Museum
www.toaster.org
Website of The Toaster Museum
Foundation.

Towbees Hoosierware
www.towbees.com
An online museum of Hoosier
cabinet glassware manufactured
from 1905–41 for Hoosier-style
kitchen cabinets.

**The Vintage Tablecloth Lover's
Club (TLC)**
www.vintagetableclothsclub.com
An online collectors club dedicated
to the education and preservation
of vintage tablecloths and other
kitchen linens.

Directory of Markets & Centres

UNITED KINGDOM

Berkshire
Stables Antiques Centre, 1a Merchant Place (off Friar Street), Reading, RG1 1DT Tel: 0118 959 0290
Over 30 dealers.

Buckinghamshire
Jackdaw Antiques Centres Ltd, 25 West Street, Marlow, SL7 2LS Tel: 01628 898285 sales@jackdaw-antiques.co.uk www.jackdaw-antiques.co.uk
Approx 1,500 sq ft of furniture, collectables, silver, china, specialist areas, books, Victorian glass, Quimper, coins, fishing tackle.

Marlow Antique Centre, 35 Station Road, Marlow, SL7 1NW Tel: 01628 473223
Wide range of antique and collectable items from over 30 dealers. Georgian, Victorian and Edwardian furniture, country pine, decorative furniture, silverware, glass, china, Art Deco, bedsteads, cameras, old tools, garden items, jewellery, pens, cufflinks, vintage toys. Also a secondhand book section.

Derbyshire
Alfreton Antique Centre, 11 King Street, Alfreton, DE55 7AF Tel: 01773 520781
30 dealers on 2 floors. Antiques, collectables, furniture, books, militaria, postcards and silverware.

Chappells Antiques Centre, King Street, Bakewell, DE45 1DZ Tel: 01629 812496 ask@chappellsantiquescentre.com www.chappellsantiques centre.com
Over 30 dealers including BADA and LAPADA members. Quality period furniture, ceramics, silver, plate, metals, treen, clocks, barometers, books, pictures, maps, prints, textiles, kitchenalia, lighting, furnishing accessories, scientific, pharmaceutical and sporting antiques from the 17th–20thC.

Heanor Antiques Centre, 1–3 Ilkeston Road, Heanor, DE75 7AE Tel: 01773 531181/762783 sales@heanorantiquescentre.co.uk www.heanorantiques.co.uk
200 independent dealers in new 3 storey extension with stylish cafe.

Matlock Antiques, Collectables & Riverside Café, 7 Dale Road, Matlock, DE4 3LT Tel: 01629 760808 bmatlockantiques@aol.com www.matlock-antiques-collectable.cwc.net
Over 70 dealers.

Devon
Quay Centre, Topsham, Nr Exeter, EX3 0JA Tel: 01392 874006 office@antiquesontopshamquay.co.uk www.antiquesontopshamquay.co.uk
80 dealers on 3 floors. Antiques, collectables and traditional furnishings. Ample parking.

Essex
Gallerie Antiques, 62–70 Fowler Road, Hainault, IG6 3XE Tel: 020 8501 2229/020 8500 6979
Over 80 dealers in 10,000 sq ft. Everything from furniture, porcelain, glass, pictures, militaria and much more.

Gloucestershire
Cirencester Arcade & Ann's Pantry, 25 Market Place, Cirencester, GL7 2NX Tel: 01285 644214
Antiques, gifts, furnishings, etc. Restaurant/Tearooms, private room for hire.

Durham House Antiques, Sheep Street, Stow-on-the-Wold, GL54 1AA Tel: 01451 870404
30+ dealers. Town and country furniture, metalware, books, ceramics, kitchenalia, sewing ephemera, silver, jewellery and samplers.

Greater Manchester
The Ginnell Gallery Antique Centre, 18–22 Lloyd Street, M2 5WA Tel: 0161 833 9037
Extensive stock of antiques and collectables covering periods from 1200BC to 1970AD, Art Deco to fishing tackle and comprehensive book section. Large stock of 1950's and 60's glass and ceramics. 8,000 sq ft including restaurant.

Hampshire
Dolphin Quay Antique Centre, Queen Street, Emsworth, PO10 7BU Tel: 01243 379994
Marine, naval antiques, paintings, watercolours, prints, antique clocks, decorative arts, furniture, sporting apparel, luggage, specialist period lighting, conservatory, garden antiques, fine antique/country furniture, French/antique beds.

Lymington Antiques Centre, 76 High Street, Lymington, SO41 9AL Tel: 01590 670934
30 dealers, clocks, watches, silver, glass, jewellery, toys & dolls, books, furniture, textiles.

Herefordshire
The Hay Antique Market, 6 Market Street, Hay-on-Wye, HR3 5AF Tel: 01497 820175
17 separate units on 2 floors selling pine, country and period furniture. Rural and rustic items. China, glass, jewellery, linen and period clothes. Pictures, lighting, brass and collectables.

Mulberry's Antiques & Vintage Costumes, Hereford, HR1 2NN Tel: 01432 350101 mulberrysantiques@hotmail.com
A wide range of antiques and collectables on 2 floors. Furniture, fine china, porcelain, silver, jewellery, textiles, pre-1930's clothing and accessories, objets d'art, prints, oils and watercolours. Trade welcome.

The Old Merchant's House Antique Centre & Victorian Tearooms, 10 Corn Square, Leominster Tel: 01568 616141
Dealers in a wide variety of antiques, collectables and memorabilia. Licensed tearooms.

Hertfordshire
Herts & Essex Antiques Centre, The Maltings, Station Road, Sawbridgeworth, CM21 9JX Tel: 01279 722044
30 antique shops and 90 showcases. Over 10,000 items of antiques, furniture, jewellery, porcelain, collectables, stamps, coins, postcards, costume, paintings, glass, ceramics and ephemera. All in pleasant, well lit showrooms serviced by friendly staff.

Kent
Castle Antiques, 1 London Road (opposite Library), Westerham, TN16 1BB Tel: 01959 562492

4 rooms of antiques, small furniture, collectables, rural bygones, costume, glass, books, linens, jewellery, chandeliers, cat collectables. Services: advice, valuations, theatre props, house clearance, talks on antiques.

Copperfields Antiques & Craft Centre, 3c–4 Copperfields, Spital Street, Dartford, DA9 2DE Tel: 01322 281445
Antiques, bygones, collectables, stamps, Wade, SylvaC, Beswick, Royal Doulton, clocks, Victoriana, 1930's–60's, Art Deco, craft, handmade toys, dolls houses & miniatures, jewellery, glass, china, furniture, Kevin Francis character jugs, silk, lace and lots more. American-style Bistro.

Heirloom Antiques, 68 High Street, Tenterden, TN30 6AU Tel: 01580 765535

Malthouse Arcade, High Street, Hythe, CT21 5BW Tel: 01303 260103
37 stalls and cafe. Furniture, china and glass, jewellery, plated brass, picture postcards, framing etc.

Nightingales, 89–91 High Street, West Wickham, BR4 0LS Tel: 020 8777 0335
Over 5,000 sq ft of antiques, furniture and collectors items, including ceramics, glass, silver, furniture and decorative ware.

Tenterden Antiques Centre, 66–66A High Street, Tenterden, TN30 6AU Tel: 01580 765655/765885

Lancashire
The Antique & Decorative Design Centre, 56 Garstang Road, Preston, PR1 1NA Tel: 01772 882078
info@paulallisonantiques.co.uk
www.paulallisonantiques.co.uk
25,000 sq ft of quality antiques, objects d'art, clocks, pine, silverware, porcelain, upholstery, French furniture for the home and garden.

GB Antiques Centre, Lancaster Leisure Park, (the former Hornsea Pottery), Wyresdale Road, Lancaster, LA1 3LA Tel: 01524 844734
140 dealers in 40,000 sq ft of space. Porcelain, pottery, Art Deco, glass, books, linen, mahogany, oak and pine furniture.

Lincolnshire
Sue's Collectables, 61 Victoria Road, Mablethorpe, LN12 2AF Tel: 01507 472406
20,000 collectable items including old glass lampshades, gas and electrical fittings. Breweriana, kitchenalia, Bakelite, chalk figures, Xmas lights and decorations. Pendelfin bought and sold.

London
Alfie's Antique Market, 13 Church Street, Marylebone, NW8 8DT Tel: 020 7723 6066 www.alfiesantiques.com
London's biggest and busiest antique market.

Covent Garden Antiques Market, Jubilee Market Hall, Covent Garden, WC2 Tel: 020 7240 7405
Visit the famous Covent Garden Antiques Market. 150 traders selling jewellery, silver, prints, porcelain, objets d'art and numerous other collectables.

Grays Antique Markets, South Molton Lane, W1K 5AB Tel: 020 7629 7034 grays@clara.net
www.graysantiques.com
Over 200 specialist antique dealers selling beautiful and unusual antiques and collectables.

Northcote Road Antique Market, 155a Northcote Road, Battersea, SW11 6QB Tel: 020 7228 6850
gillikins@ntlworld.com www.spectrumsoft.net/nam
Indoor arcade 30 dealers offering a wide variety of antiques and collectables.

Palmers Green Antiques Centre, 472 Green Lanes, Palmers Green, N13 5PA Tel: 020 8350 0878
Over 40 dealers. Specializing in furniture, jewellery, clocks, pictures, porcelain, china, glass, silver & plate, metalware, kitchenalia and lighting, etc. Removals and house clearances, probate valuations undertaken, quality antiques and collectables.

Norfolk
Tombland Antiques Centre, Augustine Steward House, 14 Tombland, Norwich, NR3 1HF Tel: 01603 761906 or 619129 www.tomblandantiques.co.uk
Huge selection on three floors. Ideally situated opposite Norwich Cathedral.

Northamptonshire
Magpies Antiques and Collectables Centre, 1 East Grove, Rushden, NN10 0AP Tel: 01933 411404
Three floor Victorian factory building 3,800 sq ft on Rectory Road, A6, Rushden, Northants. 10 minutes Finedon, 15 minutes Bedford (1st Left after Old Railway Station, transport museum). We have a wide selection including a superb range of glass. A bargain hunter's paradise.

Nottinghamshire
Occleshaw Antiques Centre, The Old Major Cinema, 11 Mansfield Road, Edwinstowe, NG21 9NL Tel: 01623 825370
Large centre with a wide range of furniture, jewellery, militaria, cameras and collectables. Services include bookbinding, furniture restoration and French polishing.

Oxfordshire
Antiques on High, 85 High Street, Oxford, OX1 4BG Tel: 01865 251075
35 friendly dealers with a wide range of quality stock.

Jackdaw Antiques Centres Ltd, 5 Reading Road, Henley-on-Thames, RG9 0AS Tel: 01491 572289
sales@jackdaw-antiques.co.uk
www.jackdaw-antiques.co.uk
Approx 1,000 sq ft of collectables (modern and discontinued), furniture, books, specialist areas, Carlton Ware, Doulton and Beswick.

Lamb Arcade Antiques Centre, High Street, Wallingford, OX10 0BX Tel: 01491 835156
Furniture, silver, porcelain, glass, books, boxes, crafts, rugs, jewellery, lace and linens, pictures, tin toys, motoring and aviation memorabilia, sports and fishing items, decorative and ornamental items.

Shropshire
Stretton Antiques Market, Sandford Avenue, Church Stretton, SY6 6BH Tel: 01694 723718
60 dealers under one roof.

East Sussex
Church Hill Antique Centre, 6 Station Street, Lewes, BN7 2DA Tel: 01273 474842
churchhilllewes@aol.com
www.church-hill-antiques.co.uk

Wales

Afonwen Craft & Antique Centre, Afonwen, Nr Caerwys, Nr Mold, Flintshire, CH7 5UB Tel: 01352 720965
The largest antique and craft centre in north Wales and the Borders. 14,000 sq ft, 40 dealers, fabulous selection of antiques, china, silver, crystal, quality collectables. Fine furniture, oak, walnut, mahogany and pine from around the world.

Offa's Dyke Antique Centre, 4 High Street, Knighton, Powys, LD7 1AT Tel: 01547 520145
18th and 19thC pottery, 20thC country and Studio pottery, small country furniture, treen and bygones.

Romantiques Antique Centre, Bryn Seion Chapel, Station Road, Trevor, Nr Llangollen, LL20 7TP Tel: 01978 822879 SATKIN1057@aol.com www.romantiques.co.uk
2,500 sq ft displaying a wide range of antiques/collectables. Parking. Trade welcome. Services – furniture restoration, upholstery, clock repairs and valuations.

Warwickshire

Barn Antiques Centre, Station Road, Long Marston, Nr Stratford-upon-Avon, CV37 8RB Tel: 01789 721399 www.barnantique.co.uk
One of the largest traditional Antique Centres in the Midlands. Now over 13,000 sq ft. Large selection of antique furniture, antique pine, linen and lace, old fireplaces and surrounds, collectables, pictures & prints, silver, china, ceramics and objet d'art.

Dunchurch Antiques Centre, 16a Daventry Road, Dunchurch (Nr Rugby) Tel: 01788 522450
11 dealers specializing in furniture, china, glass, books, postcards, stamps, clocks, toys, trains, etc.

Malthouse Antiques Centre, 4 Market Place, Alcester, B49 5AE Tel: 01789 764032
Good selection of furniture, ceramics, pictures and collectables.

The Stables Antique Centre, Hatton Country World, Dark Lane, Hatton, Warwick, CV35 7LD Tel: 01926 842405
25 independent dealers. Come and browse in friendly surroundings. Home-baked refreshments. Free parking. Farm Park and adventure playground for children.

Stratford Antiques Centre, 59–60 Ely Street, Stratford-upon-Avon, CV37 6LN Tel: 01789 204180
A one-stop collectors experience with 2 floors and courtyard full of shops.

Worcestershire

Worcester Antiques Centre, Reindeer Court, Mealcheapen Street, Worcester, WR1 4DF Tel: 01905 610680 WorcsAntiques@aol.com
Porcelain & pottery, furniture, silver & dining room accessories, jewellery, period watches & clocks, scientific instrumentation, Arts & Crafts, Nouveau, Deco, antique boxes & treen, books, ephemera, militaria and kitchenalia with full restoration and repair services on all of the above.

Yorkshire

Cavendish Antique & Collectors Centre, 44 Stonegate, York, YO1 8AS Tel: 01904 621666
sales@cavendishantiques.com www.cavendishantiques.com
Over 50 dealers on 3 floors.

The Chapel Antiques Centre, 99 Broadfield Road, Heeley, Sheffield, S8 0XQ Tel: 0114 2588 288
enquiries@antiquesinsheffield.com www.antiquesinsheffield.com

Over 25 dealers displaying a wide range of antiques and collectables including specialists in clocks, Art Deco, French furniture, books, pine, fabrics, porcelain, and much more. Services: upholstery, furniture restoration, re-caning, pottery restoration, French polishing and delivery.

The Mall Antique Centre, 400 Wincolmlee, Hull, HU2 0QL Tel: 01482 327858
60 local antique dealers. 12,500 sq ft of Georgian, Victorian, Edwardian, reproduction, 1930's furniture, silver, china, clocks, hardware, etc.

Stonegate Antiques Centre, 41 Stonegate, York, YO1 8AW Tel: 01904 613888 sales@yorkantiquescentre.co.uk www.yorkantiquescentre.co.uk
Over 110 dealers on 2 floors.

USA

Antique Center I, II, III at Historic Savage Mill, Savage, Maryland Tel: 410 880 0918 or 301 369 4650 antiquec@aol.com
225 plus select quality dealers representing 15 states.

Antique Village, North of Richmond, Virginia, on Historic US 301, 4 miles North of 1-295 Tel: 804 746 8914
50 dealers specializing in Art Pottery, country & primitives, Civil War artifacts, paper memorabilia, African art, toys, advertising, occupied Japan, tobacco tins, glassware, china, holiday collectibles, jewelry and postcards.

Antiques at Colony Mill Marketplace, 222 West Street, Keene, New Hampshire 03431 Tel: 603 358 6343
Over 200 booths. Period to country furniture, paintings and prints, Art Pottery, glass, china, silver, jewelry, toys, dolls, quilts, etc.

Fern Eldridge & Friends, 800 First NH Turnpike (Rte. 4), Northwood, New Hampshire 03261 Tel: 603 942 5602/8131 FernEldridgeAndFriends@NHantiqueAlley.com
30 dealers on 2 levels. Shipping available in USA.

The Hayloft Antique Center, 1190 First NH Turnpike (Rte. 4), Northwood, New Hampshire 03261 Tel: 603 942 5153 TheHayloftAntiqueCenter@NHantiqueAlley.com
Over 150 dealers offering Estate jewelry, sterling silver, rare books, glass, porcelain, pottery, art, primitives, furniture, toys, ephemera, linens, military, sporting collectibles and much more.

Morningside Antiques, 6443 Biscayne Blvd., Miami, Florida Tel: 305 751 2828
The city's newest antiques market specializing in English, French and American furniture and collectibles in a mall setting with many different vendors.

Parker-French Antique Center, 1182 First NH Turnpike (Rte. 4), Northwood, New Hampshire 03261 Tel: 603 942 8852 ParkerFrenchAntiqueCenter@NHantiqueAlley.com
135 antique dealers all on one level offering a good mix of sterling silver, jewelry, glassware, pottery, early primitives. No crafts, reproductions or new items.

Quechee Gorge Antiques & Collectibles Center, Located in Quechee Gorge Village Tel: 800 438 5565
450 dealers. Depression glass, ephemera, tools, toys, collectibles, Deco, primitives, prints, silver and fine china.

Showcase Antique Center, PO Box 1122, Sturbridge, MA 01566 Tel: 508 347 7190 www.showcaseantiques.com
170 dealers.

Key to Illustrations

Each illustration and descriptive caption is accompanied by a letter code. By referring to the following list of Auctioneers (denoted by ✦) and Dealers (⊞), the source of any item may be immediately determined. Inclusion in this edition in no way constitutes or implies a contract or binding offer on the part of any of our contributors to supply or sell the goods illustrated, or similar articles, at the prices stated. Advertisers in this year's directory are denoted by (†).

If you require a valuation for an item, it is advisable to check whether the dealer or specialist will carry out this service and if there is a charge. Please mention Miller's when making an enquiry. Having found a specialist who will carry out your valuation it is best to send a photograph and description of the item to the specialist together with a stamped addressed envelope for the reply. A valuation by telephone is not possible. Most dealers are only too happy to help you with your enquiry; however, they are very busy people and consideration of the above points would be welcomed.

AL ⊞ Ann Lingard, Ropewalk Antiques, Rye, East Sussex TN31 7NA Tel: 01797 223486 ann-lingard@ropewalkantiques.freeserve.co.uk

B&R ⊞† Bread & Roses Tel: 01926 817342

BAC ⊞ The Brackley Antique Cellar, Drayman's Walk, Brackley, Northamptonshire NN13 6BE Tel: 01280 841841 antiquecellar@tesco.net

BD ⊞ Banana Dance Ltd, 155A Northcote Road, Battersea, London SW11 6QT Tel: 01634 364539 jonathan@bananadance.com www.bananadance.com

BET ⊞ Beth, GO 43–44, Alfies Antique Market, 13–25 Church Street, Marylebone, London NW8 8DT Tel: 020 7723 5613

BEV ⊞ Beverley, 30 Church Street, Marylebone, London NW8 8EP Tel: 020 7262 1576

BrL ⊞ The Brighton Lanes Antique Centre, 12 Meeting House Lane, Brighton, East Sussex BN1 1HB Tel: 01273 823121 peter@brightonlanes-antiquecentre.co.uk www.brightonlanes-antiquecentre.co.uk

BS ⊞ Below Stairs, 103 High Street, Hungerford, Berkshire RG17 0NB Tel: 01488 682317 hofgartner@belowstairs.co.uk www.belowstairs.co.uk

ByI ⊞ Bygones of Ireland Ltd, Lodge Road, Westport, County Mayo, Republic of Ireland Tel: 353 98 26132/25701 bygones@anu.ie www.bygones-of-ireland.com

CAL ⊞ Cedar Antiques Ltd, High Street, Hartley Wintney, Hampshire RG27 8NY Tel: 01252 843222 or 01189 326628 ca@cedar-antiques.com www.cedar-antiques.com

CCO ⊞ Collectable Costume, Showroom South, Gloucester Antiques Centre, 1 Severn Road, Gloucester GL1 2LE Tel: 01989 562188

CCs ⊞ Coco's Corner, Unit 4, Cirencester Antique Centre, Cirencester, Gloucestershire Tel: 01452 556 308 cocos-corner@blueyonder.co.uk

CHAC ⊞ Church Hill Antiques Centre, 6 Station Street, Lewes, East Sussex BN7 2DA Tel: 01273 474 842 churchhilllewes@aol.com www.church-hill-antiques.com

CHI ⊞† Chinasearch, Ltd, 4 Princes Drive, Kenilworth, Warwickshire CV8 2FD Tel: 01926 512402 helen.rush@chinasearch.uk.com www.chinasearch.uk.com

CHTR ✦ Charterhouse, The Long Street Salerooms, Sherborne, Dorset DT9 3BS Tel: 01935 812277 enquiry@charterhouse-auctions.co.uk www.charterhouse-auctions.co.uk

COB ⊞ Cobwebs, 78 Northam Road, Southampton, Hampshire SO14 0PB Tel: 023 8022 7458 www.cobwebs.uk.com

COBB ✦ Cobbs Auctioneers LLC, Noone Falls Mill, 50 Jaffrey Rd, Peterborough, NH 03458, USA Tel: 603 924 6361 info@thecobbs.com www.thecobbs.com

CoCo ⊞ Country Collector, 11–12 Birdgate, Pickering, Yorkshire YO18 7AL Tel: 01751 477481 www.country-collector.co.uk

CoHA ⊞ Corner House Antiques and Ffoxe Antiques, Gardners Cottage, Broughton Poggs, Filkins, Lechlade-on-Thames, Gloucestershire GL7 3JH Tel: 01367 860078 jdhis007@btopenworld.com www.corner-house-antiques.co.uk

CoS ⊞ Corrine Soffe Tel: 01295 730317 soffe@btinternet.com

Cot ⊞ Cottage Collectibles, Long Street Antiques, 14 Long Street, Tetbury, Gloucestershire G18 8AQ Tel: 01666 500850 sheila@cottagecollectibles.co.uk www.cottagecollectibles.co.uk

DaM ⊞ Martin's Antiques & Collectibles, The Shed Antiques Collectibles Centre Tel: 01386 438387/ 0795 1600573 Jackiem743710633@aol.com www.martinsantiquescollectibles.co.uk

DAN ⊞ Andrew Dando, 34 Market Street, Bradford-on-Avon, Wiltshire BA15 1LL Tel: 01225 865444 andrew@andrewdando.co.uk www.andrewdando.co.uk

DEB ⊞ Debden Antiques, Elder Street, Debden, Saffron Walden, Essex CB11 3JY Tel: 01799 543007 info@debden-antiques.co.uk debden-antiques.co.uk

DgC ⊞ Dragonlee Collectables Tel: 01622 729502

DHA ⊞ Durham House Antiques, Sheep Street, Stow-on-the-Wold, Gloucestershire GL54 1AA Tel: 01451 870404

DN ✦ Dreweatt Neate, Donnington Priory, Donnington, Newbury, Berkshire RG14 2JE Tel: 01635 553553 donnington@dnfa.com www.dnfa.com/donnington

Do ⊞ Liz Farrow T/As Dodo, Stand F071/73, Alfie's Antique Market, 13–25 Church Street, London NW8 8DT Tel: 020 7706 1545

DSG ⊞ Delf Stream Gallery, Bournemouth, Dorset Tel: 07974 926137 nic19422000@yahoo.co.uk www.delfstreamgallery.com

EXC ⊞ Excalibur Antiques, Taunton Antique Centre, 27–29 Silver Street, Taunton, Somerset TA1 3DH Tel: 01823 289327/07774 627409 pwright777@btopenworld.com www.excaliburantiques.com

F&F ⊞ Fenwick & Fenwick, 88–90 High Street, Broadway, Worcestershire WR12 7AJ Tel: 01386 853227/ 841724

FLD ⊞ Flying Duck, 320/322 Creek Road, Greenwich, London SE10 9SW Tel: 020 8858 1964

FMN ⊞ Forget-Me-Knot Antiques, Antiques at Over the Moon, 27 High Street, St Albans, Hertfordshire AL3 4EH Tel: 01923 261172 sharpffocus@hotmail.com

FOX ⊞ Fox Cottage Antiques, Digbeth Street, Stow-on-the-Wold, Gloucestershire GL54 1BN Tel: 01451 870307

FST ⊞ Curiosities and Collectables, Gloucester Antiques Centre, The Historic Docks, 1 Severn Road, Gloucester GL1 2LE Tel: 01452 529716

G(L) 🔨 Gorringes inc Julian Dawson, 15 North Street, Lewes, East Sussex BN7 2PD Tel: 01273 478221 auctions@gorringes.co.uk www.gorringes.co.uk

GAK 🔨 Keys, Off Palmers Lane, Aylsham, Norfolk NR11 6JA Tel: 01263 733195 www.aylshamsalerooms.co.uk

GLAS ⊞ Glasstastique (by appointment only) Tel: 0113 287 9308 office or 07967 337795/07967 345952 glasstastique@aol.com www.glasstastique.com

GLB ⊞ Glebe Antiques, Scottish Antique Centre, Doune, Scotland FK16 6HG Tel: 01259 214559 RRGlebe@aol.com

GN ⊞ Gillian Neale Antiques, PO Box 247, Aylesbury, Buckinghamshire HP20 1JZ Tel: 01296 423754/07860 638700 gillianneale@aol.com www.gillannealeantiques.co.uk

GoW ⊞ Gordon Watson Ltd, 50 Fulham Road, London SW3 6HH Tel: 020 7589 3108

GRe ⊞ Greystoke Antiques, 4 Swan Yard, (off Cheap Street), Sherborne, Dorset DT9 3AX Tel: 01935 812833

GRI ⊞ Grimes House Antiques, High Street, Moreton-in-Marsh, Gloucestershire GL56 0AT Tel: 01608 651029 grimes_house@cix.co.uk www.grimeshouse.co.uk www.cranberryglass.co.uk www.collectglass.com

GRo ⊞ Geoffrey Robinson, GO77–78, GO91–92 (Ground floor), Alfies Antique Market, 13–25 Church Street, Marylebone, London NW8 8DT Tel: 020 7723 0449 info@alfiesantiques.com www.alfiesantiques.com

HarC ⊞ Hardy's Collectables Tel: 07970 613077 www.poolepotteryjohn.com

HEI ⊞ Heirloom Antiques, 68 High Street, Tenterden, Kent TN30 6AU Tel: 01580 765535

HEW ⊞ Muir Hewitt Art Deco Originals, Halifax Antiques Centre, Queens Road Mills, Queens Road/Gibbet Street, Halifax, Yorkshire HX1 4LR Tel: 01422 347377 muir.hewitt@virgin.net www.muirhewitt.com

HO ⊞ Houghton Antiques, Houghton, Cambridgeshire Tel: 01480 461887

HON ⊞ Honan's Antiques, Crowe Street, Gort, Co Galway, Republic of Ireland Tel: 353 91 631407 www.honansantiques.com

HOP ⊞ The Antique Garden, Grosvenor Garden Centre, Wrexham Road, Belgrave, Chester, Cheshire CH4 9EB Tel: 01244 629191/07976 539 990 antigard@btopenworld.com

HRQ ⊞ Harlequin Antiques, 79–81 Mansfield Road, Daybrook, Nottingham NG5 6BH Tel: 0115 967 4590 sales@antiquepine.net www.antiquepine.net

HSt ⊞ High Street Retro, 39 High Street, Old Town, Hastings, East Sussex TN34 3ER Tel: 01424 460068

HUM ⊞ Humbleyard Fine Art, Unit 32 Admiral Vernon Arcade, Portobello Road, London W11 2DY Tel: 01362 637793

HUX ⊞ David Huxtable, Saturdays at: Portobello Road, Basement Stall 11/12, 288 Westbourne Grove, London W11 Tel: 07710 132200 david@huxtins.com www.huxtins.com

HYP ⊞ Hyperion Collectables

JAS ⊞ Jasmin Cameron, Antiquarius, 131–141 King's Road, London SW3 4PW Tel: 020 7351 4154 or 07774 871257 jasmin.cameron@mail.com

JAZZ ⊞ Jazz Art Deco Tel: 07721 032277 jazzartdeco@btinternet.com www.jazzartdeco.com

JFME ⊞ James Ferguson & Mark Evans Tel: 0141 950 2452 or 077 699 72935/01388 768108 or 07979 0189214 james@dec-art.freeserve.co.uk mark@evanscollectables.co.uk www.evanscollectables.co.uk

JOA ⊞ Joan Gale Antiques Dealer, Tombland Antiques Centre, 14 Tombland, Norwich NR3 1HF Tel: 01603 619129 joan.gale@ukgateway.net

JUP ⊞ Jupiter Antiques, PO Box 609, Rottingdean, East Sussex BN2 7FW Tel: 01273 302865

JWK ⊞† Jane Wicks Kitchenalia, Country Ways, Strand Quay, Rye, East Sussex TN31 Tel: 01424 713635 or 07754 308269 Janes_kitchen@hotmail.com

LaF ⊞ La Femme Tel: 07971 844279 jewels@joancorder.freeserve.co.uk

LBM Not currently trading

LUNA ⊞ Luna, 23 George Street, Nottingham NG1 3BH Tel: 0115 924 3267 info@luna-online.co.uk www.luna-online.co.uk

MARK ⊞ 20th Century Marks, Whitegates, Rectory Road, Little Burstead, Near Billericay, Essex CM12 9TR Tel: 01268 411 000 or 07831 778992 info@20thcenturymarks.co.uk www.20thcenturymarks.co.uk

MCC ⊞ M. C. Chapman Antiques, Bell Hill, Finedon, Northamptonshire NN9 5NB Tel: 01933 681260

MFB ⊞ Manor Farm Barn Antiques Tel: 01296 658941 or 07720 286607 mfbn@btinternet.com btwebworld.com/mfbantiques

MLa ⊞ Marion Langham Limited Tel: 028 895 41247 marion@ladymarion.co.uk www.ladymarion.co.uk

MLL ⊞ Millers Antiques Ltd, Netherbrook House, 86 Christchurch Road, Ringwood, Hampshire BH24 1DR Tel: 01425 472062 mail@millers-antiques.co.uk www.millers-antiques.co.uk

Mo ⊞ Mr Moore

MRW ⊞ Malcolm Welch Antiques, Wild Jebbett, Pudding Bag Lane, Thurlaston, Nr Rugby, Warwickshire CV23 9JZ Tel: 01788 810 616 www.rb33.co.uk

MSB ⊞ Marilynn and Sheila Brass, PO Box 380503, Cambridge, MA 02238-0503, USA Tel: 617 492 1491 shelmardesign1@aol.com

NEW ⊞ Newsum Antiques, 2 High Street, Winchcombe, Gloucestershire GL54 5HT Tel: 01242 603446/ 07968 196668 mark@newsumantiques.co.uk www.newsumantiques.co.uk

NFR ⊞ The 40's Room, Unit 40 Rugeley Antiques Centre, Main Road, Brereton, Rugeley, Staffordshire WS15 1DX Tel: 01889 577166 info@cc41homefrontdisplays.co.uk

NOR ⊞ Nortonbury Antiques, BMC Box 5345, London WC1N 3XX Tel: 01984 631668 nortonbury.antiques@virgin.net www.antiquesnet.co.uk

NS ⊞ Nicholas Shaw Antiques, Virginia Cottage, Lombard Street, Petworth, West Sussex GU28 0AG Tel: 01798 345146/01798 345147 silver@nicholas-shaw.com www.nicholas-shaw.com

OPB ⊞ Olde Port Bookshop, 18 State Street, Newburyport, Massachusetts 01950, USA Tel: 978 462 0100 Oldeport@ttlc.net

PGO ⊞ Pamela Goodwin, 11 The Pantiles, Royal Tunbridge Wells, Kent TN2 5TD Tel: 01892 618200 mail@goodwinantiques.co.uk www.goodwinantiques.co.uk

PICA ⊞ Piccadilly Antiques, 280 High Street, Batheaston, Bath BA1 7RA Tel: 01225 851494 piccadillyantiques@ukonline.co.uk

POS ⊞ Gazebo, Pierrpoint Row, Camden Passage, Angel Islington, London

PrB ⊞ Pretty Bizarre, 170 High Street, Deal, Kent CT14 6BQ Tel: 07973 794537

RdeR ⊞ Rogers de Rin, 76 Royal Hospital Road, London SW3 4HN Tel: 020 7352 9007

RGa ⊞ Richard Gardner Antiques, Swanhouse, Market Square, Petworth, West Sussex GU28 0AN Tel: 01798 343411

RH ⊞ Rick Hubbard Art Deco, 3 Tee Court, Bell Street, Romsey, Hampshire SO51 8GY Tel: 01794 513133 rick@rickhubbard-artdeco.co.uk www.rickhubbard-artdeco.co.uk

RTo ⚒ Rupert Toovey & Co Ltd, Spring Gardens, Washington, West Sussex RH20 3BS Tel: 01903 891955 auctions@rupert-toovey.com www.rupert-toovey.com

RTT ⊞ Rin Tin Tin, 34 North Road, Brighton, East Sussex BN1 1YB Tel: 01273 672424 rick@rintintin.freeserve.co.uk

SCH ⊞ Scherazade Tel: 01708 641117 or 07855 383996 scherz1@yahoo.com

SCO ⊞ Peter Scott Tel: 0117 986 8468 or 07850 639770

SDA ⊞ Stephanie Davison Antiques, Bakewell Antiques Centre, King Street, Bakewell, Derbyshire DE45 1DZ Tel: 01629 812496 or 07771 564 993 bacc@chappells-antiques.co.uk www.chappells-antiques.co.uk

SEA ⊞ Mark Seabrook Antiques, PO Box 396, Huntingdon, Cambridgeshire PE28 0ZA Tel: 01480 861935 enquiries@markseabrook.com www.markseabrook.com

SHa ⊞ Shapiro & Co, Stand 380, Gray's Antique Market, 58 Davies Street, London W1K 5LP Tel: 020 7491 2710

SJH ⚒ S. J. Hales, 87 Fore Street, Bovey Tracey, Devon TQ13 9AB Tel: 01626 836684

SMI ⊞† Skip & Janie Smithson Antiques Tel: 01754 810265 or 07831 399180 smithsonantiques@hotmail.com

STA ⊞ George Stacpoole, Main Street, Adare, Co Limerick, Republic of Ireland Tel: 6139 6409 stacpoole@iol.ie www.georgestacpooleantiques.com

SWN ⊞ Swan Antiques

SWO ⚒ Sworders, 14 Cambridge Road, Stansted Mountfitchet, Essex CM24 8BZ Tel: 01279 817778 auctions@sworder.co.uk www.sworder.co.uk

TAC ⊞ Tenterden Antiques Centre, 66–66A High Street, Tenterden, Kent TN30 6AU Tel: 01580 765655/ 765885

TASV ⊞ Tenterden Antiques & Silver Vaults, 66 High Street, Tenterden, Kent TN30 6AU Tel: 01580 765885

TDG ⊞ The Design Gallery 1850–1950, 5 The Green, Westerham, Kent TN16 1AS Tel: 01959 561234 sales@thedesigngalleryuk.com www.thedesigngalleryuk.com

TMA ⚒ Tring Market Auctions, The Market Premises, Brook Street, Tring, Hertfordshire HP23 5EF Tel: 01442 826446 sales@tringmarketauctions.co.uk www.tringmarketauctions.co.uk

TOP ⊞ The Top Banana Antiques Mall, 1 New Church Street, Tetbury, Gloucestershire GL8 8DS Tel: 0871 288 1102 info@topbananaantiques.com www.topbananaantiques.com

TRA ⊞ Tramps, 8 Market Place, Tuxford, Newark, Nottinghamshire NG22 0LL Tel: 01777 872 543 info@trampsuk.com

TWI ⊞ Twinkled, 1st Floor, Old Petrol Station, 11–17 Stockwell Street, Greenwich, London SE10 9JN Tel: 020 8269 0864 info@twinkled.net www.twinkled.net

VS ⚒ T. Vennett-Smith, 11 Nottingham Road, Gotham, Nottinghamshire NG11 0HE Tel: 0115 983 0541 info@vennett-smith.com www.vennett-smith.com

WAC ⊞ Worcester Antiques Centre, Reindeer Court, Mealcheapen Street, Worcester WR1 4DF Tel: 01905 610680 WorcsAntiques@aol.com

WeA ⊞ Wenderton Antiques (by appointment only) Tel: 01227 720295

WiB ⊞ Wish Barn Antiques, Wish Street, Rye, East Sussex TN31 7DA Tel: 01797 226797

WW ⚒ Woolley & Wallis, Salisbury Salerooms, 51–61 Castle Street, Salisbury, Wiltshire SP1 3SU Tel: 01722 424500/411854 junebarrett@woolleyandwallis.co.uk www.woolleyandwallis.co.uk

YC ⊞ Yesterday Child Tel: 01908 583403 djbarrington@btinternet.com

YT ⊞ Yew Tree Antiques, Woburn Abbey Antiques Centre, Woburn, Bedfordshire MK17 9WA Tel: 01525 872514

Picture Acknowledgements

p.1 OPG/RS/DaM (p.290 br); p.2 OPG/MN/CB; p.5 OPG/EG; p.18x2 OPG/MN/CB; p.19 t OPG/MN/AM, cr & b OPG/MN/CB; p.20 t OPG/TR/FDE, bl OPG/TR/Z, br OPG/MN/JF; p.21 OPG/MN/CB; p.22 t & bl OPG/MN/AM, br OPG/MN/CB; p.24 OPG/MN/CB; p.25x5 OPG/MN/CB; p.26 t & cl OPG/MN/CB, b OPG/MN/B; p.27 t OPG/MN/B, c & b OPG/MN/CB; p.28 tl & tr OPG/MN/CB, b OPG/IB/A; p.29x3 OPG/MN/CB; p.30 OPG/MN/RK; p.31 OPG/MN/CB; p.32x2 OPG/MN/CB; p.33x3 OPG/MN/CB; p.34 tl OPG/MN/RW, tr & b OPG/MN/CB; p.36 t OPG/MN/CB, b OPG/MN/CDW; p.38x2 OPG/MN/CB; p.39x2 OPG/MN/CB; p.40 OPG/MN/CB; p.41x2 OPG/MN/CB; p.42x2 OPG/MN/CB; p.43 bl OPG/MN/CB, br OPG/MN/AM; p.44x2 OPG/MN/CB; p.45 c OPG/MN/CB&CDW, b OPG/MN/AM; p.46 t & b OPG/MN/CB, c OPG/MN/CDW; p.47 t OPG/MN/CDW, b OPG/MN/CB; p.48 OPG/MN/CB; p.49 OPG/MN/CB; p.50 OPG/MN/CB; p.51 OPG/MN/AM; p.52 OPG/MN/CB; p.53 OPG/MN/CB; p.54 OPG/MN/CB; p.55 t OPG/MN/CB, c OPG/MN/CB&CDW; p.56 OPG/MN/CB; p.57 OPG/MN/CB; p.58x2 OPG/MN/CB; p.59x2 OPG/MN/AM; p.60 OPG/MN/AM; p.61 t OPG/MN/CDW, b OPG/MN/CB; p.62x2 OPG/MN/CB; p.63 OPG/MN/CB&CL; p.65 t OPG/RS/BAC (p253 br), c F&F (p251 tr), b OPG/RS/DAN (p255 tc); p.66 t OPG/RS/BS (p255 br), b OPG/RS/VS (p259 tl); p.67 OPG/RS/FOX (p260 cl); p.68 WeA (p260 b); p.69 t OPG/RS/RdeR (p263 cl), b OPG/RS/SMI (p268 tl); p.70 OPG/RS/JWK; p.71 l OPG/RS/RH (p278 cl), r OPG/RS/SCH (p277 tl); p.72 OPG/RS/TDG (p281 tr); p.73 OPG/RS/CAL (p284 tl); p.74 bl OPG/RS/JOA (p287 cbl), br OPG/RS/HYP (p287 br); p.75 t OPG/RS/AL (p288 ct), b OPG/RS/AL (p288 cb); p.76x2 OPG/MN/CB; p.77x2 OPG/MN/CB; p.78 OPG/RS/SMI (p292 br); p.79 tl DO/MSB p293 cr), tr OPG/RS/HON (p292 bl), b OPG/RS/YT (p294 tc); p.80 t & br OPG/MN/CB, bl OPG/RS/HOP (p297 tl); p.81 OPG/RS/JWK (p300 ct); p.82 DO/MSB; p.83 t OPG/MN/HB, bl DO/MSB, br DO/MSB; p.84 t & bl OPG/MN/S, br OPG/MN/BFC

Key: OPG – © Octopus Publishing Group
Photographers: IB – Ian Booth, MN – Martin Norris, TR – Tim Ridley, RS – Robin Saker, DO – Dennis O'Reilly, EG – Emma Gillingham
A – Alfies, AM – Annie Marchant, B – Bazar, BFC – Books For Cooks, CDW – Clarissa Dickson-Wright, CB – Christina Bishop, CL – Caroline Liddell, FDE – Flying Duck Enterprises, HB – Harington Brothers, JF – Josephine Fairley, RK – Rosie Kindersley, RW – Robin Weir, S – Sotheby's, Z – Zambesi

Bibliography

Atterbury, Paul, *Cornish Ware*, Somerset: Richard Dennis, 1996.

Bishop, Christina, *Miller's Collecting Kitchenware*, London: Octopus Publishing Group Limited, 1996

Collecting Carlton Ware, London: Francis Joseph Publications, 1994.

Collecting Susie Cooper, London: Francis Joseph Publications, 1994.

Griffin, Leonard and Pear Meisel, Louis K. and Susan, *Clarice Cliff The Bizarre Affair*, London: Thames and Hudson, 1989.

Hopwood, Irene and Gordon, *Denby Pottery 1809–1997*, Somerset: Richard Dennis, 1997.

Jenkins, Steven, *Midwinter Pottery*, Somerset: Richard Dennis, 1997.

Jenkins, Steven and McKay, Stephen P., *Portmeirion Pottery*, Somerset: Richard Dennis, 2000.

Marsh, Madeleine, *Miller's Collectables Price Guide 2004/5*, London: Octopus Publishing Group Limited, 2004.

Watson, Howard and Pat, *The Colourful World of Clarice Cliff*, London: Kevin Francis Publishing, 1992.

Index to Advertisers

Index

Bold numbers refer to information and pointer boxes